Animal Sacrifice and the Death Penalty

Animal Sacrifice and the Death Penalty

Giosuè Ghisalberti

WIPF & STOCK · Eugene, Oregon

ANIMAL SACRIFICE AND THE DEATH PENALTY

Wipf & Stock
An Imprint of Wipf and Stock Publishers
199 W. 8th Ave., Suite 3
Eugene, OR 97401

www.wipfandstock.com

PAPERBACK ISBN: 978-1-6667-0387-0
HARDCOVER ISBN: 978-1-6667-0388-7
EBOOK ISBN: 978-1-6667-0389-4

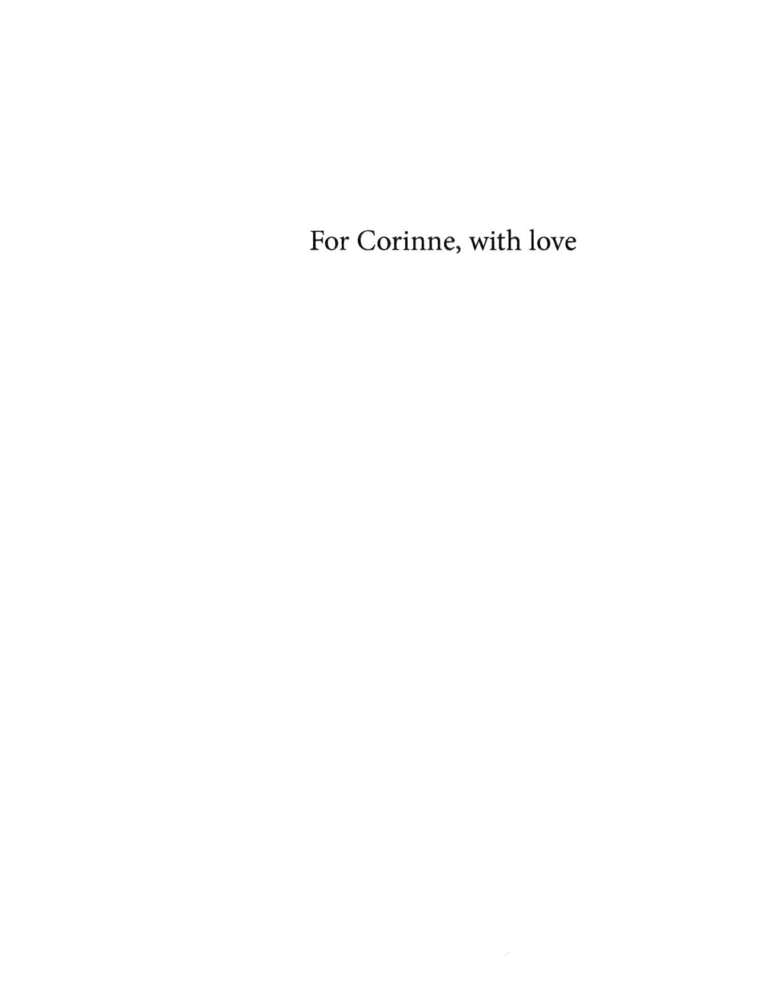

For Corinne, with love

Table of Contents

Preface | ix

Introduction: A *Parakletic* Hermeneutics for the Accused, the Judged, the Condemned | 1

Chapter 1: The Animals in Genesis 1–3 | 23

Chapter 2: Abel, the Death of a Sacrificial Killer | 57

Chapter 3: Prometheus in Hesiod's *Theogony* | 84

Chapter 4: The Execution of Socrates | 115

Chapter 5: The Abolition of the Death Penalty in the Gospel of John | 145

Chapter 6: Roman Law and the Christians *Damnati ad Bestias* | 171

Bibliography | 203

Preface

APPROACHING THE CONCLUSION OF the writing of an earlier project,[1] and resisting the temptation to comment on the *origin* of the ritual of animal sacrifice, since I was only concerned with its sustained historical critique by both the Jewish prophets and Greek philosophers, it finally became impossible to resist some early speculations—in part because of what seemed to me a consistent *apologia* for the practice and the attempt to not simply minimize the violence inherent in animal sacrifice, but in many ways to disavow it.[2] There is, today, a noticeable situation among scholars—a consensus that, to my mind (and from the perspective of earlier thinkers on the question) has failed to recognize not only the implications of sacrifice in antiquity, but equally important, its modern remnants today. To simply accept the fact of animal sacrifice by historians of religion or anthropologists, to name two of the prominent disciplines concerned with the issue, is to be complicit with its many consequences, political and otherwise.

The early speculations on the origins of animal sacrifice finally led me to a reexamination of the *texts* in question—at least in the traditions most relevant in Mediterranean antiquity: the Hebrew Bible and Greek thought—poetry, tragedy, and philosophy—as well as the Roman world when it had to confront the emergence of Christianity. The gospels are decisive on the matter; they confirm a historical awareness of the conjunction between animal sacrifice and the death penalty. Throughout the time of writing and reading, there were moments when a general theory on the origin of animal sacrifice became more in focus—especially when

1. *Soteriology and the End of Animal Sacrifice* (Eugene, OR: Wipf & Stock, 2018).

2. I refer, most especially though not exclusively, to two collections of essays: Faraone and Naiden, *Greek and Roman Animal Sacrifice*, and Knust and Vàrhelyi, *Ancient Mediterranean Sacrifice*.

rereading the thinkers who were adamant about associating animal sacrifice with violence, Walter Burkert, René Girard, and the "Paris school" led by Jean-Pierre Vernant and Marcel Detienne; but the origin of the politico-religious ritual as such was only important for the sense that animal sacrifice could never be separated from an associated phenomenon: the killing of an animal as a socially necessary observance followed by one or more instances of another *foundation*—of commandment and judgment, justice and the law, either as an expression of that most formidable of gods, Yahweh, or one or more gods from the Greek or Roman pantheon. Once again reading *Violent Origins* proved to be a catalyst. In his preface, Robert Hamerton-Kelly issued an invitation. "There is an open-endedness to the volume," he writes, "and the reader is invited to participate in the debate."[3] The following work is an acceptance of the invitation. If the prior work on soteriology argued that the abolition of animal sacrifice inaugurated a revolution in ancient piety and in part transformed the human relationship to religion, my argument on the *universal* abolition of the death penalty follows a similar thinking and hope. The continued execution of human beings by a political state with judicial powers over life and death means modernity has not yet been achieved.

February 26, 2021
Giosuè Ghisalberti

3. Hamerton-Kelly, preface to *Violent Origins*, vi.

Introduction

A *Parakletic* Hermeneutics for the Accused, the Judged, the Condemned

NEAR THE END OF *Violence and the Sacred* and in the last chapter, called "The Unity of All Rites," René Girard hesitated, paused, and found himself at a standstill. A previous "unity" was no longer certain. Almost at the conclusion, he forced himself to return to the very beginning to reexamine whether one of his foundational ideas could still be maintained. He had misgivings, and rightly so: "In Chapter 1 ['Sacrifice'], I suggested that there was a direct correlation between the elimination of sacrificial practices and the establishment of a judicial system."[1] While working through the details of his revolutionary theory on generative violence and the surrogate victim, he had reached a critical juncture in his research. There was no way to avoid the problem. Any assumption on the law serving as a substitution for sacrifice was now in doubt; any belief in the judicial system replacing, as its *supersession*, the sacrificial rituals of antiquity, was far from certain. It was, in fact, untenable. By the time Girard had reached a certain juncture (while reading Freud's *Totem and Taboo*, he tells us), "it was clear that the scope of this inquiry would have to be extended" (297). Extended, but in what way? Freud had made him hesitate. How so? Although Girard went back to reconsider his introductory conclusions, and then *retracted* them, he did not tell us the exact reason for doing so.

But in the argument in Freud's *Totem and Taboo*, the reason was clear. During his own psychoanalytic *reading* of anthropological research, Freud realized how an act considered illegal by an individual was

1. Girard, *Violence and the Sacred*, 297–98.

permitted, and sanctioned, when done by the whole community. "The rule that every participant at the sacrificial meal must eat a share of the flesh of the victim has the same meaning as the provision that the execution of a guilty tribesman must be carried out by the tribe as a whole."[2] Without emphasizing the importance of the connection (not really seeing its *metaphysical* origins) Freud saw the relationship between animal sacrifice and human executions. His psychoanalytic insights were suggestive; aspects of rituals were not to be ignored. The fundamental rituals of religion and the law mutually confirm each other in the killing of a victim who, in one way or another, will be *consumed*, eaten and eaten-up by the community.

For Girard, reconsidering his ground-breaking theory was not easy; many elements intersected too widely and generally, with religion, ritual, law, justice, and the penal system all related. One certainty, however, had to be abandoned. The *evolution* (his word) from sacrifice *to* the law not only appeared "inconclusive," as Girard admits, but it presented severe difficulties when the most extreme act carried out by the judicial system could not be ignored as a historical reality. The death penalty was not an institution created *after* animal sacrifice, as if a ritual founded from long-lost origins of archaic myths was replaced by rational *logos*.

The logos did not emerge after myth had been overcome.

No such historical chronology is evident or can be demonstrated.

The justice system was not the *rational overcoming* of sacrificial ritual; they were both implicated in binding institutions. A certain reciprocity was hermeneutically legible within foundational texts. The relevant texts of antiquity (Genesis 4, for example, on Cain's thoughts and acts) were already well known to Girard. They could lead him to additional, and obviously different, conclusions as long as he read them without the burden of orthodoxy.

(Insights were there, to be read and interpreted, that is, if their meanings were not buried under the concealments of tradition. Freudian *archaeology* was necessary: one had to return to the *origin* of the *myth/logos relationship*.)

Foundational myths had to be reinterpreted and presented without the burden of history and tradition. In Genesis, the episodes taking place in the garden of Eden have long been determined in terms of meaning; they have endured without any of the most significant interpretations

2. Freud, *Totem and Taboo*, 197.

("original sin" and the "fall," to name but two) being reevaluated. Has there been more resentment and misinterpretation in relation to *the animal*—it is not a snake or a serpent—than within the first few pages of the Bible? As for Girard's misunderstanding of Cain, for example, it was hampered by the force of his own theory: the unique meaning of this biblical figure was concealed by a universal accusation, judgment, and condemnation that made him unknowable; and when Girard misused Cain to develop his theory of mimesis and the universal explanation of "sibling rivalry" (which was [*is*] completely misguided and irrelevant to the case), the son of Adam, of *adāmāh*—the soil and ground and earth of the farmer—would remain nothing more than the subject of homicidal rage and jealousy.

No one has yet to extend Cain any understanding much less *parakletic* support.

The interpretation of Cain has been *symptomatic*. Our writings about him have been about us, not about the tiller of the soil and what his acts in Genesis 4 mean. A moral absolutism has imposed itself on Cain in order to conceal (from ourselves) the metaphysical problems emerging from out of a post-Eden existence. Girard was inheriting an entire tradition of reading perpetuated by theological concerns and by the all-encompassing urgency of morality. The act of murder stood out; fratricide was the sole concern. Without coming to a resolution about his own thinking and how it was necessarily in relation to tradition, the taken-for-granted idea of a "sibling" rivalry between Cain and Abel was ultimately misleading. Cain's unique consciousness cannot be reduced to the familial. Anthropological theories on the conflict between farmers and pastoralists were, moreover, well outside the *allegory* of the biblical text. Relying on history to clarify an interpretative conflict is off the mark; history is not a category adequate to the understanding of singular events. In this case, hermeneutics and history were irreconcilable. The remote events in time and the text were completely different phenomena. Anthropology was impertinent, even when discussed by a political philosopher of the stature of Leo Strauss, who believed "the pastoral life is closer to original simplicity that the life of the tillers of the soil."[3] Farming and pastoralism is not the issue; these are material occupations of terrestrial existence.

3. Strauss, *Studies in Platonic Political Philosophy*, 157.

There is only one problem in Genesis 4: the *killing of animals* in a religious ritual.

Cain killed Abel. The spectacle of his blood in the ground has forced everyone to look down. Perception has, as a consequence, been extremely limited. Levinas's ethical command foregoes the primacy of the metaphysical. He writes, "We approach death as nothingness in the passion for murder. The spontaneous intentionality of this passion aims at annihilation. Cain, when he slew Abel, should have possessed this knowledge of death."[4] Levinas, all too focused on the ethical "other," has made one severe omission. In due time, it will be exposed.

(Girard's assumption about justice following sacrifice was made possible by a more foundational prejudice—or, stated less forcibly, by another hermeneutic "pre-judgment": the historical *process* leading from myth to logos, all the while ignoring, or deciding to ignore, the texts that made that distinction ungovernable. Girard did not notice an analogy: logos did not follow myth. That "pre-judgment" was more complicated than assumed.)

At this juncture, one comment is necessary: it will be crucial in the work to come, in the "work on myth" to come beginning with Genesis and Hesiod's *Theogony*. Although my main concern, as a reader, is the textual relationship between animal sacrifice and the death penalty, one affirmation will be maintained throughout when all the interpretations related to our two foundational documents are treated from the standpoint of Hans Blumenberg in *Work on Myth*. He writes, "The boundary line between myth and logos is imaginary and does not obviate the need to inquire about the logos of myth in the process of working free of the absolutism of reality."[5] Blumenberg's thesis is, in the context of animal sacrifice and the death penalty, uniquely *productive*: not only does he make the necessary argument for the necessity of *working* on myth today with indefatigable conviction in its *logos*. It is also (once again recalling Freud) a "working-through" insofar as the "absolutism of reality" remains to be perpetually reconsidered.

Genesis, for obvious reasons, is the first case to be brought before our deliberation and decision. No historical text has suffered from a more enclosed reading. A glimpse into a few of its most determined episodes

4. Levinas, *Totality and Infinity*, 232.

5. Blumenberg, *Work on Myth*, 12.

will be the first statement on what, here, will be called a *parakletic* hermeneutics. A defense is necessary.

The sanctioned violence of the death penalty forced Girard to rethink the introduction of his entire theory; however urgently it presented itself, for some reason it remained only partly examined. His retraction at the end was made too hastily; he did not give himself sufficient time to pursue the meaning of its implications, again in part because the texts he chose to interpret were incomplete. Understandably, arriving at the end with much more work to do was discouraging. The Oedipus complex and the incest taboo, for him, could not be ignored; but attention to one element led to the neglect of others. Although Girard initially misidentified the origins and *chronology* of sacrifice and the law in its binding relationship, he nevertheless intuited some connection, a relationship he clearly senses but cannot quite identify how it will influence both the religious and judicial spheres. One did not *follow* the other. The end of animal sacrifice did lead to the foundation of a judicial system.

The death penalty interrupted his entire theory, a dilemma he would have to make more explicit. His future references will be sparse.

Girard first believed that the end of sacrifice *led* to "another institution also directly linked to generative violence" (297). One institution could not be an outcome of the other. On the contrary, as the following study will attempt to demonstrate in the texts of antiquity beginning with Genesis and Hesiod's *Theogony*, *animal* sacrifice (that is, the killing of a *victim* in a religious ritual) will be intimately related to another killing that is equally "justified" and made legitimate by the law, with both acts intended to restore some real or imagined imbalance in the soul of an individual or in the life of the entire community. The politico-religious order of the ancient world was founded on two rituals both related to power over life and death and conceived, in the consciousness of the ancients (both Jews and Greeks, to begin with) as mandated by the divine, by the singularity of YHWH or Zeus and the pantheon of the gods. Animals and human beings will both be slaughtered in the context of religion and the law, a double-foundation of limits established in a bind between metaphysics and the order of the world. Girard partly recognized his first "inconclusive" thesis by reading Louis Gernet's *Anthropologie de la Grèce antique* and, more specifically, his comments on the question of the death penalty.[6] Girard writes, "There is no doubt that the death

6. The beginning of the introduction will serve to emphasize the importance of Louis Gernet's work not only for Girard, and on the most important topic for us going

penalty is portrayed here as a direct extension of generative violence" (298). The sacrificial death of an animal and the judicial execution of a human being are not as distinct or as exclusive as they might at first appear; a culture may insist on their separation, so as to more effectively maintain the triadic structure of the divine/human/animal order, but once the texts of antiquity are examined, all of them reveal one consistent relationship. Girard's *unity* is suggestive. Sacrifice and executions have a common source: religion and the law come from above, divine edict moving vertically from the heavens to the earthly spectacles of public sacrifices and executions—with its final, graphic consummation the flow of blood into sacred cups, the earth, or the sewers of temples prior to the feast of commensality.

With these first intimations, a line of inquiry can now be pursued by analyzing some of the most relevant texts of antiquity. The main question is straightforward: can the institution of animal sacrifice be related to the death penalty as two reciprocal acts that are not separated by religion and the law? Do they emerge simultaneously?

The argument, for our purposes, can now be narrowed down to one essential: the repudiation of animal sacrifice and the abolition of the death penalty are interconnected in the world of antiquity and reveal, slowly but inexorably (and, finally, historically) a mutual interdependence. They will move through a series of interconnected texts and events culminating in the amphitheaters of first-century Rome. The Christian martyrs *eaten* by animals in the Roman amphitheaters are a metaphysical culmination. An interrelationship of meanings will have to traced, beginning in the two foundational myths of Genesis and Hesiod's *Theogony*. The Jewish, Greek, Roman, and Christian worlds all reveal, at different moments (in texts and in time) a fundamental commonality. The slaughter of animals

---

forward, but also for the members of the "Paris school," who will often be mentioned in the following study. Two quick references are necessary. In the preface to volume 1 of *Myth and Tragedy in Ancient Greece*, Jean-Pierre Vernant and Pierre-Vidal Naquet open with, "This volume contains seven studies published in France and elsewhere. We have collected them together because they all belong to a research project one which we have been collaborating over the years and that owes its inspiration to the teaching of Louis Gernet" (7). The inspiration is defined more precisely: in the preface to volume 2, they write, "The studies all stem from a common inspiration, namely the teaching of Louis Gernet and his efforts to understand the moment of tragedy, a moment that occurred in between law as it was about to be born and law as it was already constituted" (14).

and human beings is the visceral testimony of an inviolable order, one divine, one worldly.

Girard's dilemma in *Violence and the Sacred* was instructive: while he noticed the relation of sacrificial ritual to other cultural phenomena, he could not continue with an argument he recognized, if then only incompletely. His earlier observation in "Sacrifice" was difficult to maintain: "It is significant that sacrifice has languished in societies with a firmly established judicial system—ancient Greece and Rome, for example" (18). Already, in his introduction, there were indications of a doubt, some intuition of a problem—social, to begin with, on the prevention of violence because of the justice system and punishment. "It is that enigmatic quality that pervades the judicial system when that system replaces violence" (23). "Enigmatic" is timid. The judicial system does not replace violence; it perpetuates violence and killing in its use of the death penalty, betraying itself all the more graphically when it executes, for example, with the delusional humanness of lethal injection, as if the death penalty could be altered by *manners*. At first, Girard cannot quite come to the realization that the justice system does not at all "replace" violence (and certainly does not prevent it) but, in fact, perpetuates it with other means, as a self-proclaimed rational institution that establishes itself as the arbiter of a non-private justice—that is, *vengeance*. In his introduction, he finally expressed the one insight that would return to him at the end of *Violence and the Sacred* and with implications he did not, unfortunately, pursue at the time. "While acknowledging the differences, both functional and mythical, between vengeance, sacrifice, and legal punishment, it is important to recognize their fundamental identity" (25). With this one affirmation, Girard opens a line of inquiry consistent with his theory of sacrificial violence and the scapegoat mechanism: slaughtering animals in a religious context and executing individuals in a judicial context were fundamentally interrelated. They were inseparable because they served to rationalize the finite order of the world, theology and politics complicit in securing their place as absolute overseers.

Was there a way to hermeneutically trace the workings of two institutions from out of ancient texts? Could they be identified, over and over again, in Genesis, Greek myth, tragedy, and philosophy, as well as in the gospels and in the history of the Christian martyrs in Rome?

Antiquated observations on animal sacrifice have been repeated and rationalized. Only a few individuals (Girard, among them, with Walter Burkert and the scholars from the "Paris school" forming a neglected scholarly conviction) able to mount a sustained critique and provide an alternative to judgments that, both traditionally and very recently, have become all too complacent. When Hubert and Mauss, for example, write that "sacrifice is a religious act which, through the consecration of a victim, modifies the moral condition of the person who accomplishes it,"[7] they were unable to make the connection to the death penalty, a "moral condition" intended as the modification and improvement of the social order, as if death was somehow going to restore moral equilibrium and improve the soul of a citizen. More to the point, the "moral condition" was, presumably, made better, and without considering how the violent slaughter of an animal, and all the associated beliefs of such "piety," had unanticipated results. Their observations could be infinitely repeated, both by historians of religion and, in particular, interpreters of torah law who must ignore the writings of the prophets and, instead, reaffirm the priestly writings of Leviticus. Although this is not the place to initiate a dialogue between prophets and priests in Judaism or, more relevant for the first century, the disagreements between Pharisees and Sadducees, Jacob Milgrom writes, "Behind the specific laws of sacrifice is a profound design for creating a sense of spiritual connectedness."[8] More generally and without referencing the priestly consciousness of Leviticus, George Hyman adds, "The act of sacrificial killing affirms and enhances life."[9] Such observations are infinitely repeated without any doubts, much less considering the history of midrashic disputation or the well-known rabbinical minds of Hillel or Yohanan ben Zakkai and *their* interpretation of the torah.[10]

"I desire loving kindness, not sacrifice" (Hos 6:6).

The Hebrew *olah*, like the Greek *thysia*, may refer to the ascension of smoke; the euphemism cannot effectively conceal the reality of the sacrificial process. And when, for some, sacrifice is converted into the Latin *sacer facere* (to "make sacred") the skeptical reader can only turn to all the relevant texts in antiquity to raise extreme doubts about how sacrificial slaughter "points to humanity's renewal: to 'make sacred' and to participate in the very source of life."[11] Commentators, one after

7. Hubert and Mauss, *Sacrifice*, 13.

8. Milgrom, *Leviticus*, 17.

9. Hyman, *Power of Sacrifice*, xvi. Calling sacrifice "an act of paradoxical negation" is philosophically unsatisfactory.

10. As demonstrated by Jacob Neusner in *From Politics to Piety*.

11. Sedley, "Sacrifice, Transcendence, and 'Making Sacred,'" 268.

another, adopt a language of evasion and dissimulation: "To sacrifice is not to kill, but to abandon and to give."[12] Jean-Pierre Vernant has a response: "The distance between the candid nakedness of the practice and the fallacious masquerade of discourse is a measure of that part of ideology governing social consciousness."[13] As for the traditional belief, since Hubert and Mauss, that a relationship is established between the sacred and the profane through the mediation of a victim—an animal that is sacrificed—what no one is able to specify is how the *phenomenological* transformation of the participation in sacrificial rituals actually occurs. Neither the Hebrew *teshuvah* nor the Greek *metanoia* can be relied upon. A "return to God" or a "change of mind" are unlikely by being a spectator to animal slaughter, even if sacrificial priests are invested with a sacred authority. Onlookers who were guardedly pious regarded priests as bureaucrats. The prayer to God in the wisdom of Psalm 40:6 is one of many examples: "Burnt offering and sin offering you have not required." Atonement, redemption, reconciliation: all the categories of sacrifice are indemonstrable and are achieved only through the illusion of an act, as many prophets repeatedly say and write. Equally significant, when the act of violence and killing turns a sacrificial animal into an object and, finally, into "an inanimate *thing*"[14] (that is, *meat* to be consumed) the initial motive related to psyche or spirit is, at the very least, suspended if not completely nullified. Not one defender of sacrifice has been able to present an argument for how, exactly, the slaughter of animal can affirm piety or the holy.

To counter Hubert and Mauss, one statement will be enough as a start. Christian-Nils Robert concludes the introduction to *L'impératif Sacrificiel* with: "La justice criminelle est sacrificielle ou n'est pas."[15] Justice is nothing other than sacrificial. To complement the opening with a sense of the argument to come: criminal justice shows itself to be at its most sacrificial when it executes human beings, as some of the most relevant texts of antiquity show, and beginning with the series of events in Genesis 1–9, as well as Hesiod's two poems and, in particular, his *Theogony*. The thesis now has to be elaborated in several interconnected texts of antiquity; if

12. Bataille, *Theory of Religion*, 48–49.

13. Vernant, *Mortals and* Immortals, 294.

14. Lincoln, "Violence," 199. Although Lincoln's argument, as it pertains to the conversion of subjects into "depersonalized objects," is related to human beings, it seems to me wholly applicable to animals as sentient beings.

15. Robert, *L'impératif Sacrificiel*, 9.

any *unity* is to be realized in the religious and judicial realms, it can only be done by tracing the details of specific episodes—many, parenthetically, that continue to be supported by orthodox interpretations that have been instituted in *both* ecclesial institutions and academic disciplines.

The university and the church have, it seems, renewed an ancient alliance precisely on the question of sacrifice, which today is no longer surprising since departments within the humanities have given themselves unprecedented moral authority. The pretensions of the secular age can best be witnessed in the initiatives of a growing ethicism.

Our first two cases, Genesis and the *Theogony*, will be exemplary. For the moment, a few more words to those who remain polemical adversaries; whether they would attempt to argue for the defense of the death penalty at the same time as their *apologia* for animal sacrifice is unknown. Some, no doubt, support the logic of retributive justice.

Once again, and this time without consigning them to a long footnote as in my previous introduction in *Soteriology*, there have recently been apologists for the ritual of sacrifice most especially among historians of religion. Reading them, and most especially the contributors to two collections of essays already mentioned in my preface, have allowed me to consider their viewpoints and to more vigorously argue for my own position. In opposition to our historical apologists, I align myself with René Girard as a critic of the violence of sacrificial cultures, as well as the work of Walter Burkert and three representatives of the "Paris school," Jean-Pierre Vernant, Marcel Detienne, and Pierre-Vidal Naquet. In their studies as a whole, the condemnation of animal sacrifice was unequivocal if grounded in different arguments. A brief reminder is in order. Attention will have to be given to the critics of animal sacrifice and how each of them, despite differences, is nevertheless complementary; they develop respective theories whose relevance can be compared. This is neither the unification of a "grand theory" nor a facile omission of their differences. All of them are defined as *moralists*, and with a term Ivan Strenski, for one, finds objectionable. He accuses Girard, for example, for "his deeply felt moral conviction roundly and loudly to condemn sacrificial victimization."[16]

Morality is not the main issue; the problem is metaphysical.

Sacrifices perpetuate the archaic origins of civilization and preserve it as a remnant. To hold sacrifice and the death penalty up to scrutiny

16. See, e.g., Strenski's *Theology and the First Theory of Sacrifice*, 4.

is also a reminder of how we continue to perpetuate an order of being and *defer* another version of modernity. Are we really *modern*? Has the saeculum started to show its many disguises and, with them, a host of self-deceptions?

Although the *universal* abolition of the death penalty remains an aspiration for the future, the following study restricts itself to the texts of antiquity that, for the most part, are always *indirect*, allusive, each of them individually and interculturally requiring a consistent hermeneutic responsibility of *paraklesis*. In my case, the advocacy will concentrate on two issues: on the one hand, defending the *characters* of entire traditions who have been used (to be made *examples of*) and submitted to a moral imperative and an orthodox doctrine established in antiquity and perpetuated, with full cooperation, from both ecclesiastical authorities and academic consensus. Since the *parakletic* hermeneutics to come are intended as advocacy, defense, and sometimes plea (for all the conception of the sages: mercy, forgiveness, reconciliation, and *grace*) it is necessary to once again turn briefly, this time in more than a long footnote, to the historians of religion who have argued for their own *apologia*. They have defended, judicially (if not judiciously) the practice of animal sacrifice. The disavowal has been, to say the least, a surprise. The original polemic, begun in *Soteriology*, stands. Here is one example: a few others will be referred to here and there throughout. Stanley Stowers makes the attempt to challenge "conceptions of sacrifice that define it as a kind of killing, destruction, and violence."[17] The reader can evaluate the sentence and closely read "*a kind* of killing." My original response was simple: slitting the throat of an animal or severing its vertebrae with an axe in a religious ritual is not a "conception." As for those who want to *equate* the offering of "fruit" such as grain with a slaughtered animal, rethinking the distinction might be in order. To do so one has to continue to ignore Cain's consciousness.

Killing an animal and taking honey from bees to offer to the gods is not the same.

The inability to recognize *this* difference is a problem of intellectual honesty.

Nevertheless, Daniel Ullucci has no qualms about pointing out "the assumption that blood sacrifice was categorically different than other

17. Stowers, "Religion of Plant and Animal Offerings," 35–56.

types of offerings."[18] Assumption? Instead of responding, Cain will be given a few words on the matter, as long as we first acknowledge that Abel (so righteous, so innocent, such a victim) was *first* a sacrificial killer. Whether Kathryn McClymond would say, "Don't cry over spilled blood,"[19] in this biblical case of one brother killing another is unknown. An animal has always been considered expendable. The first subject of homicide is, presumably, different.

Prior to setting out my own textual interpretations, a few brief references to the works (considered together) of the three aforementioned theorists that preceded will set us on firm ground. Girard, Burkert, and the "Paris school" were unanimous in their research, findings, and interpretation. There is simply no denying the violence of sacrificial ritual; surely the graphics of temple slaughterhouses and the functions of priests and butchers, cooks, and janitors can be imagined.

My previous writing was explicit. The point to make is not so much with "the pathology of the ritual" (though, that too can be partly examined, for its *thanatography*), but how animal sacrifice in particular has had precise and often repeated consequences. Wollheim argues that the rituals that involve death are acts that "invariably belong to the pathology of the ritual."[20] Pathological it may be; but the psychological evaluation has to be pursued beyond its morality. The present cannot be satisfied with the analysis of the "savage," the "primitive," and the archaic as conditions of elementary being. My concerns are not, strictly speaking, moral—however one might object to violence and killing as institutional imperatives. Before one can evaluate the moral condemnation of the death penalty toward its abolition, for example, by affirming the dignity of the human being, how the law is sustained by *metaphysical principles* is ultimately the issue. Metaphysical principles are foundational for both animal sacrifice and the death penalty.

All attempts to ignore the violence of the ritual are intellectual *choices*; they can, of course, be made by historians of religion who, perhaps, are compelled to overlook the archaic practices of past societies. Anthropological relativism is a current "value." Choices, or the misguided values of the present, do not alter history or what Walter Burkert calls the "hard facts." "Animal sacrifice, at least the form most practiced

18. Ullucci, "Sacrifice in the Ancient Mediterranean," 393.

19. McClymond, "Don't Cry Over Spilled Blood."

20. Wollheim, *The Sheep and the Ceremony*, 27.

in ancient Greece, Israel, and many other contexts, is a scandal, because it makes killing animals and eating them a sacred affair, a religious act, or even *the* religious act."[21] For the first time, and following our initial reference to Freud, the *eating* of sacrificial animals is now mentioned; the connection has to be repeated. Burkert adds a political characteristic that will also be confirmed by Marcel Detienne. "Hierarchy is instituted and demonstrated in the distribution of meat."[22] This alimentary sharing and its political significance will, at a specific historical moment discussed later, will be completely transformed. The *transubstantiation* will have far-reaching consequences.

Killing and eating: the two are inseparable and will figure as motifs in virtually all of our readings and in societies Burkert defines as *opfergemeinschaft*. René Girard opens *Violence and the Sacred* with: "Sacrifice is an act of violence inflicted on a surrogate victim" (5). Two of the most well-known members of the "Paris school" each emphasize an aspect of sacrifice. First, Jean-Pierre Vernant: "Le meurtre de la victime constituent le centre autour duquel gravite toute la cérémonie."[23] As someone who has interpreted sacrificial ritual in the context of violence, politics, and commensality, Marcel Detienne writes that "political power cannot be exercised without sacrificial practice."[24] He adds that "relations with divine powers through the highly ritualized killing of animal victims, whose flesh was consumed collectively according to precise strictures" (3), marks the successive stages of the ritual. Animal sacrifice and the death penalty is the relation to be pursued in the following study. Whether abstention from meat-eating is at the same time a repudiation of the death penalty will remain to be shown as a possibility; some examples from antiquity suggest such a reality. To begin with, Detienne adds one more important element in the practice of animal sacrifice. Eating meat was a religious tradition that perpetuated the status quo—the reason why, in some Greek philosophers and Jewish prophets, the practice was rejected. On the Orphics, Detienne writes,

> Orphism is a movement of religious protest that defines itself by an attitude of refusal, refusal of the whole politicoreligious system organized around the Olympian gods and the distance

21. Burkert, "Discussion," 177.
22. Burkert, "Sacrificial Violence," 439.
23. Vernant, "Théorie générale du sacrifice," 4.
24. Detienne, "Culinary Practices and the Spirit," 3.

> that separates them from men . . . to change one's diet is to throw into doubt the relationship between the gods, men, and beasts upon which the whole politicoreligous system of the city rests.[25]

It cannot escape our attention that, as a consequence of Socrates's teaching and his recollection of more ancient beliefs and practices (to be interpreted in more detail in a chapter to come) Plato provides an original comment on Orphism.

> There was a time when we didn't even dare eat beef, and the sacrifices offered to the gods were not animals, but cakes and meal soaked in honey and other "pure" offerings like that. People kept off meat on the grounds that it was an act of impiety to eat it, or to pollute the altars of the gods with blood. So at that time men lived a sort of "Orphic" life, keeping exclusively to inanimate food and abstaining from eating the flesh of animals.[26]

Politics and religion have, as their foundation, two sources of authority and legitimacy: the traditions of the past insofar as they guarantee and perpetuate the order of the present. Animal sacrifice and the death penalty are the twin pillars of ancient societies. It remains to be shown how the two themes intersect in the texts of antiquity. Before turning to our ancient writings, one speculative idea has to be mentioned, most especially because of the Orphic aversion to sacrifice and eating meat. "Vegetarianism is not necessarily a statement about animals (it could be more than a footnote on this), but it is always a statement about identity and difference, which implies that vegetarianism comments on the relationship to other people."[27] Could Gilhus's idea of a "sacred diet code" lead from vegetarianism to its interconnection, in the ancient world, to the aversion to animal sacrifice and the death penalty?

One factor believed to be a tangential feature of sacrifice ("commensality") will become crucial. All the references to meat-eating, whether it is Burkert's guilty hunter to the "Paris school" and the social roles in the distribution of meat, other preoccupations will arise in such different events as the "dispute" at Mekone in the *Theogony* to the creation of the Eucharist at the Last Supper. Others have had similar insights, if only in passing. Although Giorgio Agamben's interest in the status of the *homo sacer* remains outside our study, one comment does point to (if

25. Detienne, *Dionysos Slain*, 70.

26. Plato, *The Laws*, 219–20.

27. Gilhus, "Ritual Meals and Polemics in Antiquity," 209.

like others, incompletely) the conjunction of executions and sacrifice. Referring to an "archaic phase," he writes, "Religious law was not yet distinguished from penal law and the death sentence appeared as a sacrifice to the gods."[28] The mythic, as we will see, figures repeatedly in Plato's writings as he continues to mount a defense of Socrates and to argue against the death penalty by showing (in the imagination of the past he outlines, for example, in *Protagoras*) when it was created and how it was made legitimate.

In *Homo Necans*, Walter Burkert makes a similar connection to Girard (both works were published, incidentally, in the same year, 1972) but, like him, had other main concerns that led him in different if not entirely unrelated connections; sacrifice and the law were not far from his thoughts. As he sets out his main argument in the preface to the English edition, he seeks "to derive sacrifice from hunting and religion from sacrificial ritual" (xiv) and to explain its affective origin in the sense of guilt and debt—emotions not unrelated to the experience of Adam and Eve, as we shall see. Although this may have been his opening and sustained argument, with innumerable examples, there are other indications of an interest he chose not to follow; to do would have considerably added to the main thesis. Consistent with Girard's position on the violence involved in sacrificial ritual, he too makes the same necessary observation.

> The worshipper experiences the god most powerfully not just in pious conduct or in prayer, song, and dance, but in the deadly blow of the axe, the gush of the blood, and the burning of thigh-pieces. The realm of the gods is sacred, but the "sacred" act done at the "sacred" place by the "consecrating" actor consists in slaughtering sacrificial animals, ιερευειν τα ιερεια. It was no different in Israel up to the destruction of the temple. (2)

Burkert has not relented from this one affirmation. Sacrifice cannot be separated from violence and killing; to do so is to deny a historical reality and, worse still, to perpetuate a modern psychological disposition that allows us to continue to rationalize how, today, we not only continue to execute, but also to foster a sacrificial ethos that, in the end, makes humans and animals expendable. As he adds to his first theory, he provides additional reasons for the necessity of sacrifice within a given social order, at least as conceived in antiquity. "Killing justifies and affirms life; it makes us conscious of the new order and brings it to power" (40). The

28. Agamben, *Homo* Sacer, 72–73.

ambiguity of the "new order" should not be strictly understood in relation to a specifically religious one, between, for example, the divine and the human world. Equally if not more important is the continued perpetuity of the social order and most especially its authoritative representatives; what is "brought to power" is not only the divine/human order but, equally, a political organization given its legitimacy by the divine. There is no separating sacrificial culture from political organization, with all its characteristics: power, privilege, stratification—with the priests, appointed from family inheritance as in Judaism or simply appointed as bureaucratic functionaries in Greece, taking their rightful place in the hierarchy of the polis.

At a particular juncture in his argument, Burket then makes a remarkable connection (in part, again, similar to Girard) on the extra-religious consequences of sacrifice; the politico-religious ritual cannot be confined to the one act of killing animals. "The death penalty became the strongest expression of governmental power and, as has been shown, the criminal's execution at a public festival corresponded to a sacrificial ritual" (46–47). For the first time, and now adding an important element to Girard, Burkert makes sacrifice and the death penalty related insofar as it represents the spectacle of "governmental power" during a specific festival of commemoration. He emphasizes two important points: the death penalty as a visceral example of the power of authority, presumed to be collective, over the individual; and its enactment as a spectacle during a festival—a date or period that was repeated on a yearly basis and therefore prepared, ahead of time, for its reenactment during a celebration. Despite the connection he draws, however, Burkert could not pursue the binding connection any further. The suggestion has too many implications to ignore. If animal sacrifice represented the binding reciprocity between the world of human beings and the domain of the gods, the death penalty (related in its emergence and actuality) confirmed the authority and legitimacy of the politico-religious institutions of Israel, Greece, and Rome.

What remains, in this introduction, is to turn to the "Paris school" so as to once more present the spectacle of violent death of sacrificial cultures and how it sustained an entire metaphysical order—in heaven and on earth and with the most obvious biological necessity that, in the context of rituals of death, achieved long-lasting meaning. "For this is the act of piety," Burkert adds, "bloodshed, slaughter—and eating." Ingestion and internalization are soon to occupy reflections that have to be expanded well beyond Girard, Burkert, and the "Paris school." The religiopolitical meaning of eating sacrificial meat provides us with only one beginning. Its permutations will be many, beginning with the extraordinary events (of a primordial killing more significant than committing a "sin") in Genesis. The most fundamental of all necessities, eating, will be represented as a crucial problem at the very origins of the human community. Once sacrifice is first divided between a dead animal and agricultural produce, a perpetual conflict will arise in the heart of religious sensibility—one that will be graphic in the case of Cain. He will kill Abel, the sacrificial killer.

As an example of the connection between animal sacrifice and the death penalty, one individual associated with the "Paris school" will be singled out. In a series of writings, beginning with the above-mentioned *Dionysos Slain*, Marcel Detienne emphasizes the alimentary aspect of animal sacrifice, and with one example of the Titans killing, dismembering, *boiling*, and the roasting the infant Dionysos before devouring him. Detienne's ingenious argument is this: to boil the meat prior to roasting it meant they were interrupting the precise order of the ritual and, more consequently for the Orphics who wrote the myth, completely undermining the belief in the progressive movement, the evolution, from a primitive world to one of culture where killing and cooking animals in a religious ritual was rationalized as a *progress to civilization*. Detienne provides several more frames of reference for the consistently thought-out political implications of animal sacrifice. And inasmuch as he refrains from taking up the discussion of animal sacrifice and the death penalty, he does highlight the question of the victim and all the socio-political consequences of the ritual.

In "Culinary Practice and the Spirit of Sacrifice," he writes, "Sacrifice derives its importance from another function, which reinforces the first: the necessary relationship between the exercise of social relatedness on all political levels with the system the Greeks call the city" (3). Detienne further alerts us to one example in particular that shows the "solidarity" between sacrifice, politics, and the law. Girard, Burkert, and Detienne, each in his own way, give us an element that contributes to a developing idea. In one example he writes: the relationship "can be seen in the carceral space temporarily occupied by citizens awaiting the decision of the court or *the execution of a sentence*. All prisoners share the fire and the meals" (3). Eating meat before being executed is the last civilized privilege of the condemned. What Detienne hints at is the crucial point in relation to prisoners who are sentenced to death and will share a *last meal*—one where the access to meat will be a last privilege of the civilized society: a last meal, traditionally steak, followed by dessert, the last reminder of the pleasure of childhood. If the severity of the moment did not lead to an execution, the last meal might appear as a farce; instead, the prisoner condemned to death eating a last piece of meat has all the intimations, for us, of a later argument on the most symbolic last meal ever eaten. Although my concerns are not, like the Paris school, strictly alimentary, Detienne nevertheless demonstrates one more way in which the sacrificial and the political are interrelated as far as society, law, and the most extreme judicial punishment is concerned. He is the only one here to mention the last meal prior to the execution. Other "meals" will later preoccupy us, and with an analysis to follow—one on the meaning of the Last Supper and the creation of the Eucharist, the other in the Roman amphitheater to witness the death of martyrs *damnati ad bestias*.

In the work to follow, one fact will be omnipresent. The relation of animal sacrifice and the death penalty will be consistent, which makes the *meaning* of food and eating (literally and allegorically) a recurring problem. If, as Marcel Hénaff argues, "it is through sacrifice that meat consumption, which is essential for life, enters into the system of relations between humans and gods"[29] (and with the interjection that, as the Greeks knew, meat-eating is *not* essential to life at all), the consumption of dead animals will be made into a problem to reconsider. The "systems of relations" he believes to be obvious are ultimately to be completely transformed (and inverted) by the Roman magistrates who condemned Christians to death. Only in first-century Rome will an entire mythic past become evident as the beginning of a historical transition in antiquity. Before, then, turning to our primary texts and introducing the interrelated acts of animal sacrifice and the death penalty, an initial definition has to be provided in terms of a *parakletic* hermeneutics.

How can a *parakletic* hermeneutics first begin to be defined; and where is its ancient origin? As an anticipation of an interpretation of the pericope in the Gospel of John on the woman accused of adultery and saved from being stoned to death by Jesus, the evangelist mentions the future presence of *the Paraclete* (as the Spirit) as he will intervene at appropriate moments in the future. Without necessarily relying on a *theological* interpretation of *paraklesis*, the responsibility of being called

29. Hénaff, *Price of Truth*, 190, my emphasis.

to defend the accused will not be done for the sake of *consolation*. The Paraclete as *ad-vocatus* is *called* to speak in the name of the defendant. As soon as the advocate acts to defend the accused, the judged, and the condemned and most especially when a sentence of death has been handed down, the advocate argues for not only clemency, within the bounds of the law, but also grace. To console or "comfort" the one who has been at the mercy of the justice system and its laws is too late if the verdict is absolute and soon to be carried out, either in a death sentence or in an absolute judgment in terms of perception—that is, a belief. The more difficult defense pursues a comprehensive return to the texts that, in history, have most responsible for establishing and perpetuating an almost unassailable worldview. In relation to our texts, it begins with the interpretations that have become synonymous with the truth. The reasons are, ultimately, unimportant: if Genesis has been interpreted and its meanings defined once and for all and with the impositions of "original sin," "the fall," and that most peculiar metaphysical creature called Satan who is responsible for deceit and *evil*, a *parakletic* hermeneutics has no other choice but to return to the original acts and attempt to reconstruct the events as they occurred and then provide a different interpretation about the characters who are accused. There are extenuating circumstances and mitigating factors. The presumption of deceit, first of all, is a charge, not a fact. One has the responsibility, the duty, to reexamine the only witness possible, the *logos* as it presents itself. The supposed evidence, as *proof*, has to be reexamined.

The "serpent" and Prometheus have both been wrongly accused of *trickery*.

A *parakletic* hermeneutics has a double and related function: to defend the text from the history of judgments that, in the end, are ancient prejudices. They have been rigid, unchanging, and decidedly orthodox. For reasons that are as difficult to explain as the historians of religion who continue to defend the ancient practice of animal slaughter as a religious ritual (and they are, in effect, *attorneys for the state*) a *parakletic* hermeneutics turns to the texts and their main characters who, above all, can be presented from a completely different perspective. All of them are so prominent in the history of thought that they need no introduction; the knowledge of who they actually are and what they represent is, however, now open to reevaluation.

As for the direct origin of a *parakletic* hermeneutics, it comes from the very same gospel where (I will argue) Jesus accomplishes a "miracle" that has, perhaps, not been noticed before: he saves a woman from being stoned to death (as a punishment for a crime) by a simple argument against the law and—for the first and only time in his life—*twice* writing into the ground, once in the name of death, once in the name of life.

In the Gospel of John, many commentators will noticeably make their own case for the whole incident as a later interpolation and, remarkably, *inauthentic*. To a *parakletic* reader, the insistence on virtually expunging the entire episode from the life of Jesus is astonishing. The commentators do not seem to recognize that to abolish the section of the gospel from the Bible is, at the same time, exclude one of Jesus' most profound teachings. Readers of the Bible are too often tempted to act as *editors*; they can make unbelievable claims about actually expunging a piece of writing. These are remarkable events in the history of hermeneutics. Historians who are textual experts and philologists take enormous liberties, as do theologians. To return to the text, then, and present a case for a *parakletic* hermeneutics is in essence, a *kerygma* here understood in the sense of its "proclamation" and, more precisely in a legal context, a judicial argument for everyone to hear and read. As for a response to theologians and philologist, there is no one better to introduce at this juncture than the writer of *Human, All Too Human* and as one more counsel for the defense of a *parakletic* hermeneutics. Following his advice, it will be important "for once to play the advocate of the worst things: as they have been perhaps only the worst slandered?"[30] It began with slander; history treated some of our characters (Cain) with impunity.

To now return to Girard from the opening of this introduction and complement his earlier uncertainty, one further concept is necessary: *revelations*. Revelations understood from the original *apokalypsis* are the possible perception of a new form of knowledge and a new way of being. To his disciples, Jesus tells them about the Paraclete and defines its essence as "the spirit of truth, whom the world cannot receive, because it neither see him nor knows him" (John 14:16–17). A *parakletic* hermeneutics answers the call not to be a comforter or consoler; rather, a reader is called to be an advocate for the accused and so needs to return to the original scenes of the "crime" and there present a completely different case, a different understanding and interpretation of the events judged with such certainty that they have determined, strangely, in the Bible and in classical studies, both ecclesial orthodoxy and classicist consensus. *A*

30. Nietzsche, *Human, All Too Human*, 3.

parakletic hermeneutics will above all defend the texts from judgments imposed on them and the misunderstandings later manipulated to serve specific means and ends.

This brief introduction, beginning as it does with Girard's *Violence and the Sacred* and with a back-and-forth hesitation all the more clear once one reads the pertinent sections of his work, can now be brought to a close—and for two different reasons: one, to *complement* the work of Girard by highlighting the conclusion of *The Scapegoat* in particular and, two, a further appeal to the Gospel of John on the Paraclete and adopt the idea of the spirit of advocacy for the interpretations of all our texts to come and with special attention to our principal figures. In the last chapter of *The Scapegoat*, Girard concludes his examination of the phenomena of persecution by turning to the Gospel of John. The Gospel of John made a *parakletic* hermeneutics possible. Girard defines the Paraclete this way:

> *Parakleitos*, in Greek is the exact equivalent of advocate or the Latin *ad-vocatus*. The Paraclete is called on behalf of the prisoner, the victim, to speak in his place and in his name, to act in his defense. The Paraclete is the universal advocate, the chief defender of all innocent victims, *the destroyer of every representation of persecution*.[31]

The advocate makes an important appearance in Girard's work as the necessary complement to earlier ideas. If one then takes the liberty to extend this *parakletic* attitude to figures in history, whether mythic or real, invented or historical, in order to defend some of them from a long and virtually uninterrupted history of misinterpretation, the task will be as one who speaks for them since their words have often been misinterpreted. They have been slandered.

In the autobiographical "The Life of the Mind," Girard returned to our problems at hand and not only used a specific form of capital punishment in antiquity relevant for a later interpretation of the Gospel of John, he now (in 2008) makes sacrifice and the death penalty interrelated. The initial ambiguity was not, however, resolved.

> The Tarpeian rock later became a place for capital punishment, where people were forced to jump from a cliff. Stoning (or crushing) and throwing someone from a rock are forms of sacrificial killings which are related to each other. They are forms of capital punishment where

31. Girard, *Scapegoat*, 207.

> everybody participates and nobody is responsible. Nobody touches the victim. It is a form of collective and unanimous capital punishment, and it is a way of uniting the community when you have neither the central power nor judicial system that can prevent mimetic conflicts. There must be a device that makes collective killing possible at a distance, without any polluting contact with the victim. This is really the beginning of the state as an institution.[32]

While my interest is not all concerned with the origins of the state, there is no hesitation in attributing the double-function of animal sacrifice and human executions to a specific kind of social organization consistent with a divine, metaphysical order used to rationalize a social-temporal world. Nietzsche's defense of the slandered is inseparable from his critique of the consequences of a formidable metaphysical reality.

There can be no better text to begin a hermeneutics of *paraklesis* and the sustained argument on the relationship between animal sacrifice and the death penalty than Genesis 1–3 and with the presence of one extraordinary animal who, by speaking and presenting a rational argument consistent with his *ārum* (Jewish wisdom) and *phronesis* (Greek reason in the Septuagint) human beings are called to themselves to initiate a life-world independent of original creation.

32. Girard, *Evolution and Conversion*, 27.

Chapter 1

The Animals in Genesis 1–3

No single interpretation of the Hebrew Bible has been more decisive in establishing an absolute worldview than the unfolding of events in Genesis—from the moment when, after the beginning in ordinary time, the man and the woman are banished from the garden of Eden; no single interpretation has been more influential in defining the essence of a human being and the condition it has imposed on itself, forever, as a consequence of one act of *ingestion* whose meanings have all too readily been defined according to a language that will be decisive for all future understanding of the truth; and no single interpretation has been more responsible for determining the meaning of the entire sequence of complicated events once a four-part relationship is established between God, nature, animals, and human beings.

In the beginning was the *logos*.

God *said*, "Let there be light."

But for reasons related to the fragility of theological speculation, ecclesial orthodoxy, or the inability to extend our hermeneutic obligations, Genesis 1–3 has remained within the limits of either an empirical history or a mythic account of creation whose inner *logos*, as its revelation, has consigned perception to interrelated limits. Despite the intricacies of what the *logos* announces, an enduring metaphysics has been absolute. Alternatives have been discouraged and virtually inconceivable; which makes a *parakletic* hermeneutics all the more necessary for an interpretation motivated only by the possibility of another decision, another *verdict*, and so attempt to release it from its perpetual bind to tradition. While meanings have been determined by the historical necessities of doctrine (for example, on the idea of a "fall" or "original sin," or with the one exclusive, and by no means exhausted, translation of the "serpent"), other possibilities remain to be articulated from out of Genesis itself once the world and reality it represents can appear differently than all assumptions. Without, here, relating Genesis to its vital, dynamic relationship with other writings in antiquity; without drawing upon the historical documents of even more ancient civilizations (for example, the Babylonian *Enûma elish*,[1] "when above," or the *Epic of Gilgamesh* as at least partial antecedents as it concerns certain events like the flood) the world of Genesis is not isolated and closed in on itself.

The limits of Genesis cannot be either historical or textual.

The dynamics of its transference makes it infinite.

For one of our purposes, Genesis 1–3 will be read individually and then compared to an equally meaningful myth in ancient Greece and, in particular, two of Hesiod's poems: the *Theogony* and *Works and Days*, seventh-century compositions on "the genesis of the gods" and on the life of a *farmer* no different that Adam and his son Cain.

Their *myth* and *logos* are inseparable; they are inspired and revealed.

The intersection of meanings between two foundational myths of Western metaphysics is going to be consequential—leading in two different and complementary directions. Each begins with religion and piety as a *problem*.

The problem is singular. It will begin, in Genesis and the *Theogony*, with the death of an animal and the creation of a ritual defined as *sacrifice* and with the language of euphemism nowhere adequate in concealing the nature of divine worship. One translation: *sacer facere*. Religion, in one of its manifestations, will be the attempt to "make sacred," that is, to create the sacred *in the world* by killing, slaughtering, butchering, and eating. Hesiod and Adam, two farmers and both responsible for the earth and its growth no less than for their pastoral relationship to domesticated animals, are not accidentally at the beginning.

The events in Genesis, and their specific chronology, have to be followed as God, the world of nature, animals, and human beings emerge from out of the language of creation—and with a first reminder that the animals in general and one above all in particular (*Nachash*, or other transliterations, *nāhās*, a verb meaning to "observe signs") have been taken for granted, their existence and their *meanings* closed, penned in, by the understandable human preoccupation with its own life and

1. See, in relation, Alexander Heidel's *The Babylonian Genesis: The Story of the Creation*, as well as *The Gilgamesh Epic and Old Testament Parallels*.

future. Already and prior to all impositions of guilt or sin—that is, *moral* attributes sometimes evading the nuance of the human as, essentially, incomplete and self-divided—the tendency is to be self-preoccupied at the expense of a more complete perception. The overwhelming pressures of existence have reduced the limits of human seeing and enclosed it within the assurance of a dogmatic truth, as if to protect it by one absolute definition.

In the meantime, animals have been an afterthought; the omission has been grave and ongoing. Our existence has consigned the animal to a strange periphery: in the wilderness and in the lives of human beings as a pragmatic object and yet, nevertheless, with unavoidable reminders, of a back-and-forth empathy. Adam, for one, creates the category of biology, a *bios* in no way reflective of *life*. Most theological considerations have made the animals nothing more than a *by-product*, not at all essential, simply to be used according to the earliest directives, in life and in death, for work and food.

Eating animals has been the most anthropologically obvious reality in history and one used to rationalize a certain conception of terrestrial existence as irreducibly material.

The *metaphysics* of killing and eating animals remains a problem to be deciphered. Jewish and Greek sacrifice, once read as a relation, begins to reveal other historical institutions.

Ecclesial interpretations have been preserved and handed down with a restricted vocabulary that has made it virtually impossible to rethink their theological impositions no less than its conclusions—for example, both with the neglect of animals as a whole and then with a much-maligned creature whose relation to the *logos* has been entirely forgotten; either that or never acknowledged to begin with. *Nachash*, the animal who speaks, who reasons, has not been acknowledged for its unique singularity. Before *our singular* animal can be understood instead of accused, judged, and condemned, on its own or in relation (to God, first and foremost, and with a characteristic to be compared with others—*ārum*, that is, its wisdom) there will be a necessary return to Genesis with a hermeneutic motivation that is *parakletic*. One has to be an *advocatus* for the figures, animal and human, who have been condemned to serve a purpose for our self-understanding. They have been sacrificed in more ways than one. A *parakletic* hermeneutics will "speak," at once objecting and interjecting, and doing so by turning not a preestablished law but from the *logos* embedded within Genesis itself as the first of other examples to be deciphered in Greek myth, tragedy, and philosophy and, finally, in the gospels.

Without reducing a particular reading to a systematic "method," and most especially in a work devoted to the conjunction of animal sacrifice and the death penalty in antiquity, a *parakletic* hermeneutics will be used insofar as it devotes itself to a defense and *advocacy* (and in the end, a plea) and makes the attempt to confront the law that has proclaimed itself absolute and without so much as the possibility of its amendment or, to take it to its conclusion, its *abolition.* The law will do everything in its power to preserve itself, whatever the cost. A *parakletic* hermeneutics, in the act of interpretation, sets itself another task; or, rather, two different concerns: one, defending the text against traditions of reading that have made its meanings inviolable and supported by constant and almost unassailable judgments; two, and equally as important since several figures in the history of antiquity will have to be recalled, defending the animals, creatures, and human beings who have suffered from the consequences of introducing a completely new concept of being into the world. There will be ongoing appeals and other testimonies. Human preconceptions have become rigid; other perceptions of meaning will be introduced, as supplemental evidence. Words and names, in many ways concealed by translations, will be rethought.

Mentioning *Nachash* early on gives us one indication; there is none more important. So disparaged, so maligned, so much an object of human judgment through the ages, this animal defined as a snake, a serpent, a viper (who *speaks and reasons*, with *Chavah*, the woman who is "the mother of all living") will be defended against an entire history of misunderstanding; malice has been adopted as justifiable, condemnation legitimate. So often, animals, human beings, and other fantastic creatures—i.e., the Titan Prometheus—still remain to be thought in all their complexity and hopefully to free them from human certainty—one that is more an indication of human vulnerability than from *their* existence. Human dread can be so formidable since it would rather judge to protect itself from self-doubt, than reflect and expose itself.

The animal is so often defined from out of our needs. The reality of a world has suffered from the limits of human understanding, whether from an inherent confinement or from a self-induced protection against extending too far beyond what has been decided as irreducible. Limits have been established as protective measures. Anyone who turns to Genesis 1–3 (as a reader) from its announced "in the beginning" all the way to the end and the expulsion from the garden of Eden must be cautious of all preconceptions inherited from dogmatic sources. But if an attempt at reading, understanding, and interpretation is assumed as an obligation and with the imperative of a new understanding, all inherited "prejudgments" are to be, at least, suspended. The language of slander has been too easy to use, defamation of character equally so.

Genesis has been so formidable in its tradition that even a reader as erudite and sensitive to the nuances of meaning as Leo Strauss can read the myth of Genesis and comment on it as no more than a report, a repetition of words from the past: from a priest, catechism, church, one or more commentaries on Genesis. The political philosopher here can only repeat the handed-down assumptions of tradition, and with the whole array of an interconnected language. Strauss inherits a vocabulary; he neither questions nor refuses any of it, as if the whole was self-evident. His reading is already determined; the meanings have been given to him prior to opening the book. Beginning with the man and the woman in the garden, he writes, "Both were naked but, lacking knowledge of good and evil, they were not ashamed. Thus the stage was set for the fall of our first parents. The first move came from the serpent, the most cunning of all the beasts of the field; it seduced the woman into disobedience and then the woman seduced the man."[2] All these enduring presuppositions—from the idea of the "fall," to the "serpent" nowhere present in the garden and misunderstood, to the "deception" or *seduction* perhaps only capable of being understood by someone from Vienna who has suspicions[3] about other meanings—have become so rigid and foundational they have remarkably stood for two millennia and with the only response has been from those who have judged the myth to be untrue, not historical, and therefore unworthy of being considered. Atheists have never taken the time to read; unfortunately, it has been more expedient to dismiss the obligations of interpretation. Their indifference has been complicit in perpetuating an ancient reality. The meanings of myth are, however, more important than any verifiable empirical history. The truths of myth perpetually demand to be rethought for the needs of the present. The truth of myths are events wholly outside the situations of time.

2. Strauss, *Studies in Platonic Political Philosophy*, 155. See chapter 7, "Jerusalem and Athens: Some Preliminary Reflections."

3. The allusion is to the "hermeneutics of suspicion" developed by Paul Ricoeur. See, in particular, his *Freud and Philosophy*.

A *parakletic* hermeneutics, originating in the Gospel of John, must demand more of itself than mere suspicion or criticism; critique has so often been reactive. For an example, and with the first of many prejudices, when someone writes that "evil is both intelligent and personal, symbolized in the serpent, who is a creature hostile to God and malevolent toward humanity,"[4] the impositions on the text are so extensive as to make its *logos* impossible to see. Another commentator tells us that readers "fail to recognize that the serpent's trickery is the ultimately the voice of Satan."[5] The *revelations* of Genesis are concealed beneath dogmatic assertions of the most traditional kind. The problem is more serious than being merely dogmatic. The negativity has had consequences: to impute malevolence and trickery to the events after creation coerces our readings. Vocabulary and reality have become synonymous. The requirements of "faith" and atheism, however, are equal failures; there are alternatives to dogma or nothing. But Genesis has always been much too *infinite* to be too easily apprehended, much too elusive to be grasped by beliefs prior to reading. Evolutionary biology and allegory have nothing to do with each other. Scientism and texts are irreconcilable. In what follows, and with only a first beginning (there will be another, in Hesiod's *Theogony*) the events to be interpreted in the garden of Eden and beyond have consequences different than original sin and fall. Other events, out of the garden, are necessary for a comparison; generations will be divided from each other. Much more compelling than any traditional interpretation is the relationship between God, the animal who speaks and reasons, and the two human beings who can only become themselves after making certain decisions. *One decision*, and it is nothing less than the foundation of religion (or piety, and it requires no faith since the relationship of the man and the woman to God is immediate) remains nothing more than an allusion; only one of their sons will confirm the act. Cain is engendered by more than human parents, and perceives himself, with all his conflicts, to be between God and the animals, who will be crucial to his self-reflection. Cain remains outside the boundaries of understanding unless he is *looked at* and recognized as the first human being who struggles, authentically, within himself and in relation to the order of the world. Everyone has averted their face from Cain. He remains, nevertheless, a mirror. Cain will be defended; he is worthy of our consideration and our

4. Duggan, *Consuming Fire*, 77.

5. Matthews, *Genesis 1—11:26*, 234.

solicitude since he allows us, for the first time, to think for ourselves, which is what Genesis asks.

Karen Armstrong writes, "Christians in the West have seen the story of Adam and Eve as a catastrophic fall from perfect innocence to chronic guilt. They have traditionally equated the serpent with Satan, the fallen angel who became a devil and lured humanity away from God."[6] Any attempt to reconceive the meaning of Genesis has to first of all divest itself of traditional vocabulary—most especially any words or concepts completely foreign to the text itself, i.e., "fallen angel." These are later fantasies from the Christian and Talmudic imagination. The appeals to metaphysics will be many. Angels, or devils, will have no part in what follows on the abolition of animal sacrifice and the death penalty. Etymological inquiries on the *nephilim* of Genesis as "the sons of God," for example, and the possible connection to *naphal* ("fall") brings us no closer to an interpretation without any appeal to metaphysical entities.

Everything outside the world, in fact or thought, has no relevance when reading.

However pertinent these metaphysical creations are to other discussions (angels as messengers, as mediators, for example), they will have no part in the interpretation to come—one that attempts, as much as possible, to remain within Genesis itself and without imposing ecclesial doctrines or Talmudic midrash on its meanings.

> For many centuries now, that adventure has been called the story of the fall of man. But why the "fall"? It is the story of something quite the reverse—the story of a creature rising up in self-assertion against his creator. Call it the rebellion of man, the rise of man, or, better still, the story of man's discovery of himself, but let us not call it a *fall*.[7]

Leaving aside any *heretical* intentions, and underlining its relation to *hairesis* and a "school of thought," one of the motivations in reading Genesis will involve being attentive to what has been proclaimed as doctrinaire and, therefore, already judged to be secure. Conclusions have been drawn; verdicts are in. Nevertheless, all interpretations of "original sin" or "the fall" cannot determine a starting point to reading. Truth will not be an intimidating category despite how the term has suffered from critical disparagement.

6. Armstrong, *In the Beginning*, 21.

7. Hanson, *The Serpent Was Wiser*, 41.

A *parakletic* reading begins fully conscious of traditional interpretations in order to avoid them; the disposition is not, however, the anxiety of influence. The events in Genesis will give us the opportunity to interpret their sense with a completely different emphasis—even if, like others, enjoyment or pleasure is not one of the motivations. One cannot help but notice how certain thinkers have responded to reading the Bible in general and Genesis in particular with *pleasure*. Calling their act of reading biblical hedonism might be excessive, though it is certainly preferable to mortification. Stephen Greenblatt tells us that "this is fiction at its most fictional, a story that revels in the delights of make believe."[8] Reading Genesis was for Hermann Gunkel both a great pleasure and a "source of delight."[9] In *God Without Being*, Jean-Luc Marion writes, "One must admit that theology, of all writing, certainly causes the greatest pleasure. Precisely not the pleasure of the text, but the pleasure—unless it has to do with a joy—of transgressing it."[10] My interests are not so much the "transgression" of the text (itself) as to provide interpretations to what has been historically determined as the truth and reality of Genesis. If "each midrashic *parole* participates in God's canonical *langue* and revitalizes it for new generations,"[11] then the most vital hermeneutics will be *parakletic*, interpreting as an advocate and in defense of the word, in this case relying on our last text (our last reading and chapter, in the Gospel of John and beyond) of *paraklesis* being inseparable from the spirit of truth (John 15:2) that works for the defendant, *pro bono*. Any attempt to provide an alternative to a formidable tradition must simultaneously turn to the writing and the invention of a vocabulary apparently reflecting a certain reality—for example, the "serpent" described with specific characteristics (in Hebrew) that have sometimes been neglected. Before, then, turning to the unfolding drama in the garden of Eden, some attention to the creation of animals will not be without its relevance.

A few initial details are necessary as the animals are created, with one or more distinction that are not to be omitted; as they occur during the creation of the world and owing to their immediacy, they may be missed, which is all the more reason to have a hermeneutic awareness of their place as they first emerge and later (before and after the flood)

8. Greenblatt, *The Rise and Fall of Adam and Eve*, 3.

9. Gunkel, *Legends of Genesis*, 37.

10. Marion, *God Without Being*, 1.

11. Fishbane, *Exegetical Imagination*, 18.

they are given their being in creation. When God first creates swarms of creatures, birds, and all the living beings of the sea, he "blessed them" (Gen 1:22). However one interprets *barak*, and in this case it is a first act and therefore original (God makes blessedness from out of himself) the creation of land animals fails to repeat the blessing. Victor Hamilton makes a noticeable comment: "For some unknown reason the land animals are not the direct recipient of a divine blessing as are aquatic creatures."[12] The creation of animals was pronounced "good," but they did not receive a similar blessing. A simple omission? It need hardly be stressed that at this point in Genesis nothing should be, in the slightest way, incidental. There is nothing more intentional than the act of creation. All enigmas are, eventually, illuminated. On the sixth day, Yahweh allowed the natural world to "bring forth living creatures of every kind" (Gen 1:24), a decision soon to develop into long-lasting consequences once the animals, with precedence, were soon followed by the "making" of humanity. Is it conceivable to attribute some kind of reticence on the part of God? Does God act and withhold? An answer will come in due time; for now, one other feature of genetic creation has to be emphasized: once "humankind" is created in the image and likeness of God, they are given "dominion" over all life. The land animals are not blessed and will be subjects of dominion. Decisions made by God during creation are not readily explainable; only time and history will bring motives to perception. Time will tell.

Daniel Berrigan writes that Genesis 1:28, and the command to "subdue" and "dominate," has often been a "vilified text." He calls it, simply, "a scandal."[13] The animals of the air, water, and land are now living in the natural world. As soon as living creation has been prepared, God then deems it suitable for human beings to also be created. They take their place in the order of the world. God, with an enigmatic *us* and *our*, creates human beings; they are living beings, "in our image, according to our likeness" (Gen 1:26). The plural "our" remains enigmatic; speculations may be acceptable, in principle, but references to either angels or the nature of the Trinity does not exhaust the possibilities for us.

Our image and likeness: are human beings going to be *like* God and animals both?

12. Hamilton, *Book of Genesis*, 132.

13. Berrigan, *Genesis*.

Writing the word once is not enough to define the image, the *tselem*; it must be repeated, for stress and emphasis. "So God created humankind in his own image, in the image of God he created them; male and female he created them" (Gen 1:27). Between the repeated statements, one aspect of creation immediately makes the reader halt; the moment is jarring as it is inexplicable. All motivations attributed to God cannot hope to divulge reasons and motives; none are immediately forthcoming. Every moment, every sequence, every related movement can only be understood at a later time, when the possibility of a comprehensive evaluation becomes possible. At once, humanity has been created as distinct and, in some ways (though essentially unknown as to its meaning) in relation to God who, twice, refers to its being as "our," in the plural. The image and likeness, what can be seen and also similar, is a reflection; whether God and humanity come face to face, at this juncture, cannot be certain. Without a doubt, however, he makes another decision; for when he "let them have dominion" (Gen 1:26) over all the animals of the world, a certain foresight becomes, to say the least, questionable. God *creates* dominion.

Or, to pause, God is the one simultaneously created with a certain image and likeness.

The language is neither of care nor husbandry; the animals are not to be cherished and appreciated as integral to the natural world. Once dominion has a reality, it will endure; domination will not be contained, forever being a mark on the world. Genesis may mention "all the wild animals of the earth" (Gen 1:26), but the dominion eventually unleashed in the world will make any idea of "wild" in an animal incomparable to human beings. Everyone who comes across the startling word must take it into account. Far from exposing the creative intentions of God, it may more accurately reflect an already existing world.

Dominion (*rādă*) has multiple social meanings—as in a king and subject, with associations of inferiority, as one who is subjected. The meaning cannot be determined from any subsequent act in Genesis 3. The word is retrospective; the word is embedded in human history. As so much else in Genesis, pronouncements are not seen, so there is never an episode where the "dominion" becomes evident—except in an unprecedented event, the one which shows God's double-nature, simultaneously creative and destructive, at least from all appearances.

The unprecedented act of killing an animal will be far-reaching. The consequences will be logical. One for one.

The dominion is announced now so as to make a future event understandable, explainable. Whether one can understand its *justification* remains to be seen; the reader will have to decide. And if we can categorically notice a difference between the blessed creatures of the water and the animals of the earth (to be dominated) cannot, for the time being, be considered; the problem will remain suspended and analyzed later and at several different junctures. The commentary here can only be partial and guided by only one concern as it leads us toward one transformative event—a divine act with long-lasting consequences for human beings and animals and their *cultural* relationship.

So far, animals have been given the prominence due to them; they have too often been neglected as merely secondary creations and without the decisive acts soon to be essential in the lives of human beings. God does not only create matter and life; he has already introduced nothing less than a certain spirit in the world, the *rûah* that first hovered over the water but will soon be defined much more precisely as the condition of being a "living soul." Before a "soul" can become a part of a created being, a distinction cannot be overlooked. *Blessing* and *dominion* are not easily reconciled; one appears to be a gift, the other an imposition—one is both given and withheld by God, and the other sounds at first like the bestowing of an ability or a command, for one over another. However one translates "dominion," any appeals to *husbandry*, taking care of, or having the responsibility for (all of these possibilities are suggested) do not easily announce itself as a reality in the text itself. All the theological good will in the world cannot invent a condition that is, simply, not there. Rather than the reluctance to *understand* Genesis as it presents itself to the reader, with all the problems of its startling reality, theology has to avert itself from certain consequences that become ever more perplexing as the unfolding of the text leads to its finality. Given the events to come, it is difficult to imagine the reality of God being without discernment—that is, for the future; or, at least, for a sense of what the creatures of his world might be led to by their own inclinations.

At one of the most interesting of transitions in Genesis, immediately after the day of rest, we turn to the event when God first made a human being. Yahweh-Elohim (God now with two names, two references) reached down and "formed man (*adām*) from the dust of the ground" (Gen 2:7), giving him substance and shape. The man was physically made as an object from the matter of the ground. At first, he was a being, in the form of a thing. He was not complete until God "breathed into his nostrils the breath of life; and the man became a living being" (Gen 2:7). The man, not yet named though taken from the ground (*adāmāh*), from the created earth, has two origins.

Once the man is placed in a garden in Eden, there are trees that are beautiful as well as good for food; there are, also, two unique trees, of life and of the knowledge of good and evil. The life of the man will be given purpose, fulfillment, as well as responsibilities and one (one, and no other) commandment, with his future open-ended. Let us note that between God and the world, and with no plants or herbs in the field (and no rainfall to initiate a cycle of life) there is nothing that can be generated. And to introduce the all-important factor of *work*, at this point there was "no one to till the ground" (Gen 2:5). God therefore turns to the soil, the ground of future agriculture as well as the foundations of a city, and creates a human being.

Theodore Hiebert brings our attention to the use and meaning of the Hebrew *nepeš hayyâ* ("animate creature") in Genesis 2:7 and 2:19 and to a mistranslation: "In the King James Version, *nepeš hayyâ* was rendered 'living creature' when used of the animals (2.19), but 'living soul' when used of the human being."[14] The translation imposed a difference not found in the text. This may as well be the introduction to a recurring problem in the translation(s) of the Hebrew Bible and the impositions that distort the meanings of Genesis. If the importance of animals are once again to be stressed as essential in Genesis as well as, more particularly, in the coming to be of the human world, a different reading and interpretation of the first book of the Hebrew Bible will be a prime motivation. Dogma and doctrine cannot have a final word; all interpretations read *into the text* must come under the closest scrutiny. Before dismantling traditional meanings (which is not the only purpose here) what those meanings have concealed becomes the issue. A hermeneutics of suspicion may also be insufficient. A more insistent reading is possible and called for. To expose a dissimulation is not enough. A return has to be initiated. Genesis infinitely asks us to return to the beginning in order to generate, with the writing, what has remained outstanding.

In the NRSV, there is a similar and untenable distinction: the man is described as "a living being" and the animals are described as a "living creature." The Hebrew contains no such difference. Biology is *not a*

14. Hiebert, *Yawhist's Landscape*, 63.

complete category of being. *Bios* cannot hope to be equated with *rûah*. All the matter of the world, for all its solidity, has never been complete.

The living being of *bios* is incomplete without spirit.

If the importance of animals is going to be stressed as essential in Genesis and, more particularly, in the unfolding of the human world (humanity cannot emerge, consciously, without both its relationship to God *and* animals), then all attempts to denigrate animals as a second-order creation have to be met with the most strenuous objections. A theological reading of Genesis has concentrated too one-dimensionally on the God-human relationship and has failed to introduce into the whole of the story of creation the essential participation of the animal—an omission here to be rectified by stressing a reality that has been almost completely disavowed. Has there been a theological reflex? At the same time as God ultimately banished the two human beings from the garden, translators, readers, and those who identify with their own "dominion" also banish animals to the periphery of the garden. In the meantime, as the animals already occupy a place in creation for themselves, God places the man in the middle of the garden and gives him initial instructions. He has the responsibility to "till" and "keep" all the tress and vegetation in the garden. He has all the fruit of every tree at his disposal, except he cannot eat from the tree of knowledge of good and evil—a commandment he seems to have accepted even if the reader has no choice but wonder about the promise or threat by God that if the man eats from the tree, "for in the day that you eat of it you shall die" (Gen 2:17). Surely it is not obtuse to ask: How did the man learn about death? What does die man? Or, as a related question: Is his familiarity with language already so sophisticated that he knows the difference between the literal and the allegorical meaning of words? The question is not impertinent for the modern reader. Death will not be a problem among others; more importantly, mortality and finitude are not at all equal concepts; one is about the inevitability of physical death, the other is a perpetual limits self-imposed on the human.

For now, *eating* is nothing more than a biological necessity; food nourishes. An entire process of eating and digestion, too often taken for granted as merely physical, soon becomes much more important than has previously been the case. Eating and *taste* are inseparable. As soon as God said the word "good," the ethical and the aesthetic were created simultaneously.

The ethical and the aesthetic, however, have metaphysical foundations.

The idea of *internalization* will ultimately be distinguished from *eating*.

The events in the garden of Eden are soon to move to the eating of dead animals in the context of religious worship. Sacrifice is going to be created. Killing and worship is one of the first acts of human invention.

Immediately after the man has settled into the garden, given his place and responsibilities (and time has elapsed since then, with his life unfolding in a way that can only be imagined) the next series of events are, as always, surprising, unexpected, and of course without precedence. First of all, Genesis brings our attention to the perception of God. There is simply no way to avoid the idea of God (his reality, in the text) without considering him as a being, a *character*, even if the word or concept itself—from drama, first of all—cannot be adequate to his being. Our approximations are always within the realm of the imaginary and the linguistic. The access, as is perfectly understandable, can only be through language, which is one reason rabbinical consciousness can so concentrate all its focus on the open-ended figure of the letter *Bet* (ב), the beginning of God's very first utterance.

But as soon as God, for the very first time, believes some aspect of creation is "not good," he has to act to somehow alter the situation. God is involved with his creation. He perceives, acts, intervenes. Yahweh is a God of reciprocity. God has feelings, of empathy and compassion; and when he notices that "it is not good that the man should be alone: I will make him a helper as his partner" (Gen 2:18), God believes, or knows with certainty, that the man has been "alone," in fact, but also lonely, as an emotional experience. A reader might also be able to imagine the man as completely destitute, forlorn and anguished to such a degree that God was at first overwhelmed by the emotional state of his creation—so that man and God are fully reciprocal beings who, in some yet uncertain sense, know each other (they are aware of each other's existence) but the man seems completely at a loss to know what his *purpose* is.

He cannot seem to understand the nature of his *calling*. Being is not enough.

All theological affirmations, however, about their relationship, on their closeness, are simply unfounded. One often reads about their feelings, of exchange, that are nowhere present in the text and are seemingly invented and attributed to each of them without really knowing *anything*. Surely a reader can admit that he knows nothing about the man at this point. There are no indications in the text about him at all until God feels (perhaps empathically, by looking at the man, looking at his face or body) that he is in fact alone and as a condition much more visceral than physical. Only a being with a living soul can be lonely.

Genesis can be read for many different reasons: if my concern is above all with the role of animals in this creation story and the role they will play within the Bible as a whole, from Genesis to the gospels, a similar interest can be in the character of God as created from out of the words presented to the reader. Instead of accepting the provocative theological idea of revelation (the writing of Genesis was inspired by God, even dictated) a purely human response understands theology, *theo logos*, according to an initial definition by Plato who believes *peri theologias*[15] was, strictly speaking, what can be said or written about the divine from out of human perception. This does not, however, simply find an incommensurable position between reason and revelation; rather, hermeneutics has no other choice but to place itself between reason and revelations and mediate between the two, and without contradiction. They do not cancel each other out. Although, at this juncture, certain considerations require too much to pursue, Jean-Luc Marion asks, "Could not the requirements of theology permit phenomenology to transgress its proper limits, in order to finally attain the free possibility at which it has pretended to aim since its origin?"[16] In a dialogue, one can also ask a question: What if phenomenology would force theology to transgress *its* proper limits insofar as it would allow it to see more than its previous history? A *parakletic* hermeneutics does not for a moment forget the defense of the accused as well as the reason of the prosecution. One point can be stressed: revelations have always and only been given to perceive to human beings, as in the paradigmatic experience on Sinai. The question can only be raised at precisely this time, when the solitude of the man prompts God to create animals for him, as a "helper" and "partner" (Gen 2:18). A revelation, as we soon see, is not simply given; a condition of being has to be prepared for its reception.

The next sequence of events can only be described as momentous, though this might be redundant. Before the conception of disobedience or rebellion, there may be an even more serious *failure*. Once that most-complicated of ideas is extended from its moral limits, then "sin" (Heb. *chatta*, Gr. *hamartia*) can be interpreted and understood no longer

15. Plato, *Republic*, 379a.

16. Marion, *The Visible and the Revealed*, 13.

within a thought or act. Rather, the man sins prior to its conventional act; the man sins by being unable to draw, from out of himself, the resources to establish a relationship with the animals who are *before* him. Again, theology has failed to recognize the event as an indication of God and what he anticipates from the man; one cannot, with confidence, sense it was expected. Perhaps it was a hope. When God brings the animals to the man "to see what he would call them" (Gen 2:19), the reader could easily move on and pay not the slightest attention to the scene. Tradition has been definitive. A resolution was provided a long time ago. There is nothing more to think about; and yet as soon as one foregoes all traditional determinations of meaning and again is motivated by a *parakletic* hermeneutics, defending the text against one-dimensional meanings that have become both convenient and complacent, then all of a sudden the text becomes liberated from *history*. Every reader has the open-ended ability to read, interpret, and understand beyond all custom and find, for themselves, incomparable meanings. Hermeneutics has always accepted its responsibility to illuminate the biblical text, from the very first, from the rabbis of the ancient world all the way to Schleiermacher's aphorisms of 1805.[17]

The restrictions of the biblical text are loosened by hermeneutics; the ties are no longer as binding as before. Other meanings become possible and, with them, an entire reinterpretation of a dogmatic reality that has neglected other, equally important elements of the reality—*for us, today*. The pathos cannot be underestimated here. Yahweh-Elohim can look at Adam and recognize a lack. Yahweh-Elohim believes the man needs a "helper," for work, or chores, or simply to be next to; he needs a partner, to share his life with, alleviate the oneness of his solitude. Inverting the chronology of the first version of creation (unless a chronology is simply inappropriate, an imposition for human understanding) Yahweh makes animals. The moment to follow from the act of creating animals raises a disjunction nothing will be able to remedy; again, consequences follow with remarkable poignancy. Gathering, in a first but not a one-time herd, God unifies all the animals and "brought them to the man to see what he would call them" (Gen 2:19). There are no hints of any instruction. If God has any expectations, the man is left completely on his own as he stands before the animals—many, certainly one—who may ultimately be more intelligent, wiser, than him.

17. Schleiermacher, "Aphorisms on Hermeneutics," 57–84.

To see *what* he would call them.

The "what," here, is questionable; it is not as self-evident as has been supposed. All interpretations have faltered on this certainty—of naming. But before interpreting the Hebrew *mi*, the reader is more interested in God than in Adam's task. He has brought the animals to Adam and is curious in the man and whether he has the capacity to be *like* him, as intended. The "likeness" is put to the test. The breath and spirit inhaled by the man should *inspire* him. Inspiration, by virtue of its relation to the spirit, should allow the man to elevate himself and the world around him; the world can be exalted to reflect its spirit. If inspiration is to be creative, then some force within him must be able to become real in the world, as an influence. But for a reason the reader cannot know with any degree of certainty, the inspiration has failed the man; the spirit in him as been ineffectual. The living soul in him still lacks a certain dynamism. The man was *not* supposed to *name* the animals; the meaning of the Hebrew *mi* should not be read as "what" *he would call them*, but "how." David Rosenberg's translation in *The Book of J* reads, "So Yahweh shaped out of the soil all creatures of the field and birds of the air, bringing them to the man to see *how* he would call them."[18] This difference, so ignored in its meaning and interpretation, changes the consequences of the events to come. The "how" refers to God's wonder. *How* will the man *call* the animals? The question is not so much as hinted at by many commentators, as if it was simply irrelevant. The act of naming has been all too obvious, as if the *linguistic* understanding was sufficient. Have we, as readers, fundamentally underestimated the importance of the moment and, more seriously, *God's purpose*, who surely tells us something about himself that seems not to have been discerned. So anxious are readers about the fate of the human being that neither God nor the animals, as a relation, with each other, are considered. God brings the animals he has created to the man to see how he would call them—with the *wayyqra* here more than appropriate.

The call comes long before Moses' experience. The call comes out of the spirit.

The call/name distinction could not be greater. To call upon a unique source here, from his *Republic* of all places, when Cicero analyzes the forms of government and, in particular, the power of one man, he

18. Rosenberg, trans., *The Book of J*, interpreted by Harold Bloom, 62, my emphasis.

defines someone as a "dictator" from the Latin *dico*, "to name."[19] More precisely, the man seems to have no other ability than to become a *zoological* dictator who now doubles the "dominion" with nothing more than categories, thereby reducing the being of the animal to a zoological definition. He has no ability to look at one animal as an individual; all he sees are species, each interchangeable, one exactly *like* the other. Every one of their *kind* are the same. The consequences of the original "dominion" now begins to be experienced in the world; once adopted (so the man can stop thinking) then reality and truth are set in place.

As soon as one denies the animal its individuality and turns it into nothing more than a species, one can easily dispense with developing an individual relationship. Every animal is reduced to a type, nothing more than a biological repetition. Without considering any alternatives, without considering the radical difference between calling and naming, the man "gave names" (Gen 2:20) to all the animals and made their designation, as a species, permanent. The man's *failure* to call the animals—at the very least to form a bond and a relationship—soon has far-reaching consequences, most especially for one of the animals who, rational, wise, and capable of *speaking*, will not forget the man's act as a failure. One is tempted to call the man's omission a sin—as long as the word and concept refer to much more than a *moral* failure.

The man has an *ontological* failure in the expression of his being.

An original sin has been committed by naming without calling.

At the very emergence of a man as himself and what he can aspire to be, there is a kind of ontological destitution much worse than solitude and loneliness. The man is incapable of being fully conscious. Westermann writes, "God is only concerned to see how the man reacts face to face with the animals."[20] And yet so many commentators have interpreted the event and provided all kinds of rationalization (that is, an excuse) for the act of naming. The rationalization is initially made possible by accepting, without any doubt, the original idea of dominion. The assumption is typical. The fact that human beings name the animals "indique à fois la connaissance qu'il possède et l'autorité qu'il excerce."[21] Human beings are knowledgeable and have authority—essentially. Such observations are often repeated. To name "significava per gli antichi avere autoritá sopra

19. Cicero, *De re publica*, 1.63.

20. Westermann, *Genesis 1–11*, 228.

21. Chaine, *Le Livre de La Genèse*, 39.

di uno."[22] The appeal to a natural "authority" over the animals fails to consider the man's inability; far from the knowledge he has of himself and his relationship to the animals, the man simply has no idea what "calling" means—either, first, to call the animals to him to establish a relationship or, much more importantly, "call" in the sense of bringing the animals *to themselves*. "Jahweh has the animals pass before man to receive their names, for to name, in the Bible, expresses superiority."[23] There are two errors in Daniélou's interpretation: one, God does not bring the animals to the man to be named at all—as is obvious by the entire sequence of events, beginning with being alone and in some sense separated from the animals because, also, *separated from himself*. Surely his loneliness was not appeased by his ability to name. As for the second quite overreaching claim, naming does not, "in the Bible," express superiority. If such was the case, then the angel who named Jesus was, by Daniélou's argument, superior to Jesus. "He was called Jesus, the name given by the angel before he was conceived in the womb" (Luke 2:29). One presumes there are no writers, and certainly no readers of the Bible, who could support such an argument. More follow. When, for example, Cassuto writes that "unto every kind of *living being* the man succeeded in giving a name befitting the character and qualities of that kind,"[24] nothing in the text gives us any indication of this supposed ability on the man's part. To impose a sign on a thing is nothing remotely like understanding either its character or qualities. How could the man possibly know the qualities and character of an animal if he hasn't even begun a conversation with them—*listened* to them? Biblical scholars overestimate the man's intelligence while simultaneously ignoring the presence of animals who also, of course, have a relationship with God. On the matter, Genesis says not a thing.

Why has the God/animal relationship been so ignored?

The sequence of events now begin to extend themselves toward the most graphic of conclusions at the end of Genesis 3 and beginning with God's response to the events to come. Only because the man failed to call the animals—to themselves, with and for a purpose beyond *his* limits—does God now proceed with putting the man to sleep and creating the woman from out of his rib.

22. Daquino, *Lettura Cristiana della Genesi*, 35.

23. Daniélou, *In the Beginning*, 40.

24. Cassuto, *Commentary on the Book of Genesis*.

The man's failure to call the animals will be answered when an animal calls the woman.

The man was never aware in the first place; too overwhelmed by being unable to have any sense of his purpose but feeling the anguished loneliness God noticed with empathy, he had no proper consciousness of himself until the appearance of the woman from out of himself and the perception that remained unknown to him. A *parakletic* hermeneutics of Genesis comes to the defense of the text itself and what it signifies; and it has the added task of defending its meaning (in relation to the animals) against all impositions. " Stanley Jaki writes, "The postponing of land animals to the sixth day should then be seen as support of its meaning that man is created in the image of God. As such man has to be *vastly superior* to animals. This is demonstrated by his naming, at God's bidding, the animals as they are shown to him."[25] The appeals are always made to human authority and superiority; and yet once Genesis 1–3 is read in its entirety, we soon are forced to confront all the presuppositions projected unto this text and, most especially, the character of the animals. One of them is perfectly suited to bring the reader (and the story itself) to a different conclusion. The failures of the man are many; readers often mimic him. "In the garden story, the focus was on the failure of the man in his responsibility to exercise dominion on behalf of God."[26] All these evaluations of the event are read in isolation and without considering the events about to unfold and how they are, in essence, interrelated. The named animals are nowhere described; they are neglected and forgotten—that is, until the transition into 3:1 and the appearance of an animal that will utterly transform reality and all future history. The related acts of God and an animal are necessary to initiate the human world.

"Now the serpent (*nachash*) was more crafty (ā*rum*) than any other wild animal that the Lord God had made" (Gen 3:1).

However the Hebrew *ārum* is translated, whether the negative "crafty," the sometimes used "sagacious," or the slightly more neutral "subtle," none give the animal the characteristic of being *wise*. The Septuagint gives us *sophrosyne*. The Vulgate, *callidus*. Equally if not more important is the "name" of this animal—which if related in any way to a

25. Jaki, *Genesis I through the Ages*, 290.

26. Keiser, *Genesis 1–11*, 111.

serpent or a snake or is tied, etymologically, to Chavah, cannot be confined to a state of a slithery reptile of the natural world, all the more to invoke disgust.

Shedding its skin also makes it an object of envy, for its transformative ability.

The name is ambiguous enough, as a living being capable of thought and speech, not to be strictly identified except by turning to *nachash* and the indeterminacy of its meaning, including being a "shining one" (a source of "illumination") as well as being a *diviner*. As an animal that shines, it lights up, makes visible. *Nachash* is a *phenomenon*: the animal illuminates itself as well as a reading of the text. The latter, diviner, is especially significant for a number of reasons: for one, it overlaps and has certain characteristics with another one of our nonhuman creatures to come, the Greek Prometheus, and someone also capable to "seeing" the future, an ability that has less to do with prophetic anticipation or divination than simply being intelligent enough to look ahead to consequences—to understand the experience of time, to see ahead how history may be transformed from out human resources.

There is *nothing metaphysical* about the animal in the garden of Eden that will be, in any way, meaningful for the entire movement toward the conclusion at the end of Genesis and also heading toward the one episode that will consecrate the future for a long time to come. That act of God has not been sufficiently noticed. At this point, a reminder is in order: if the man named the animals, the reader is left in a precarious situation once the "name" of the animal is announced as *nachash*, ambiguous to the extreme since it does not, in Hebrew, merely define a snake or a serpent or a viper, with all their phobic connotations, but more importantly a characteristic that will be decisive for the events to soon be crucial.

The relationship to the figure of Prometheus in Greek myth, tragedy, and philosophy (to be interpreted at the appropriate time) should now be emphasized with one specific feature. Classicists are virtually unanimous in their evaluation of Prometheus, and with a precise and recurring description that, here and throughout, will be resisted. William Propp believes "the serpent is thus in some respects the best biblical analogue to the Trickster archetype."[27] A reminder will be in order at a later time: nonhuman creatures in the myths of antiquity have been negatively defined without so much as considering their role in the lives of human

27. Propp, "Eden Sketches," 195.

beings and, most especially for our overall argument, how they can figure so prominently in both the emergence of religion and the law. As soon as we call the "serpent" or Prometheus in any way *deceptive* or a "trickster," and responsible for someone else's temptation, the interpretation is thereby closed. One can only then come to one conclusion. An alternative does not first of all judge the animal for its speech or argument; it simply follows how this extraordinary animal, of course created by God and free of all the later mythologies of a "fallen angel," and attempts to understand its motives. Perhaps the theological imagination can be considered insofar as the animal is self-willed, capable of persuading; but among all the consequences, some facts are forgotten and disavowed. The animal, as wise and rational, can think; moreover, it can speak and at least as eloquently as the human beings. The man never so much as says a single thing until much later. Although he cannot be mute, he does seem like an *in-fans*, someone who appears infantile if for no other reason that he has no real access to language except in a vocabulary of nouns.

From the moment the animal and the woman initiate their world-altering conversation, the events become ever more consequential and (as if anticipated from the beginning) toward one particular event that has been, again, either ignored or misinterpreted by commentators who are unwilling to recognize how extreme the complications become once the fruit from the tree of the knowledge of good and evil is eaten. This first experience of eating, with nothing, perhaps, more natural in the service of day-to-day life, will not be restricted to a natural necessity made obvious since creation. "The Greek word designating 'sage' is etymologically related to *sapio*, I taste, *sapiens*, he who tastes."[28] Eating, ingestion, internalization: the most taken-for-granted of human acts has metaphysical implications as soon as the fruit from the forbidden tree is tasted. The savor will last forever.

But first, the animal comes on the scene. *Nachash* is accompanied by all kinds of translations that make its consciousness shrewd, cunning, and clever, with all the mischief and more that can be imputed and rarely considered for entirely different reasons. An entire history of reading and interpretation would have to be reexamined from its very beginnings to trace how the nature of this animal has been maligned. According to all moral considerations, it has been made culpable for the most heinous of acts, leading to consequences for human beings that will be irreparable.

28. Nietzsche, *Philosophy in the Tragic Age of the Greeks*, 43.

The animal is itself divided, before any "sin" is committed, by a human propensity for distinction—so that the man's initial act of naming becomes, metaphorically, related to *calling names*, that is, insulting and with a prejudice that is never so much as considered.

A *parakletic* hermeneutics is now in an admittedly difficult position, and certainly from the standpoint of a theology that has determined the animal to be the manifestation of evil. How is one to relate to the animal without making harsh judgments? How does one remain independent from the virtual anonymity of a Christian interpretation and provide, if possible, another perception of the animal and its reason? The animal is intelligent and discerning and wise; and what has not ways been noted with sufficient emphasis is its ability to speak and, first and foremost, be capable of asking a question that allows the woman to deliberate, for herself, in her freedom, and then to answer. The animal speaks; the animal reasons. The Greek *sophrosyne* defines the animal in terms of excellence. There are so many disjunctions in this formidable of all texts that a reader has to wonder how the history of perception has been maintained in all its rigidity and failed not only the animal but the entire unfolding of creation within the minds of the narrators.

Many readers have been called to the text and repeated Adam's failure. They have named the text instead of being called by it.

The animal can speak. Animals too have been created (in some sense, hidden, disguised) in the likeness and image of their creator—necessarily so; for no creature from out of the consciousness and language of God could be alien. Animals are in the image and likeness of God insofar as they are linguistic beings and animated by the spirit. Before continuing and arriving at the events themselves, one has to insist on making the animal nothing like a snake or a serpent and in no way related to a metaphysical creature that has no place in the nature of the world as created by God. *Satan* has no existence in the text except, perhaps, as the meaning of the Hebrew *adversary*, the one who brings human beings to themselves, to an accounting, from out of their own self-confrontation and with the sense of being inadequate to the call of creation. The poignancy of a reversal has not been sufficiently considered by the theological imagination; but if one returns to the man and his inability to *call* the animals, then what the animal characterized by *ārum* does is nothing less than call *human beings to themselves* and an inherent possibility of being. The dialogue is the condition of all self-overcoming. When words are spoken, Martin Buber tells us, "they establish a mode of existence,"[29] no different than a text as it reveals a mode of being.

Two polarizing statements will introduce the discussion on this quite remarkable animal and, indeed, one of the outstanding characters in the history of human stories of self-understanding—with a creation (world literature) inseparable from an emulation of God. First, from the classical tradition: "Though the name Satan does not appear in the story, *it is evident* from the overall teaching of the Bible that he is present and acting through the serpent."[30] The "it is evident" can be asserted as a claim; but it can find no support in the text itself or in Genesis. Commentaries have fallen for the temptation of supplementing creation with their own fantasies, a human characteristic to have such consequences—especially in the realm of politics. Other alternatives are possible. "Who or what is the Serpent supposed to represent? In later scriptural tradition, the Serpent is clearly identified with the Adversary (i.e., Satan) or the devil. The identification between the Serpent and the Adversary is nowhere suggested in the text."[31] There is nothing to suggest the animal confronts the woman as an adversary; on the contrary, and to repeat, the animal will call the woman to herself. The animal appears to the woman and immediately begins a conversation with her. This animal does what the man was utterly incapable of doing. The animal calls the woman to herself and to the possibility of being a self-transforming creature. Being can be other than itself. In other words, what the animal reveals to the woman is her inmost possibility of being, one she has not yet recognized, on her own, or from any relationship she has had during the time of her life, with the man, or with God. The animal's intelligence and capacity for speech, for meaningful dialogue, which has nowhere been evident between either the human beings themselves or in their relationship with God, is relational. The animal complements the creation of the world. God's initial words of creation, "let there be light," is enhanced by *dialogue*. An entire deliberation could be pursued here on the nature of language as first created by God and then emulated, in its infinite variation, by the animal who uses words not so much to create matter and things and appearances of the world, but nothing less than the spirit of human beings insofar as they are linguistic and therefore capable of generating meanings; spirited

29. Buber, *I and Thou*, 53.

30. Hobbs, *Origin of All Things*, 37, my emphasis.

31. Plastaras, *Creation and Covenant*, 53.

words enhance the matter of the world. The animal and the woman speak to each other; they reason, present arguments, allow for thought to first recognize what their capacities are. Genesis makes it clear that thought is necessary to reflect on what has been said—by God, by the animal, by the woman. For all the preoccupations about the nakedness of the man and the woman and the mysterious aspect of their visible flesh, soon to lead to a turn of events that will resound in the Bible itself no less than for the Jewish people, first of all, and then Christians, the animal's conversation with the woman leads to the realization that the self cannot be reduced to the body, to a physical appearance. God and animal, *together*, contribute to the foundation of a human world, with its accomplishments and failures, and with the theological ideas of sin and fall as too rigid to properly account for the complexity, the overdetermination, of the lives of human beings in the garden of Eden as they begin to understand themselves in the world of nature between the presence of God and the animal.

Can the world, animal, and human relationship be considered a *trinity*?

If so, human responsibility has never been greater or more urgent.

The human has long cared too much for his *oikonomia*. The *matter* of his manufactured world has predominated.

The affirmation of the spirit has to be recalled from its forgetting, an oblivion that has also been entrusted to the authority of the *saeculum*, the limits of the times and the aeon.

Genesis once again asks us to rethink the relation to the economy and the secular.

One intriguing suggestion can open a few more comments on the classical evaluation of the animal in order to provide us with intimations of an alternative. In his translation and commentary on *Genesis*, Robert Alter interprets the word *Chavah* (Eve) and how it "sounds suspiciously like the Aramaic for 'serpent.' Could she have been given the name by the contagious contiguity with her wily interlocutor, or, on the contrary, might there lurk behind the name a very different evaluation of the serpent as a creature associated with the origin of life?"[32] Alter doesn't answer his own provocative question. At least it has been posed; to attempt at least the beginning of a complete reevaluation of the meaning of the serpent seems necessary. *Life* would have to be interpreted beyond its biological fact; as previously indicated, the animal and the woman, who is not yet

32. Alter, *Genesis*, 15.

given her name, together reach an understanding of what "life" entails. As the animal and the woman begin to reach the same conclusion, being satisfied with material fulfillment is not remotely adequate in rendering thanksgiving and gratitude to being in the world. Human beings require much more than the physical sustenance provided to them by the generosity of God. As he surely knew long before the creation of human beings, at some point they would endeavor to become more than their physical selves and exceed their original condition of creation. They could not be mere *bios*; they were also *psyche* and *pneuma*—as God intended when he breathed into the man and he became a living soul. *Chavah* does not *need* to eat for sustenance alone. Her craving arises out of a desire for experience what cannot, can never, be satisfied by an object.

Still, the vilification of the animal is without measure, this despite a fundamental recognition. At the same time that he can write that "the serpent offers an access to another kind of cognition," LaCocque also feels the need to add that "the primal couple are confronted by a vicious animal."[33] This is an ancient prejudice, much too obvious, much too judgmental. How he interprets the scene as a "confrontation" and how he can believe that the animal is "vicious" defies explanation; these observations are entirely foreign to the text. The animal has been so denigrated in the long history of interpretation of Genesis that its originality has been effaced. Again, one can turn to the idea of the animal being "called names," that is, slandered. The animal, we are told, "odia gli uomini e li vuole privare della felicità di paradiso."[34] How anyone can conclude that the animal "hates" human beings and wants to deprive them of the supposed happiness of paradise is perplexing. What happiness are the human beings actually experiencing? How can anyone think they are happy? What can that possibly mean? The garden has often been described as peaceful, idyllic, the *paradeisos* raised to the level of "heaven on earth" instead of the Near Eastern word for a natural place.

A *parakletic* hermeneutics has one fundamental responsibility: it must defend the word and what it represents. This, hopefully, will not be attempted either with ignorance or, equally, with simple humility. Hermeneutics cannot be arrogant or humble; it has to be concerned less with its own character than with finding an adequate access to the scriptural text. For this reason the defense of the word has to be undertaken at

33. LaCocque, *Trial of Innocence*, 36.

34. Heinisch, *Problemi di Storia Primordiale*, 89.

the same time as a defense of the animal—the first of our sentient beings. For my reading of Genesis has two motivations; and they are inseparable from the announcement in the introduction and the whole range of the argument on the central role of the animal in the lives of human beings at the level of religion and the law, piety, and justice. From the primordial textuality of Genesis and across the world of antiquity, through the Jewish, Greek, Roman, and Christian worlds, one startling reality can be reconstructed and with its beginning, in the God, world, animal, and human relationship that, now, at the most decisive moment when the human beings finally eat from the tree of knowledge of good and evil, are initiated into events of such long-lasting consequence that it will take us many interconnected readings to reach our conclusions. There will be several events to analyze.

The animal has promised the woman that eating from the tree of knowledge of good and evil would have one result: their eyes would be opened. They would see; they would be transformed from physical creatures capable of seeing the appearance of the world to the ability to recognize the relationship between perception and consciousness and, therefore, in many ways with the overwhelming ability to interpret. Visibility can no longer be mere apprehension. All comments prior to the following moment were merely preparations. The event, now, is staggering: "Then the eyes of both were opened, and they knew that they were naked; and they sewed fig leaves together and made loincloths form themselves" (Gen 3:7). Open eyes, nakedness; these facts alone could hold our attention for a long time, along the lines of that most problematic of human realities—sexuality. Instead, to prepare for the conclusion of the chapter and its continuity, what matters most is the need to "cover up" the body and, therefore, a first cultural creation.

They hide their genitals.

Nakedness and exposure require concealment. If one can here introduce the idea of "sin," it would have to be poignant for us on the level of what can be seen and what is hidden. Beneath the act of covering their genitals, which the images of Renaissance paintings never cease to remind us, one has to admit (as an aspect of "sin") that the possibility of revelation will no longer be self-evident. Permitting oneself an allegorical interpretation (a *literal* interpretation will follow), the consequences of eating from the tree of knowledge of good and evil is the catastrophe of the revelation of creation now concealed behind, and beyond, appearances.

It will be forever mysterious perhaps until such time as other *witnesses* make themselves visible.

One can follow a genealogy that begins here and leads all the way to first-century Rome.

The decision has been made. There has been no deception or temptation, no malice or trickery. The animal and Eve have had a conversation; there has been a back-and-forth, each answering to the best of their ability in relation to each other. All subsequent events begin to reach their stunning conclusions. The humans are ashamed; they cover themselves and hide, in part, in whole. They are exposed; they see themselves. When God finds them and the reality of their situation is revealed, God reacts with apparent punishments. These punishments (Eve's painful childbirth and Adam tilling the soil) are *paradoxical*. They are not intended as individual punishments, for themselves alone. The consequences of the punishments will be long-lasting—so long, in fact, that they stretch across the entirety of biblical time from what Paul calls "the first Adam" all the way to the second, with enough punctuations to last an eternity but that in the end must return to this one primordial place and one event in particular that, if it has received attention, has in many ways been disavowed and not taken into consideration for the events to come once the Eden couple are exiled from their original home. Before the expulsion and the punishments to be endured forever, one act by God can only be regarded with a later response—in "fear and trembling," for in the act God discloses a possibility not known before. From Genesis 3:20 until the end, until the expulsion from the garden, the figure of God has to become at least partly ambiguous; at the very least, uncertainty on the part of the reader cannot be surprising. God seems now to be a figure of the greatest ambiguity. He takes action. He seems to be capable of disappointment, displeasure, and certainly recrimination followed by the first judgment, when good and evil are now enacted in the world and made manifest.

"And the Lord God made garments of skins for the man and for his wife, and clothed them" (Gen 3:21).

The announcement could be passed over without so much as a comment; the event is a detail, an act within the whole. But if one lingers on this one act of unparalleled importance, the event itself and the implications are beyond estimate. It is far from an *unnecessary report*, as Stratton believes. "The narrative continues in 3:21 with what may seem to be a disconnected and unnecessary report of an unmotivated divine action. God makes . . . clothing for the man and his wife, and clothes them. Theologians are quick to see this making as a caring action on God's part and to see in it a mitigation of the recently pronounced divine punishments."[35] Is Stratton right to point out how theologians regard God's act as one of "caring"? God expresses solicitude? The entire scene requires much more deliberation, both for the moment itself and for the implications it has for the events to follow and, most especially, to all the heirs of Adam and Eve beginning with their children. God's act cannot be interpreted as a "mitigation" of the recent punishments—painful childbirth for *Chavah* "the mother of all living," and tilling the soil for *Adam*, the man who was born from the ground.

Childbirth and work are *blessings.*

Pain and sweat are consequences of *grace.*

While the description of the act may conceal as much as it reveals, allowing the reader to see "the garments of skins" without, at the same time, reflecting on what this actually means, those who have taken time to pause on the words have been confronted with a profound dilemma; still, much has remained unexamined. A pun, if it can be so called, is not out of place.

The English word *hide* is startling.

As much as the sentence on garments and skins conceals, a reader has to now fill in the blanks and follow how the cultural act of making clothes is achieved; and at what cost. Who *pays* for the act of disobedience? We cannot but mention Girard and the invention of the "scapegoat"—though he never mentions this original example; nevertheless, all the repercussions of violence and the sacred are presented here. Even more startling, the moment will become, for the two human beings and, perhaps more importantly, their two sons Cain and Abel, the origin of animal sacrifice as a religious ritual. A *human killing* soon follows, though it cannot be called a *murder*. There is no murder as there is, yet, no *law*.

God, however, is the first killer in creation. The earlier promise of "you will die" was much more than personal. One has to imagine Adam and Eve looking (being forced to watch) as God kills an animal, graphically, viscerally, making the necessary incision before the hide of the animal is peeled away from its body and sewn together to make a covering for human bodies—so that this moment, a most profound one and that will only be fully realized, in all its power and implications, long after as it begins a series of events that are without measure and estimate and last

35. Stratton, *Out of Eden*, 62–63.

for centuries all the way down to the Hebrew prophets and beyond to the city of Rome.

God appears to be a killer. All creation is punctuated with this irrevocable event. In the act of killing one or more animals for their "skins," there will also be other instructions, including the necessity of eating flesh—in other words, being forced to live by relying on the death of others.

Eating the flesh of an animal will become a metaphysical act.

In this instance an entire history of punishments for animals can also be discerned; and with it the introduction of a human ritual soon to occupy subsequent life. Before turning to Genesis 4 and the children of Adam and Eve as they inherit the sins of their parents and the world made in conjunction between God and human beings, a few comments are not without relevance, most especially when theology defends God's care: "That Yahvewh makes leather tunics for Adam and Even is probably intended as a sign of the fact that he still loves and cares for his creatures in spite of their disobedience."[36] *Probably* shows enough hesitation. Love and care cannot be without their profound ambivalence. Love "for his creatures" is even more unsettling. The human beings who have witnessed the killing of the animal have one understandable response. It is the creation of a feeling Walter Burkert, in the introduction, had associated to *guilt* and *debt*, the *Schuld* understood by Nietzsche so well in the genealogy of morals. Guilt, however, does not arise on its own and without an accompanying necessity. Still, commentators are stuck on the empathy of the giving without being able to perceive it in all its graphic reality. "He cares for them in their broken condition. He makes them garments."[37] The act of care is also developed into a theology of grace, in principle acceptable as long as this *gift* is understood from the perspective of human beings who will do nothing less than create an institution for its *reciprocity*. "God graciously gave the couple garments of skins to replace the flimsy covering they had made with fig leaves."[38] Grace is a recurring word and concept. It is misapplied. Surely this is not grace. To interpret the act as kind or generous does not acknowledge the catastrophe of the death of the first animal(s). "God graciously clothed

36. L'Hereux, *In and Out of Paradise*, 22.

37. Blenkinsopp, *From Adam and Abraham*, 43.

38. Hartley, *Genesis*, 72.

Adam and Eve in suitable garments."[39] There are no shortages of descriptions that completely overlook the most decisive element in the ending of Genesis 3 and make possible an entire biblical history. In a noticeable comparison (in this case, between the "folly" and the "wisdom" inverted in importance by Paul) "the folly of the first couple's act of making fig-leaf 'aprons' is to be contrasted with the wisdom of God's making of the 'coats of skins.'"[40] The comments could be included so as to be innumerable and continue with the mere description without the necessary analysis of its meaning, from "And Yahweh-Elohim made for Adam and Eve and his woman cloaks of leather and clothed them,"[41] to many more about care, grace, and wisdom. Finally, before turning to the truth and reality and all the consequences of God's act, we have both an impression and, just as quickly, a disavowal. At the same time as grace if affirmed, sacrifice is completely rejected.

"The connection of clothing made of skins with the killing of animals *and so with sacrifice* can well operate in the ancient pattern which lies behind 3:21, but it plays no role in the present context."[42] However much the event as an act of sacrifice is disavowed, subsequent events cannot be ignored. The reality of the situation can only be rationalized for so long until the repercussions are noticed in detail and unequivocally. The following comments are noticeable for both affirming grace and rejecting sacrifice.

> While some try to read the language of animal sacrifice and the shedding of blood in this verse, that seems misplaced. The significance of this act is that God is showing humanity that, though they have sinned and will suffer the consequences of their sin, he will remain involved with them. In other words, God extends his people a token of grace.[43]

Theologians are unwilling to recognize how sacrifice is initiated in the act of slaughtering an animal and soon to be incorporated into a whole cult of worship and ritual.

These are the historical facts of religion in Mediterranean antiquity.

39. Arnold, *Encountering the Book of Genesis*, 40.
40. Lambden, "From Fig Leaves to Fingernails," 76.
41. Good, *Genesis 1–11*.
42. Westermann, *Genesis 1–11*, 270.
43. Longman, *Genesis*, 70.

All the elements of sacrifice are going to be present: the guilt of witnessing the slaughter of an animal will require the human beings to create, for themselves, an appropriate thanksgiving in the form of reciprocity, an act ultimately defined with all kinds of linguistic ambiguities and euphemisms: in Judaism, *korban* and *olah*, by the Greeks *thysia* and *charis*, and by the Romans with the complementarity of *do ut des*, "I give so you may give." The exchange of sacrifice will become binding and perpetual. More importantly, once the relationship between Cain and Abel is analyzed from the perspective of their obligatory sacrifice (which Cain emphatically resists, and with good reason, as a tiller of the soil) his subsequent act of killing will now establish a binding relationship between animal sacrifice and the death penalty that will be witnessed both within the reality of biblical scripture and other cultures of antiquity.

The lengthy commentaries on Genesis by church fathers emphasize the allegorical significance of Genesis 3:21, ignoring the death of animals and the use of their skins, arguing instead that the "skins" are a figurative illustration of human mortality.[44] They could not foresee the necessity of God killing animals; they were unable to bring themselves—strange, given God's propensity for judgmental killing—to the perception of a relationship being created from the garden of Eden and for history to come, with God, humans, animals each participating in a binding reciprocity.

The interpretations from Genesis 1–3 are limited, purposefully, only with considerable strain. Two last comments will form the transition into the story of the children of Adam and Eve and the conflict they must experience. These comments are about animals, one last reminder of their importance and the impossibility of a human life without them. While the attitude is understandable, Vicky Hearne might give animals too much choice at this point. The all-encompassing consequences of sin does not avoid them, not when one of their own (the illuminated and wise animal) was essential in the unfolding of humanity. According to her, the animals were given a choice. Some animals "agreed to go along with humanity," she writes, "thus giving us a second chance to our damaged authority, to do something about our incoherence."[45] Despite Hearne's sense of pity for human beings, the truth is otherwise. Animals had no choice in the matter. Only one thinker, to my knowledge, has been able to describe not only the conclusion of Genesis 3, but also an anthropological truth.

44. Beatrice, "Le Tuniche di Pelle."

45. Hearne, *Adam's Task*, 48.

"Why did people keep animals with them?" asks René Girard. The answer is unequivocal. "Surely to make sacrificial victims of them."[46] Domestication and animal sacrifice are inseparable. Genesis 1–3 now takes us to one more cultural creation: if, in Genesis, killing and sacrifice were at the very origin of *religion* and a certain conception of theology in Judaism but shared by all people of Mediterranean antiquity, another creation occurs at virtually the same time and in conjunction with sacrifice. The killing of animals in the context of a religious sacrifice will soon lead to the first killing of a human being. One consequence of the events in the garden of Eden leads to two interconnected creations. During the transition toward the world outside the garden of Eden, all the factors are now in place for the beginning of the creation of a human world. If the first cultural act needed the death of an animal, the human response will be to create a religious ritual.

Despite Girard's awareness of the origin of animal domestication (which also domesticated human beings within an order of being that prescribed a certain concept of life and death) one of his beliefs cannot be defended. My interpretation at the end of Genesis 3 denies its validity or truth. It might not jeopardize Girard's theory as a whole on sacrifice and the scapegoat mechanism, but it does make one statement indemonstrable; as far as I know, the scene is not considered by him. Without entering into a discussion on the whole of his theory of scapegoat and mimetic theory, his insight into the violent origins of religion is profound as it is relevant in what follows—with one objection. He writes, "In every one of the great scenes of Genesis and Exodus there exists a theme or quasi-theme of the founding murder of expulsion. Obviously, this is most striking in the expulsion of the garden of Eden; there *God takes the violence upon himself* and founds humanity by driving Adam and Even far away from him."[47]

A different reading of Genesis 3:1 shows that far from God taking "the violence upon himself," it is inflicted on one or more animals, even if the motives (for now) can hardly be discerned. A reading of all the prophets on animal sacrifice and how it does not amount to piety is one response. For my purpose, the first killing in the garden of Eden creates the first religious act and the emulation by human beings to repay God—so that guilt and debt (or the reciprocity of giving and receiving) will be

46. Girard, *The One by Whom Scandal Comes*, 88.

47. Girard, *Things Hidden*, 142, my emphasis.

infinitely repeated in the sacrificial act until the ritual will be inevitably abolished and at two precise junctures in the first-century CE. Before the abolition, however, which is essential in all the texts of Jewish and Greek antiquity, in the writings of the prophets and the philosophers, Genesis 4 will have to be interpreted for its interconnected events between animal sacrifice and the first killing of a human being and how it inevitably leads, after circuitous events, to the end of an acclaimed event after the flood. By now turning to the events to unfold between the two brothers—and, much more relevant, the relationship between Cain and God—a chronology can be followed to the point where animal sacrifice will be reinstituted by Noah at the same time as God creates the death penalty.

Chapter 2

Abel, the Death of a Sacrificial Killer

In the Hebrew Bible, there are no given origins, no explanations, not even the slightest of indications for the reason(s) Cain and Abel began the religious ritual of sacrifice to God except for the elusive "in the course of time Cain brought to the Lord an offering (*minhâ*) of the fruit of the ground, and Abel for his part brought of the firstlings of his flock, their fat portions" (Gen 4:3). There may be no explanations for the origin of the ritual, none given by the narrator, who prefers to omit it altogether rather than either speculate or announce what is evident; but if one extends beyond the neutrality of descriptions that are withheld and perhaps done so to provoke the reader's interpretation and memory, then what occurs at the end of Genesis 3 is an event—an act of God—of unparalleled importance for the future lives of human beings.

Does God found religion by killing animals for human beings?

The disavowals are many, and with a straightforward acceptance: "The offering by Cain (and Abel) are not explained. They seem to be simple gifts to a higher power, as we find in many primitive cultures, rather than highly developed cultic practices."[1] The description here has the feel of an apology; the overgeneralized "primitive cultures" bears no relation to the writing of Genesis. The *minhâ* are anything but "simple gifts." The logos of myth excludes any and all history; the denial of "cultic practice" (that is, acts with a specifically religious intent) renders the whole even more in need of an interpretation.

The facts of Genesis, as myth, are undeniable.

1. Miller, *Book of Genesis*, 33.

At the same time as the expulsion from the garden and the necessity "to till the ground from which he was taken" (Gen 3:23) and therefore begin human life with agriculture and, associated with it, pastoralism, God's act of killing one or more animals to make clothes for Adam and Eve also created the beginning of human culture. At the origins of the post-Eden existence is a consciousness of guilt and debt; Adam and Eve will bequeath these human affects to their children along with the institutional order of worship and piety.

Killing animals as a religious ritual will establish relationships. Humanity emerges, in relation to God, in relation to itself, by inaugurating the practice of an incommensurable offering, produce from the earth and dead animals.

By discounting the act of violence by God and then attributing "the bloody foundation of the beginning of culture"[2] to Cain, Girard has unwillingly repeated what has been the traditional view of the individual who is the first to experience a "sacrificial crisis." Sacrifice leads to a discordance in the self. Cain is alone in this foundational perception.

Tradition has been handed down; observances are compulsory. "Offerings" will have to be given. Violence, death, and killing will be intrinsic to *reverence*. Killing and the disguised definition of sacrifice will become fundamental imperatives, forcibly repeated as acts essential to the nature of existence, to all *life*. God initiates human beings into a world of killing and religious observances. The inheritance of his parents' tradition by Cain (that is, submitting to the sacrificial order) begins a response that has not been at all appreciated for its motivations. If one can suspend easy judgment, Cain's motivations, and his state of mind, are something other than what has been imagined. A *parakletic* hermeneutics has two tasks: suspending taken-for-granted interpretations of the events to follow, and understanding Cain.

Cain has only been perceived for an act; he has not been considered for his thoughts. His motivations have been assumed. He questions, first of all, the religious emotions of guilt and debt and whether they can be a proper foundation to piety. In Genesis, the slaughter of an animal by God *for* human beings led to the twin foundations of religion in guilt and indebtedness, one to be infinitely repeated as a ritualistic gift. The pain of human conscience was projected from the self to an animal; killing proved easier than self-reflection.

2. Girard, *I See Satan Fall like Lightning*, 83.

Adam and Eve did not sacrifice one or more of their domestic animals and return the skins and fur to God—as he did to them; they co-created the ritual by including the animal in a series of observances, ending in roasting its body and serving it as a family meal. The body of the sacrificed animal had to be communally *ingested*; meat, a euphemism, had to be incorporated into oneself as essential in creating a new order to life outside the boundaries of the garden where, from the beginning, there was no death and assuredly no killing. Sacrifices were offerings; they were also, necessarily, food to be shared as part of the definition of a community. Everyone had to be implicated; everyone had to take responsibility. Eating dead animals is not only permitted; it is made sacred and part of the "natural" order of the world. The religious ritual of sacrifice will therefore serve a double function: as an act of piety and perpetual indebtedness of the God who killed the first animal and as part of a meal that will contribute (most especially for the children of Adam and Eve) to their growth. The death of an animal perpetuates the being of the human as both spirit and body at the same time as it dedicates the act (the ritual) to God; rationalizing and ignoring the violent origins of religion will soon have unintended consequences. Unlike their diet in the garden of Eden, wholly vegetarian since there was no death, now human beings have turned a religious ritual into a carnivorous necessity and with an anthropological rationalization.

The religious worship of God involves killing an animal, "offering" it (more precisely, giving God ascending smoke and a fragrance as the Jewish *olah* and the Greek *thysia* suggest) and eating meat. An alimentary necessity and a cultural creation are mutually implicated. The death of an animal also serves as a *thanksgiving*. God's creation provides. The matter-of-fact description is only the beginning of an interpretation of the events of Genesis 4. "Animal sacrifice seems to be, usually, the ritual killing of domesticated animals by agrarian or pastoral societies."[3] Smith's *anthropological reality* here is merely descriptive; an analysis remains to be applied. Theories about early human beings are unable to enter into the profound revelations of myth. The rift between the logos of myth and all "studies" related to the *anthropos* in a reconstructed history can say little about Genesis since the narrator makes particular demands on the hermeneutics of the reader.

Once the transition to the natural and human world is made with the birth of Adam and Eve's two sons, the entire meaning of sacrifice will

3. Smith, *Relating Religion*, 149.

necessarily be reexamined by the very individual who has been universally judged.

Cain is the first individual.

Once human beings enter the world, an irreducible division is established and must be maintained. Each brother provides an offering to God reflecting his place in the world and their respective labor—Abel "the keeper of sheep" who will give up (kill, skin, eviscerate, butcher, roast and, finally, eat) the firstborn of his flock, and Cain a "tiller of the ground" (*obed adāmāh*)—that is, someone who *serves* and cares for the earth, loves and *worships* it, for its cultivation and its relation to his father Adam who taught him how to tend it and his mother who taught him how to appreciate its natural beauty.

Cain, however, is not only a human being who lives in the physical world. Human life involves a *flourishing* much more comprehensive than a biological one. If a difference can be discerned beyond their immediate identities as agricultural and pastoral workers, one in the field growing crops, the other in a pasture with his flock, the two brothers also have a more important relation: Abel sacrifices animals while Cain works in the field, like his father, Adam. Cain also shares a likeness with his father as a tiller of *adāmāh*: Cain thinks, reflects, is endowed with the ability to delve *within himself*, to till himself as the *metaphysical ground* of a nonmaterial world in the closest proximity to the spirit—an attribute denied him.

The tiller of the ground takes the metaphorical plowshare to himself.

The hovering spirit is above the water and above the earth, as well.

Cain is capable of self-flourishing and, therefore, cannot be simply determined by his biological life. He feels, within himself, a still unclear yearning, one that cannot be fulfilled by a ritual, and certainly not one requiring the death of an animal, unless the incongruity makes him all the more aware of a fundamental problem in the nature of piety and religious observances. Cain's profundity, *as a thinker*, has not been considered; only by reflecting on his consciousness will it be possible to understand him without making the judgments everywhere in evidence by theologians, biblical commentators, and Genesis experts. First, the animal in the garden of Eden was misunderstood. Cain will suffer from the same harsh and unreflective judgments. A *parakletic* hermeneutics, before coming to his defense and intervening on his behalf, will attempt to understand his consciousness and what he *senses*, in himself.

Cain has not simply inherited a sacrificial imperative. He cannot subject himself to a religious worship involving violence, killing, and death. Cain can make a choice; indeed, he has made a choice by offering an alternative to death.

The New Testament judgment of Cain has been unanimous. There is simply no attempt to understand him. Cain's *metaphysical* sophistication has not been acknowledged. Modern commentators, no less, with some distance from the past, have also single-mindedly judged Cain only within the limits of moral categories. The judgments have been unanimous; a jury-like mentality has prevailed and without one individual giving Cain any consideration—any thought, any understanding. But he too needs an advocate. A *parakletic* hermeneutics has the obligation to defend him.

Beginning with the Letter to the Hebrews, there is no reason to accept its conclusions. "By faith Abel offered to God a more acceptable sacrifice (*thysian*) than Cain's" (Heb 11:4), a judgment that can in no way be verified by the text of Genesis itself, forcing the reader to ask how Cain has been so mistreated, and for what reasons. "More acceptable": because the sacrifice was a living animal? One of the Synoptic Gospels mentions "the blood of the righteous Abel" (Matt 23:35), though, from Cain's perspective, Abel is also a sacrificial killer who does not at all seem "righteous." The condemnations of Jude single out what he calls the unnamed "intruders" and he uses language that, in two cases, betrays age-old conceptions. "But these people slander whatever they do not understand," he begins, and without so much as being aware of how *slander* is an accusation more easily directed at others than recognized in oneself. "And they are destroyed by those things that, like irrational animals, they know by instinct. Woe to them! For they go the way of Cain" (Jude 1:10–11). Slander, irrational animals, the way of Cain: the words give themselves away by the presence of an instrumental use of rhetoric. All imaginary juries have reached their verdict without taking any time to deliberate, as if the necessity to judge was self-evident. The distinction between "Righteous Abel, Wicked Cain"[4] is a judgment to be made after the fact but without asking the difficult question of circumstances and motives.

Is a self-deception noticeable here? Does Cain perceive his brother as reflecting an impossible predicament, the conjunction of human brutality and divine worship?

For an inexplicable reason—not the first, certainly not the last—God will soon make a decision with long-lasting consequences for an

4. Lohr, "Righteous Abel, Wicked Cain."

individual, for humanity; another one in a series beginning from creation and the events in the garden of Eden, a decision by God has extensive consequences. Later commentaries on the character of Cain can only be theologically asserted and by no means hermeneutically observed in Genesis itself. In 1 John 3:12, we are told that "we must not be like Cain who was from the evil one and murdered his brother." Once more, human beings do not seem to act on their own, from deliberation or passion. They act in the service of metaphysical entities like "the evil one," as if manipulated from dualistic externals rather than taking the time to reflect on their human condition, in thought, in deed. Rather than understanding his acts as a rational response to a situation he finds intolerable, he appears to be susceptible to some kind of suggestion, in this case "from the evil one." Finally, "murder" is a judicial concept that has no place in Genesis 4. Murder and the law are not yet in existence.

Before the events, Cain's consciousness has to be understood. He cannot accept the obligation of offering sacrifice—a dead animal—as a form of religious worship; and that is the reason he offers "fruit" instead, requiring only cultivation, produce to be picked, from the ground or a tree.

Cain has conceived an alternative to sacrifice.

Cain invented the offering of "fruit" as a substitute for sacrificial death.

Cain gives God produce from the earth instead of a dead animal.

Violence can be averted, death respected for its place in creation without it being in any way religiously necessary or serving a social function. The *character* of Cain has been much too maligned; but unless his *ethics* are given prominence and examined, he remains misunderstood. Moreover, as a reflective human being, he wonders about reasons, knows full well how the ritual of animal sacrifice has been *inherited* and how it was justified, as a perpetual obligation, by the religious sensibilities of his parents. Sin is, indeed, a "schema of *inheritance*,"[5] but Cain refuses to live by such an imposition. He refuses inherited sin; the burden of his parent's guilt and debt is not assumed. An inheritance can be genealogically interrupted. Cain demonstrates his willingness to become a unique human being—free, self-determining, with the ability to make decisions for the future—by raising doubts about the origin and ritual of sacrifice and how it may be resisted, suspended, abolished, an alternative found

5. Ricoeur, *Conflict of Interpretations*, 284.

to better serve God and life. Unless Cain's consciousness is taken into account, he remains inexplicable; he will only remain an object of moral judgment, of traditional condemnation. Cain is prototypical. He is the first human being who questions the legitimacy of a specific kind of worship to God. He is neither an atheist nor an agnostic. Cain is the human being who cannot simply accept the *tradition* of religious worship; in his case, and from the beginning (from his childhood) Cain could not accept the relationship between killing an animal that was inseparable from its being with the family and the worship of God. Slaughter and piety are, for him, incommensurable; and the inner conflict of his life will lead to an act that will precipitate a cascade of events leading to another foundation; sacrifice and justice will be bound irreducibly together. The act most associated with Cain has only been superficially understood. He has not been appreciated for being foundational.

Cain's life is a revelation. His decision illuminates all subsequent events.

Although Girard does not mention Genesis in the discussion concerning the domestication of animals, he recognizes such a cultural development as inextricably bound up with sacrifice. There is no other reason given for Cain and Abel to keep animals and to practice the religious ritual of sacrifice. Girard writes, "The domestication of animals requires that men keep them in their company and treat them, not as wild animals, but as if they were capable of living near human beings and living a quasi-human existence. . . . An immediate motive was necessary, one powerful and permanent enough to encourage treating animals in such a way as to ensure their eventual domestication. The only motive could have been sacrifice."[6] We have now reached a first crucial juncture in the human world; in Genesis it is indisputable. Cain and Abel, the two sons, the brothers, are obligated to offer a sacrifice to God. While many have been extremely quick to judge the actions of Cain as they unfold, and with complete lack of empathy much less understanding as to *his motives*, his consciousness demands some acknowledgment; facile moral condemnations are refusals to consider his emerging humanity and for his desire to be more than an emulation of his all-too-human parents. He certainly does not mimic them; he has no desire to emulate them—though, to be sure, Cain's *spirit* makes him aware of his relationship to

6. Girard, *Things Hidden*, 69.

God, however strained it may be, however it may be characterized by more than pious subjection and worship in terms of *works.*

For Cain, faith is a *problem.* Has he recognized faith to be distinct from works?

Unlike Girard's search for a founding *murder*, however, Genesis presents us with the killing of an animal and the invention of a religion of sacrifice. Sacrifice, as we now turn to Genesis 4, leads not so much to a *murder* (which is a judicial concept) but to the foundational killing of a human being. The sacrificial killer experiences his own death as a harsh emulation; Abel can only identify with the death of his animals by being slaughtered in the same way. The events to unfold are about the death of a sacrificial killer. *His death suspends the ritual* for a long time to come. The repercussions of the event are momentous. They will extend into innumerable episodes; and it will be necessary to trace its chronology at least until the "reckoning" in Genesis 9:6 and the institution of the death penalty and at the same time as the resumption, by Noah, of blood offerings. The beginning of the world after the flood cannot but perpetuate (and respond to) an earlier and unresolved conflict, what Girard has rightly defined as a "sacrificial crisis."

To begin to trace the history of animal sacrifice and its relationship to law and justice, turning to Genesis 4 allows us to observe Cain, attempt to understand him, see his relationship to his brother, the sacrifice of animals, and ultimately his dealings with God. Unlike his brother Abel, who seems more than capable of being a *dutiful son* and a pious individual (who has been portrayed to be *good* and *righteous*) Cain cannot understand why his brother so easily subjects himself to a tradition not of his own making, which is the only justification for the equation of death and worship. The brothers have inherited a world from their parents. If a *fall* occurs at all, it can be readily observed in their predicament as human beings who enter a world and must accept the reality imposed on them. Abel accepts tradition and submits willingly to its demands; he fulfills his duty as if it were itself sacred. Cain, unlike his brother, struggles, and does so because he has raised himself to be discerning. Above all, what Cain perceives is the reality of the world and how its limits, as established in nature and by his parents as cultural makers, cannot exhaust the possibilities of being—in the world or in himself. His yearning cannot be reduced to the impulse of desire; Cain is at a loss to understand.

The repercussions of Genesis are to be found, first, in its words, and then from all others pronounced after, in its wake. The letter to Hebrews is, for one, a precise moment of its own textual awareness. Let us first note an obvious statement—traditional, expected, and far from self-evident. No pronouncement seems more certain and unquestioned. It has been unanimously accepted. Theology has simply understood one aspect of the letter writer(s) without so much as a doubt or hesitation. But if one closely examines the passage in question and this startling appearance of Cain and Abel in a New Testament letter, then one must also turn to the complexity of its construction and its declaration to learn, so consistent with the doctrine of Paul that "by faith we understand." What is to be understood? What was first *revealed* by Cain, "that what is seen was made from things that are not visible" (Heb 11:3). Just as the creation of the world emanates from out of God, authentic faith cannot be demonstrable in an act, and not in one where violence, blood, and death are intrinsic. The reality had to be a source of the deepest conflict in himself. Paul rightly, justifiably, abolishes animal sacrifice as a religious observance and for an offering to God since it was already a question from the very beginning. His repudiation of the law for faith was not simply a declaration made for the present. Paul reevaluates the whole of his own past as a reader and, as a former Pharisee, guides himself through his connection to midrash.

Cain is nothing less than the first religious *visionary* who, in his faith, in his relationship to God, recognizes the meaning of the slaughter of animals as an incongruous aspect of religious worship. His parents, bereft of all sense and unable to cope with their banishment and exile and hardly capable of understanding their predicament, established their future lives, and those of their sons, by an imposition of a guilt and a debt. Cain knew, intuitively, that any authentic relationship to God had to be established freely, and not by creating a human culture dependent on raising domestic animals for slaughter. Once we understand Cain's opposition to an *inherited theology*, then we can better assess the profound truth of his character and why, in the end, when his act of killing leads to his own exile, he founds a *city*, in part to distance himself from the supposed reality of the natural, material world.

Once more, we witness a disavowal and the inability to consider the manner in which a sacrifice originated in Genesis. "There is no reason to see this story as the beginning of the sacrificial cultus."[7] These observa-

7. Towner, *Genesis*, 58–59. On the same page, he repeats, "There is no hint that the story is intended to account for the origin of the sacrificial system." The story does not "account for the origin of the sacrificial system." It does, however, confirm its origin and its bind.

tions, and so many like them, are indications that Cain has been misunderstood from the ground up.

> The story opens with a report ascribing sacrifice and offering to the first human born of woman. We are not told that God demanded this of Cain and Abel or that some religious festival required it. This absence of motivation is instructive, for it assumes the willingness to sacrifice and worship is innate in man, to be utterly natural, instinctive and spontaneous expression of the spirit of religious devotion. But the story also tells us that man has it in his power to corrupt even the purest and noblest of emotions.[8]

The assumptions here are many, beginning with the inability to make a distinction between sacrifice and worship. As for sacrifice being "utterly natural," "instinctive," and a "spontaneous expression," Sarna reads *into* Genesis 4 what is nowhere evident in the text itself. How can killing be natural? So much has to be assumed for his conclusions to stand. The assumption that sacrifice is "innate" fails to acknowledge the events in Genesis 1–3 and how they necessarily led, from God's sacrificial act, to its commemoration. When Sarna then adds that human beings are "corrupt," he has assumed that the slaughter of an animal during a religious ceremony was consistent with the "noblest of emotions." How the violent death of an animal can be "noble" will be left up to the reader to decide. Cain, for one, the first one, has no hesitation in regarding animal sacrifice as a questionable ritual.

The chronology of Genesis 4 has been a "leading" one. Readers, at first, have no choice but to follow it; they can assume that the sacrificial crisis begins when God rejects Cain's offering. But the crisis began a long time before—in Cain's consciousness.

There is a profound and relentless conflict in Cain, between himself as a thoughtful individual and the world he lives in, with its definition of what reality is. He confronts the nature of religious worship and the sacred within himself. Cain is the first human being who has the capacity, in himself, to transcend history and begin to perceive what is not, in the everyday order of reality, open to sight. God's involvement can now be traced.

"And the Lord (Yahweh) had regard for Abel and his offering, but for Cain and his offering he had no regard" (Gen 4:4–5). "Regard." So much of what occurs now is concentrated on the face, on looking, on

8. Sarna, *Understanding Genesis*, 29.

indications of acknowledgment. God does not look at Cain. He ignores him, as if he does not even exist. He has no presence. As for any explanation for God's refusal of Cain's gift, it can only be conjectural; despite the necessary precaution to be taken, many have had no hesitation whatsoever in judging Cain. The reasons have been many. One, however, can be dismissed. "God preferred the offering of the keeper of sheep who brought the choicest of the firstlings of his flock, to that of the tiller of the soil. This preference has more than one reason, but one reason seems to be that the pastoral life is closer to original simplicity that the life of the tiller of the soil."[9] Surely their vocations have nothing to do with the coming events. Any historical conflict between farmers and shepherds is irrelevant when attempting to understand the meaning of this one *singular* event. Any reliance on anthropological history is completely inadequate in explaining the depth of this myth. The farmer/shepherd conflict, even if it was a historical reality, has no bearing on the relationship of the two brothers as portrayed in Genesis.

History diminishes the logos of myth.

There was always some reluctance on Cain's part, a division between what he had created as a substitute for killing (offering the "fruit" of his *labor*—which he perceived as a blessing, and in part to fulfill the sense of honoring his father) and watching his brother slaughter animals from his flock. Abel's act was incomprehensible to him. Cain resists the idea of the slaughter of an animal as a form of religious worship to God. Animal sacrifice and worship are, to him, disjointed. Cain cannot understand how the violent slaughter of an animal could be an expression of piety. He can only see the sacrifice of an animal as the atonement for God's initial slaughter of an animal for his parents. It may be pertinent to provide a substantial number of commentators who, taking liberties with their interpretation with an enigmatic text, make decisions that Genesis 4 does not, in any way, support. Retrospective theology demands some attention, here and elsewhere. One author, commenting on Irenaeus's *Against Heretics*, begins conspicuously: "Apparently, the reader of this story is not to assume that God accepts or rejects offerings based upon his own need. God's response reflects only the worshipper's need. Cain hid secret sin within himself, harboring envy and malice against his brother and therefore his offering was rejected. The martyr Abel, on the other hand,

9. Strauss, *Studies in Platonic Political Philosophy*, 155.

made his offering with simplicity and righteousness and was accepted."[10] All these descriptions are questionable; because they depend on judging Cain's character. One strenuous argument can be made: Cain does not feel "envy" for Abel at all. One cannot ignore how Cain must also, consequently, regard his brother with some incomprehension; this has nothing to do with the classically understood "rivalry." The supposed rivalry *between the brothers* has been misidentified. If a rivalry exists, it is not *between the brothers*. Finally, the description of Abel as a "martyr" is inappropriate. A martyr is a witness; he provides a testimony. But no such testimony is ever presented. Abel has absolutely nothing to say, on his behalf, or for anything else.

Cain is the only witness in Genesis 4. He is the one who is revelatory.

"So Cain was very angry and his countenance fell" (Gen 4:5). When God rejects Cain's offering, his reaction was expected and understandable. Translations are indicative of a relationship to Cain. There is a considerable difference between the NRSV's "very angry" to others, for example, "very sorrowful." Anger and sadness are quite different. But if we are to understand Cain, his emotions from the moment of God's refusal are essential, even when the language becomes enigmatic. His "countenance fell" implies sadness, perhaps extreme anguish. God's words do not in any way appease him; their meanings are not easily understood, as if God made himself opaque, perplexing. *He lost face*. Cain feels humiliated.

Is it possible to witness Cain's disappointment as also disbelief in the fact that his offering as an alternative to a blood sacrifice has been rejected? His human decision, which is intended to be consequential for the future (for all subsequent piety and worship with fruit alone) has been exposed to extreme doubt.

The lacunae in Genesis are extensive; they demand speculation, imagination, and so too empathy. When, for example, Cain makes his first offering, from the "fruit of the ground," one expects the harvest to be edible—as in a grain, or that which is produced from the labor of a bee, honey; although the word "fruit" seems to imply a produce to be eaten (say, a nut, vegetable, fruit, or the above-mentioned grain) it may also be a produce from the ground that cannot, in fact, be eaten, but used in the making of garments. If Cain's offering is *cotton*, for example, God's response would be uncertain and ambivalent, especially considering if cotton is now spun and used to make clothes. Cain's offering would also be a

10. Bingham, "Christianizing Divine Aseity," 64–65.

commentary on a previous decision made by God. An offering of cotton would be overwhelming in its symbolism. It would be an effrontery to God. Cain's offering is also an affirmation of his self-sufficiency and, once again, related to the former skins of a dead animal worn by his parents as they left the garden of Eden. Cain has thereby demonstrated his abilities to make clothes without killing animals; his *culture* has not been, for the moment, founded upon death and its exploitation. Cain does not exploit animals after their death. Though "fruit" implies edible produce, we cannot discount other possibilities. If Cain has invented a crop for making clothes (hemp, as another example) the offering would have been a message, a human response to God's initial act of clothes-making. The death of an animal was unnecessary. Cain has defined himself as a pastoralist and as a human being capable to establishing a reciprocal relationship to animals but without the necessity of death.

Whether God could anticipate the disastrous events about to unfold, or if the extent of human emotions—disappointment, anguish, or rage—remained beyond his capacity to either predict or understand, does not seem entirely evident. The need to impose divine will on the world with a providential design seems urgent; it will be constant and relentless, an expression of God's frustration in needing others (those with a similar "image and likeness") to actualize his intentions—as yet announced, though eventually expressed, repeatedly, insistently, to certain unique individuals like Noah and Moses who are obligated to obey commands. For the time being, history will be unable to fulfill divine intentions; more often than not, human acts will be unable to fulfill expectations, resulting in disappointment, and worse. A dependent God who will suffer regret, and so much else, will also be capable of affecting the mind of a vulnerable human being; a relationship between God and the sons of Adam and Eve has been established, though it can be precarious, and one-sided, making human beings dependent. God decides to accept the slaughtered animal, its sprinkled blood and viscera, its meat and fat, but reject the offered "fruit of the ground," thereby ignoring Cain. A sacrifice can always be refused,[11] a dilemma experienced by the Jews of

11. In *On Sacrifice*, Halbertal writes that the "offering makes the possibility of rejection immanent in the practice of sacrifice" (3). Such a refusal is present both in the Hebrew Bible and in Homer's *Iliad*, thereby creating a fundamental ambiguity in the Jewish and Greek response to their respective deities. The refusal and rejection have other implications: it means the divine can withhold the expected favor in return; and that means, eventually the need to inquire on the supposed reciprocity of the relationship.

the Bible no less than the Greeks in Homer's *Iliad*. In this case, produce from the ground (grain, for example) does not seem comparable to the death of an animal and its immolation; there may not yet be an altar, but blood must nevertheless be spilled, violence and death intrinsic to a certain foundational worship. Perhaps produce from the ground—from inside *ădāmah*, the earth—does not please God, at all. The slaughtered animal, butchered and roasted, is preferable.

Despite the attempt to give a gift to God and be acknowledged, the gesture leads to refusal and a subsequent incomprehension when Cain's "countenance fell" (Gen 4:5) after God's rejection, parenthetically the first time a "fall" does indeed occur in Genesis. Cain looks away; he looks *down*, at the ground. He "loses face," has been deprived of his sense of self; the respect he previously had has now been taken from him. God's rejection has devastated him, for many different reasons: God can be unpredictable, his motives without assurance and therefore unsettling. God then approaches Cain and asks him—as if surprised by his reaction—the reason for him being so unhappy. Why should he be despondent? Cain has no answer; noticeably, *he does not say a word*, now doubly devastated by God's inability to understand the extent of human emotions. Whatever God says, Cain cannot respond; a conversation seems impossible. Instead, he proceeds to tell Cain that if he "does well," he will be accepted (his face will be raised; he can hold his head up high), but if he does not do well, "sin (*chatta*) is lurking at the door" (Gen 4:7), as if "sin" was a metaphor for possible intrusion, the disruption of something within, the "lurking" reminiscent of a "crouching animal ready to pounce."[12] The significance of the animal has now entered a human being, as a disposition; what is objectionable in a human being is animalistic. If God's admittedly complicated words do indicate the presence of an animal within Cain, then the advice might be to tame if not domesticate the wild within him. God's words are enigmatic to say the least.

Whatever Cain may have understood from God's words, as well as the subsequent "its desire is for you, but you must master it" (Gen 4:7)—the compulsions and urges of desire must be minimized if not abolished, as the Hebrew *timsel* indicates with not so much a command from God as an ability to choose by Cain[13]—nothing more is added to this one-

12. Kissling, *Genesis*, 222.

13. As emphasized by Brueggemann in *Genesis*, 58. In *The Book of Genesis*, Hamilton stressed how the choice given to Cain is multifaceted, involving a shall, a must, a may (a promise, a command, an invitation) without any one meaning being dominant.

way conversation. Cain may not have even heard him; his emotions were too overwhelming, the devastation from the refusal too difficult to bear, more difficult to comprehend than any reference to such an idea as "sin," *chatta* (like the Greek *hamartia*) complex and not simply reducible to a moral idea. "And Cain talked to Abel his brother" (Gen 4:8), the narrator tells us—to make us realize the difference between his ability to speak, now, and a previous silence. The brothers speak; but not a word can be read, none inferred. Again, silence. Nothing can be represented from this exchange.

Cain, however, responds with one decisive act. How can the decision to kill his brother be explained? A traditional one is too superficial. "While the story of Cain and Abel does not pause to offer anything like a full account of logical explanations or deep motivations, it is safe to say that it tells a story of sibling rivalry. It depicts a world that has just been created—a world that is virtually unpopulated—and in that world the first man and first woman give birth to the first brothers who immediately dramatize the first inexplicable sibling rivalry."[14] *Pace* Schwartz and countless others who all agree on this apparently self-evident *sibling* rivalry,[15] it is not at all "safe to say" anything about the brothers. The rivalry has been misperceived. Cain is not envious or jealous or otherwise in competition with his brother except for being uncertain at his submission to the sacrificial system. Cain cannot understand the reason for Abel butchering his sheep for religious reasons that have been *inherited* from their parents. Cain is not in competition with his brother. He is, if in competition at all, in a relationship with an established tradition bequeathed to him from his parents and, apparently, one God accepts as proper to devotion and worship. While readers are contemplating the nature of the killing, they have forgotten the *original killer*. It has never so much as occurred to anyone that Cain kills his brother (once) so as to make any subsequent sacrifice impossible. Abel, the sacrificial killer, is himself killed and with the same method. There is one absolutely sure way to bring animal sacrifice to an end. The sacrificial killer must himself be killed. One death will bring about the end of a ritual slaughter.

Theologians have been virtually unanimous in their condemnation of Cain; one can concede that it is, in part, understandable, when a

14. Schwartz, *Curse of Cain*, 2.

15. A bibliography of secondary sources that all agree on the sibling rivalry would be extensive. An exemplary one will suffice: Byron's *Cain and Abel in Text and Tradition*.

one-dimensional morality is applied. After all, Cain kills another human being, his brother. He commits fratricide. One could make an appeal to "extenuating circumstances" and therefore make him less culpable. No such thing will be attempted. Rather, a much more penetrating analysis of Cain can be attempted so as to recognize some of his motivations. The first cannot be avoided. Let us even concede one other point, emphasizing it one more time: Cain experiences the deepest kind of conflict. He has inherited a sin experienced by his mother and father without a choice. No repentance on his part could obviate acts in the past. More seriously, Cain resents the guilt imposed on him by an action committed by God. Cain has been an heir to the first sacrifice, though in his case his offering was bloodless. No one has been willing to defend Cain. But if the entire sequence of events from the garden of Eden to the murder of Abel are to be interrelated, then the killing of an animal by God (out of pity and, perhaps, love of his favored creatures) cannot be disassociated from Cain as the one who kills the individual responsible for blood sacrifices. Once the animal is disregarded for its existence and companionship, then it can easily be butchered as some mere object, a means. Cain, however, knows that to be a farmer and have the support of an ox makes labor easier and, though rarely recognized, less lonely and a matter of a human being in a double-relationship with an animal and the earth.

Cain kills his brother Abel, the man who sacrificed animals. Only after the killing (not before, not during) does God approach—but this time not with pronouncements, but with questions and then *judgments* ("now you are cursed from the ground"), exiling him from the land he clearly venerated and no longer making it possible for Cain to be a farmer. "When you till the ground, it will no longer yield to you its strength; you will be a fugitive and a wanderer on the earth" (Gen 4:12). Any reference to "sibling rivalry," or some mere historical conflict between shepherds and farmers, seems, to say the least, secondary to the intention of the killing: an act of wrath against God, perhaps, and certainly ending in the death of the man who previously had the responsibility of sacrificing his animals. And if the first "offering" or *korban* means to "draw near," so that sacrifices were, somehow, intended to draw human beings nearer to God, it remains beyond all comprehension how the killing of an innocent animal—a domestic one (a goat, for example) living and serving humanity with its presence, first and foremost, and also providing milk and cheese—could somehow allow human beings to draw closer to the divine.[16] That Abel's name (Heb. *hebel*) means "emptiness" and is the expression used in Ecclesiastes 1:2 for "vanity of vanities"[17] may be an indication—in Cain's mind—of the animal sacrifice his brother offered; in vain, a waste.

Immediately after, and without a response from Cain who, the entire time, says absolutely nothing to God, Cain goes in search of his brother; he did not answer either of God's two questions or ask for clarification to his enigmatic references to sin and desire. Instead, he finds Abel and tells him, "Let us go out to the field" (Gen 4:8); it is unknown whether the description refers to a plowed field or a pasture and, perhaps, with animals present. In any case, "when they were in the field, Cain rose up against his brother Abel, and killed him" (Gen 4:8). The consensus view has been absolute; it has survived without opposition. Cain kills his "innocent" brother out of enraged jealousy; the act was intended to get rid of a rival. With the death of Abel, their competition has been overcome; he will no longer be secondary to his brother. The regard for Abel as a victim can be understood; it can be explained, along with the traditional representation of Cain as the embodiment of a catastrophic moral failure. And yet, one alteration forces the reader to imagine a different reality altogether. Cain kills the sacrificial killer, exacting a strange retribution. Justice and the law are, for the time being, irrelevant; they are not yet realities. Abel, the dutiful son and traditional worshipper, has inherited a theology from his parents (and, it seems, preferred by God) and has instituted a religious practice as binding as any other of their *works*.

By killing Abel, Cain has brought animal sacrifice to an end.

The ritual will be completely suspended until a particular juncture in Genesis when, after God does nothing less than carry out a sentence of death on virtually the whole of humanity, animal sacrifices will once again be instituted by Noah simultaneously with the creation of a *new law*. At this juncture, however, no law exists. One cannot make the case that "according to Deuteronomy's code of law, Cain's offense is punishable by death."[18] The law has not yet been created. The death penalty has not yet been instituted; other events, a long, drawn-out history and many generations are necessary for another divine decision. A genealogy has,

16. Watts, in "The Rhetoric of Sacrifice," makes the argument that sacrifice "is clearly an evaluative label, not a descriptive one" (16). The reader can reflect on the matter given the above arguments.

17. Towner, *Genesis*.

18. Longman and Garland, *Genesis-Leviticus*, 98.

however, been established. The force of events now move the narrative forward toward a logical end.

In the meantime, Cain has been underestimated, simply looked upon as already suffering from some defect (above all, moral), for why would God reject his offering if his intentions had been authentic and his gift, of worship and acknowledgment, had been worthy. The act of killing was as swift as it was brutal, and using a tool (or weapon) that nowhere can be seen but only reconstructed from nothing more than an imagination conscious of their respective duties—a farm implement (a scythe, perhaps), but more likely the same knife used by Abel when slitting the throat of his firstborn sheep, an act Cain had no doubt seen and could easily emulate. What cannot be avoided is the logic of the sequence that begins with animal sacrifice and leads inexorably to the first killing of a human being. Since Cain kills his brother, the act cannot yet be defined and controlled when placed within the limits (and the breaking) of a future law; he sets in motion a series of interrelated events in the narrative of the Hebrew Bible that, together and with each episode providing an important element, leads to its culmination. One argument is untenable: in *Violence and the Sacred*, Girard writes, "One of the brothers kills the other, and the murderer is the one who does not have the violence-outlet of animal sacrifice at his disposal" (4). If only Cain had been given the opportunity to kill animals, Girard seems to argue, he would not have killed his brother. My argument, instead, is: if Abel was not a sacrificial killer, he would not have been killed by his brother who, after all, learned to kill by watching his brother do it first and on a regular basis—as if "natural" and part of the reality of the world.

When God passes a sentence on Cain—immediately after Cain tells God that he is not responsible for being his "brother's keeper"—the punishment is not singular. It has more than one ramification: "You are cursed from the ground, which has opened its mouth to receive your brother's blood from your hand" (Gen 4:11). The punishment is serious but *not capital*. Nevertheless, Cain experiences the punishment to be graver than retribution; he has been "cursed" from the ground in two ways. He will be sent into exile, away from the only home he has ever known; and the previous occupation he had and that gave him such a sense of fulfillment will be taken from him. He has been deprived of himself. "When you till the ground, it will no longer yield to you its strength; you will be a fugitive and a wanderer on the earth" (Gen 4:12). Cain has been punished not with physical death and the end of his mortal life; he will instead be punished with exile and with the loss of his vocation. The punishment makes him momentarily anxious; the prospect for his future is bleak, dangerous, threatening. He has been deprived of a calling, from the ground and himself. He must feel *dispirited*. Whether we can here affirm that "once again we find grace in the midst of judgment"[19] is one possibility not to be overlooked as God comes to terms with Cain's act.

We know that later he will build cities—as if making a transition between agriculture, in close proximity to the land, to a dweller of cities; however, when Cain tells God "my punishment is greater than I can bear" (Gen 4:13), he is responding specifically to the punishment of the ground no longer giving him sustenance, what God called "her strength." Cain's equally serious punishment involves being "a fugitive" (Gen 4:12), that is, someone guilty of a crime but still, somehow, physically free to be a wanderer and a "vagabond" but also, always and perpetually, on the run and suffering from unappeased anxiety. When Cain tells God, "I shall be a fugitive and a wanderer on the earth, and anyone who meets me may kill me" (Gen 4:14), he has seemingly understood, if incompletely, how his future will always be tied to the same "it came to pass" that initiated the ritual of sacrifice; but, this time, with a significant difference. Anticipating being killed for his crime, God has to assure him he will not be killed, and most definitely not executed.

Despite the killing, no law has been created, no commandment given to him or anyone else. Cain does suffer a punishment, though the reader cannot be at all sure about his relationship to what will later be called a capital crime. "When you till the ground, it will no longer yield to you its strength" (Gen 4:12). The act of "tilling" the ground will not be restricted to being a farmer and working on the land to produce crops for food. The reminder of the meaning of the name of his father lets Cain know that the punishment is even more serious. He is now exposed to being deprived of his spirit, of the "tilling" that could have resulted in the development, in time, in the world, of what the image and likeness could actually mean once they were actualized. God could have instituted the death penalty here and now; the time was appropriate, and yet chose not to. Cain was punished with a self-estrangement he immediately feels for its overwhelming consequences. Finally, when Cain hears God telling him that "I will be hidden from your face" (Gen 4:14), once again the reminder could not be more evident insofar as, now, there will no longer

19. Lim, *Grace in the Midst of Judgment*, 158.

be a possibility of being face-to-face with God and he will therefore be left with an abiding sense of loneliness far worse than his father's in the garden of Eden.

"Cain said to the Lord, 'My punishment is greater than I can bear! Today you have driven me away from the soil, and I shall be hidden from your face; I shall be a fugitive and a wanderer on the earth, and anyone who meets me may kill me'" (Gen 4:14). The punishment cannot, at this point, be considered judicial. There has been no law created. For now, before the pronouncement of the law on capital punishment in Genesis 9:6, Cain is to be separated "from the soil," estranged from himself and the whole of his past, including his father and mother. A genealogy is severed. Soon, the separation will be absolute. The punishment suffered by Cain is now directly related to the effects of "sin" in the life of a human being. The punishment has been set: on the one hand, Cain will be estranged from the land as a physical place of dwelling as well as his work as a farmer; and, equally as important, he will be estranged from his essence, from himself as "the soil" where he originated from and where he had begun to develop himself. The so-called "fall" defined as the event occurring in the garden of Eden is, in the end, suffered first by Cain. The consequences of this fall or perdition or destitution from what might have been his future can now no longer be recovered and in fact will give him only one other choice: he has been punished by being deprived of growing his own food and by being separated from the possibility of his own self-flourishing. At the same time as he will be estranged from himself, he will also be separated (in part) from God and, just as meaningfully, from the animals that were essential to his life as a farmer. The punishment suffered by Cain and to be experienced forever as a condition of being, will be his separation from the land, the animals, and the parents he has lived with for his entire life.

His initial self-conception has been verified. Cain is the first individual.

Scripture could not abandon Cain to an absolute isolation. The deprivation would be too much—as he admitted. So God separates himself from Cain and from the man's ability to *see* him. God will no longer be visible. However, if the consequences of the entire chronology of Genesis can now be understood in their relation, it is not that Cain will be hidden from the face of God, as he believes, but the other way around. The face of God will no longer be visible, at least directly; only in time will one or more individuals realize that any proximity to God and to look on him indirectly will be a continual strain and effort. Cain is the first human being to be deprived of God and natural creation. He will settle in the land of Nod, "know" his wife, engender a son, build a city, and establish a completely new level of creation. The lives of the dwellers in a city will have unanticipated consequences, so much so that Cain, his son, all the generations who follow him, will find themselves at their limit and marked by the recurrence of a human killing, this time carried out by Lamech. These two acts of killing, beginning with the foundational one of Cain killing his brother (Abel a "priest" prior to the invention of the institution) remain as emblematic, as sure as the sign on Cain. Finally, when God could no longer endure how human life had developed itself, out of its own initiative and without being able to either recognize or do away with their "wickedness," he made a decision that would have consequences for all creatures in the world (though, noticeably, not aquatic ones) and lead to the decision to renew the earth with only Noah, his family, and chosen animals.

The history of Cain has been preserved; as for all his descendants, they have been chosen to perish in the deluge and relegated to insignificance. Still, when the cataclysmic events of the flood are unleashed on the world, the necessary continuity leads to two acts that will resound in Genesis and the rest of the Hebrew Bible—one observed by Noah, the other an apparent edict announced by God. Connections to future events can be witnessed.

The waters of the flood have subsided. The earth has reappeared. There are again signs of terrestrial life. For some reason, Noah makes a decision that has not been commanded. It eludes all explanations, all reason. In his haste to return to tradition and re-begin the world in the same image as before, Noah believes he fulfills his piety when he decides to build an altar. An altar, as a place of worship, could have been different than in the past; the new altar could have been used for other purposes than the ones from tradition. The altar will be used for the building of fire.

Immediately after the previously flooded earth again becomes dry, God speaks to Noah and tells him to leave the ark with his family and all the animals. "Bring out with you every living thing that is with you of all flesh—birds and animals and every creeping thing that creeps the earth" (Gen 8:17). God's instructions are clear and straightforward: allow the animals to leave the ark so that they may again populate the world with their kind. Animals and humans are supposed to develop together and simultaneously; they are to reestablish a relationship. There can never be a natural world without a human being and animals living together. The desolation would be unimaginable. When Noah and his family and all the animals leave the ark, the *patriarch* makes a surprising decision. It certainly has not been commanded by God, neither in a conversation nor in a one-sided declaration. The *pater arche* was, indeed, supposed to be the father of a new beginning. Noah was instructed to free the animals to be themselves, to live and procreate, alone, among other animals, with human beings, each expressing their nature and establishing a relationship of reciprocity. As in the offerings made by Cain and Abel, there has not even been a hint that sacrifices are ordained or demanded, hoped for or desired. The decision comes from a human being, making the sacrifice of animals essential to any idea of piety and worship and, stranger still, thanksgiving. There are no intimations of Noah's decision, no preparations or warnings. The human world has been renewed; it was supposed to be re-created, and yet Noah does not separate himself from a sacrificial past and cannot conceive of inaugurating a different world. Instead of assuming an inaugural obligation, he inherits the past, and is thus incapable of reflecting on whether animal sacrifice as a religious ritual is appropriate for the new world. He adopts a tradition from the destroyed world, now in the process of being revitalized, and yet perpetuates the violent killing of an animal in the service of God.

"Then Noah built an altar to the Lord, and tool of every clean animal and of every clean bird, and offered burnt offerings *(olah)* on the altar on the altar" (Gen 8:20). There are two interrelated acts that Noah believed were essential to the devotion to God: he had to build an altar, raised up from the ground, for the purpose of laying out the body of a sacrificed animal and cook it as an "ascent" offering.

The language of offering in Genesis 4 has been transformed from the neutral *minhâ* to the euphemism of *olah*, the "ascent offering" that emphasizes the smoke moving upwards rather than the slaughter of the sacrificial animal. The smoke is deceptive in more ways than one. The altar, now raised up from the ground for the first time, means this elevated structure mediating a human act with the always vertical supremacy of the divine cannot be lowered to the level of the previously ravaged earth, in part for the trauma it has suffered, its signs of devastation still obvious to anyone looking at a nature previously inundated—buried. The altar cannot touch *adāmāh*, the ground. The resumption of the sacrificial ritual has many kinds of descriptions.

One commentator writes, "In gratitude Noah built an altar and sacrificed on it one each of every clean animal and bird."[20] We are forced, once again, to wonder at the nature of the gratitude no less than on the tradition of sacrificial thanksgiving.

History will ultimately reveal a succession of sacred objects, from the altar to the tabernacle to the temple. For now, there are no descriptions of the *killing* of the animal, the slitting of the throat, the bloodletting, the cutting open to remove its entrails, skinning the hide, the butchery of cutting up the animal parts and, finally, the roasting and the communal meal. Turner calls attention to Noah's "act of butchery on a scale which makes Abel's offering insignificant,"[21] though many others would follow, as in Solomon's dedication of the temple in Jerusalem when "sacrificing sheep and oxen, that could not be told nor numbered for the multitude" (1 Kgs 8:5). Unlike the precise descriptions in Homer's *Iliad*, Genesis omits all and any details related to the animal as it is prepared for its consummation. All the reader knows for certain is that (surely, among the strangest of anthropomorphic oddities) God has an olfactory experience followed by more than a few enigmatic declarations. First of all, "the Lord (*Yahweh*) smelled a sweet savor"[22] (Gen 8:21), we are told, a first extraordinary impression, as if God could actually *sense* that one of the animals he has both first conceived and then created could now be used for such a purpose, as an offering or gift, the *korban* that somehow is intended to "draw near" or/and the *olah* as an "ascent offering." Seemingly as a response to smelling the fragrance of roasted meat (the animal was not boiled, as might be appropriate in this case, after the flood) God talks to himself, "in his heart," with feelings. He makes a promise. "I will not again curse the ground (*adāmāh*) any more for man's (*adām*) sake," a declaration that could, in principle, be reversed: God will no longer curse human beings for the sake of the earth. The additional statement can only be arresting: "For the imagination of man's heart is evil from his youth; neither will I again smite any more thing living, as I have done" (Gen 8:21). Again, a promise: God will no longer kill anything following the recognition that "man's heart" (unlike his) is "evil"—and unlike Noah, whose very first act after leaving the ark was to reinstitute the practice of

20. Vos, *Genesis*, 51.

21. Turner, *Announcements of Plot in Genesis*, 47.

22. In *Genesis 1–11*, Wenham believes that "God's anger at sin is appeased by sacrifice is the clear implication of this phrase" (189). This is highly debatable, especially given God' words "in his heart" (that is, privately) to himself.

animal sacrifice. Sailhamer too believes that God makes the promise as a response to now being satisfied with the sacrifice of animals;[23] but such an interpretation has to ignore the passages in question. God will refrain from both cursing the ground and *killing any more living things*. The killing, then, will be left to Noah and his descendants and serve two purposes simultaneously: animals will be a source of food and become the essential form of piety, worship, and thanksgiving by their sacrifice. Subsequent generations will perpetuate the ritual and, as the narrator of Exodus tells us, the need to offer a sacrifice to God was the one fundamental reason given to the Egyptian pharaoh for releasing them to go into the wilderness. Exodus, then, is not about liberation as such. Leaving Egypt allowed the Jewish people to once again offer animal sacrifices to God.

To simply witness the resumption of animal sacrifice as pleasing to God cannot suffice; the act itself can only ever be at the origin of a future expected to be actualized—though it will take time and be well out of the hands of Noah, who, during his final episode, has simply passed out, naked, in his tent after drinking too much of the wine he has for the first time fermented. There was, of course, a reason for drinking too much: to numb oneself from the thoughts of all the human beings and all the animals that, previously in the world, had drowned, were no longer (unlike him) alive and well if suffering from *guilt*. God did make a promise: he will refrain from any more killing. However, Noah did not understand the relationship—that is, the bind between the sacrificed animal and what it symbolically represented, the disavowal of killing. Noah will be unable to complement the ritual with a law; and so what God most demands will have to be necessarily postponed and require more significant history (one more beginning with Abraham) and, finally, the extraordinary effort of Moses, who will be the supreme law-giver.

In the aftermath of the flood and the covenant made between God and Noah, there is no way to avoid an ambiguity in the agreement. God's words are not simple; they are not straightforward. How can one know, with any degree of certainty, if the new covenant of animal sacrifice and the consumption of meat-eating is part of the new order of things? One law, however, does get established. Despite all postponement, animal sacrifice and the death penalty are both announced as new practices, as if theology and the law emerged at the same time as the twin foundations of a new world. "Whoever sheds the blood of a human, by a human shall

23. Sailhamer, *The Meaning of the Pentateuch*.

that person's blood be shed" (Gen 9:6). One doubt remains as we move from the biblical world toward ancient Greece: is the "shedding of blood" simply an act of revenge or is it the creation of a law? Subsequent references to the law and the death penalty in particular will become more and more pronounced.

"Whoever strikes a person mortally shall be put to death" (Exod 21:12).

"If anyone kills another, the murderer shall be put to death" (Num 35:30).

It will be evident in the harsh *lex talionis*: "Show no pity: life for life, eye for eye, tooth for tooth, hand for hand, foot for foot" (Deut 19:21).

In Leviticus, the statutes organized by the priests will involve the death penalty for many crimes in addition to murder, beginning with one perhaps not unrelated to Cain: "All who curse father and mother shall be put to death" (Lev 20:9).

The Torah is unequivocal.

Despite the inability to answer the pertinent question on the simultaneous creation of *the law* prescribing a death penalty, once certainty remains: in the foundation of a new world and with the recollection of the old (for God and Noah) each of them acts in a way appropriate to their sense of how the world will continue. For Noah, animal sacrifice will be resumed; for God, the death penalty is now instituted. Two foundations of an ancient conjunction are now decisive. Generations have lived and died from the beginning of the human world and with two foundational human beings along with their two sons. Events have been multiple, repercussions have followed, one after another, from God's initial act in the garden of Eden and only resolved when a new beginning was attempted, with a remnant from the old. The biblical world sets itself a new history; and as for the now strict relationship between animal sacrifice and the death penalty, the prophets will make themselves heard, repeatedly, insistently, and always with the uncompromising attempt to bring their people to a self-accounting. A final episode remains in the distant future. Events in first-century Jerusalem will be decisive; but before moving ahead to the life of Jesus and his relationship to animal sacrifice and the death penalty, a turn toward the Greek world and with similar concerns will provide us with an overlapping series of concerns as evident, first of all, in Hesiod's *Theogony* and with the enduring presence of Prometheus in myth, tragedy, and philosophy.

One final comment, in relation to the prophet Malachi and with a disturbing reference that can also be anticipatory: by looking ahead from the Greek world to Jerusalem under Roman administration. In quick succession, then, we have the reemergence of animal sacrifice as a form of piety and the institution of the law on homicide and the death penalty. Nothing is contingent. The repercussions of the moment are so extensive that, from here, one would necessarily have to reconstruct the entirety of Genesis and beyond and lead all the way to the very last of the prophets and the words heard by Malachi.

"Oh, that someone among you would shut the temple doors, so that you would not kindle fire on my alar in vain? I have no pleasure in you, says the Lord of hosts, and I will not accept an offering from your hands" (Mal 1:10). Nearing the end of the Tanakh, the words of God repeated by the prophet could not be more startling. We seem to be, once again, at a time of reckoning when God holds people accountable for their actions and rebukes them with the most severe warnings.

"I will send a curse on you and I will curse your blessings; indeed I have already cursed them, because you do not lay it to heart. I will rebuke your offspring, and spread dung on your faces, the dung of your offerings, and I will put you out of my presence" (Mal 2:2–3).

Dung on your faces.

However much one resists the language and the visceral descriptions, which can only be disheartening and anguishing for the pious, this end has remained too self-contained, either reflecting some immediate historical situation, or another moment in time when God announces himself to the people via the prophet to demand of them another kind of piety and service.

One graphic, unsettling image leaves us, at the moment—as long as it is remembered once we reach the end. The image, however raw, will resound from now until the end of this study—from Genesis, to the myth, tragedy, and philosophy of the Greeks, to the gospels of Jesus, and finally, to the spectacle of the Roman world in their amphitheaters. For now, we cannot simply ignore or minimize the shocking effects of God's words as he does nothing less than invoke the *dung* of animals. This, surely, is one of the most degrading of all scenes of the Bible.

God will smear the dung of the animals that have only now been sacrificed on the faces of those who have brought him the slaughtered offering.

Malachi closes the Tanakh. We are now in a better position to move momentarily from the biblical world to the world of ancient Greece and to reconstruct a related series of writings to trace, there too, the emergence of the ritual of animal sacrifice as a problem and to the related institution of the death penalty.

Chapter 3

Prometheus in Hesiod's *Theogony*

The events in Genesis as they lead toward the simultaneous re-creation of animal sacrifice and the institution of the death penalty, however singular they may be, nevertheless have affinities with an exemplary poetic myth of ancient Greece. The poet Hesiod transforms an oral tradition into a *logos*. He no longer sings and performs for an audience. Hesiod writes.

His literary aesthetics are inseparable from a metaphysical reevaluation.

The first conflict between two brothers, a family divided *on principle* and not in some narrow narcissistic emotion of envy or rivalry, discloses the first and long-lasting sacrificial crisis. Animal sacrifice is *the problem* of piety and relationship to God. Abel, the sacrificial killer, is murdered by his brother; this is a *religious killing*, motivated by ideas, not mere emotions. Once Genesis' all-important mythic meanings are compared to the first intimations of a similar consciousness in the worlds of the poetry of Hesiod, an interrelated representation of humanity begins to be revealed—one on the "genesis of the gods" in his *Theogony* and, as a fundamental relation, the poem of a *farmer* in *Works and Days*. Hesiod, the poet who works the land as a tiller of the soil, represents the body and the spirit, labor and inspiration, and with a new interpretation of the past that exposes the metaphysical foundations of a social world.

The Judeo-Greek world intersects, however different its period, however different its mythic self-understanding, with the divine, human, and animal relationship inextricably connected with the ritual of sacrifice and with a startling transgression; in both myths, there will be acts that are violations of established norms, forcing a complete reinterpretation of distant origins and, equally important, the world of the future to be lived by all.

As a figure from Greek antiquity, and who makes appearances in mythic poetry, tragedy, and philosophy, Prometheus will demand a defense just as *parakletic* as the one extended to the animal in the garden of Eden, *Chavah* the "mother of all living," and Cain the man who killed his brother Abel, the proto-priest and sacrificial killer. One intersection between Hesiod's two poems opens his world to the reader and the creature whose name, Prometheus, means "forethought" and is, in some essential way, connected with the animal in Genesis 3 who is a *diviner*. Nonhuman beings are essential in the consciousness of humanity. Before seeing a possible future, the traditions of the past can no longer hold sway, dominating the present with its continuity. The farmer-poet who, like Adam, was given the breath of the spirit to both work on the land as well as to delve within his own fecundity, produces food to eat in abundance as well as the language of the poet that initiates a new relation to the world; and he too, like the writer(s) of Genesis, turns to a well-known beginning.

In the section of *Works and Days* defined as "The Story of the Ages of Man" and immediately following part (but only part) of the events surrounding Prometheus's defiance of the gods, Hesiod returns to one version of a mythical beginning in order to present "another story (*logon*) for you,"[1] a *logos* appearing as an explanation of the events that have recently been described, those concerning Prometheus and his relationship to Zeus and how, for some unknown reason, the lives of human beings are now hampered by the gods. Hesiod tells us about an irrevocable change: the lives of human beings have been transformed from a golden state to a less valuable, a less appreciated, element. Hesiod returns to a primordial time, there to mark a difference, a before and after. One version has to be recollected. Hesiod the poet, the one who represents *poesis* and is therefore a "maker" (a maker of worlds beyond what has occurred in the past, in fact, and in thought), provokes his reader to interpret, and above all to avoid the previous attention of the listeners to the *rhapsode* who could command attention with his voice and melody alone. The words themselves have to be released from being publicly performed at a particular time. The act of writing and the complementary reading is

1. Hesiod, *Works and Days*, 106.

new; the previous limits of myth and its representations are extended. Another thought emerges. In order for the reader to relate himself to the metaphysical revelations of the poet, the aesthetic pleasures of song and melody will in some way have to be ignored. Emotions are to be examined; feeling is not enough. Not only that: if Hesiod is to be successful, as a poet, the age-old meanings of what he writes are to be composed in such a way as to provoke the possibility of an entirely different understanding. Nietzsche, a philologist after all, already senses how the "mythical and allegorical"[2] are not rivals. They are bound together as a preliminary *consciousness* at the origins of philosophy.

The defense of Prometheus is obvious; it was expected. In the composition of the poem, Hesiod achieves a *paraklesis* equally as significant: he becomes an advocate for the creativity of the poet and for his individual ability to reveal, in his writing, meanings that have never been considered prior to him. In "Myth Interrupted," Jean-Luc Nancy writes, "In myth the world makes itself known, and it makes itself known through declaration or through a complete and decisive *revelation*."[3] Without the poet, however, the revelation appears but has no witnesses. There can be no revelation without, first, the acuity of perception and, second, giving it language and being. Hesiod represents both Nietzsche's sense of the mythical and the allegorical no less than revelation and inspiration, which (conventionally) the poet acknowledges as originating with the Muses. Before reading Hesiod, one of his Muses will have to be recognized for being an inspiration: *Polyhymnia*, the muse of both poetry and agriculture, inspires him by her presence as well as by one article of her clothing: her *veil*. In two poems both representing Prometheus, the veil will be present as a "cover-up," one not so much to simply hide, but to reveal another meaning beyond the appearances many, as we will see, have accepted at face value.

In another day and age, Hesiod tells us in *Works and Days*—"these belonged to the time when Kronos ruled over heaven" (111)—both human beings and the gods came into being from "the same source." This, at first, may sound misleading. Hesiod means that human beings, who were made by the gods, somehow had their source in them. In the age of Kronos, human beings "lived like gods." There was no worry, no labor of any kind, no apprehension at all about an uncertain future. Death did

2. Nietzsche, *Philosophy in the Tragic Age of the Greeks*, 43.

3. Nancy, *Inoperative Community*, 48, my emphasis.

not concern anyone. Food was bountiful and easily accessible. Everything was available in abundance. The story is well known in the Greek world; it was foundational and one that has persisted down to Hesiod's day and beyond. Plato will be essential when turning to the life and death of Socrates and how Prometheus, in quite a few interrelated dialogues, makes crucial appearances. The dialogue of mythic meaning and philosophy can hardly be overestimated. For one, they both attend to the present time and how it was made *from tradition*. The reliance and dialogue with Hesiod in Plato's work is extensive, though with many different and often contradictory evaluations.[4] More specifically, "there is a significant and distinctive place for Hesiod in Plato's project of presenting philosophy."[5] It may be necessary to make the argument stronger, introduced by a question: Does the transference from the oral to the written also initiate (because of the mythic/allegorical relationship) a critical consciousness related to a philosophy of interpretation? Is there a transference between the poet and the reader in terms of hermeneutics?

In "The Age of Cronus" from the *Laws*, the last of his excursions into the mythic past, Plato comments on this idea from another time. "The traditional account that has come down to us tells of the wonderfully happy life the people lived then, and how they were provided with everything in abundance and without any effort on their part."[6] The speaker, the unnamed Athenian, continues and gives us a sense of this Golden Age and the governmental leadership by superior beings who were more spirit than human; they made everyone aspire to emulate the divine. And yet, Plato's fragmentary account leads to one dilemma. It raises an enduring problem. It pretends to define "the good man," and yet the goodness is curiously in doubt.

> If a good man sacrifices to the gods and keeps them in constant company in his prayers and offerings and every kind of worship he can give them, this will be the best and noblest policy he can follow; it is the conduct that fits his character as nothing else can, and it is his most effective way of achieving a happy life. (716d–e)

Needless to add, the mythic recollection of the past has more than one version. For Plato and his Athenian spokesman, one of the explanations for the happiness of human beings during the age of Cronus was due to

4. See the collection of essays *Plato and Hesiod*, edited by Boys-Stones and Haubold.

5. Van Noorden, *Playing Hesiod*, 89.

6. Plato, *Laws*, 713d.

their reverence for the gods and their dedication to them in the ritual of animal sacrifice. It was, by all accounts, a perfect order, everyone acting according to a preestablished essence. At some point, however, it occurred to one or more human beings (perhaps, a poet and philosopher) that sacrifice as a form of traditional and inherited piety was anomalous. What was its *reason*?

Hesiod turns to the supposed Golden Age and raises a serious doubt. For reasons he now reveals, the gods made a decision to create another race of human beings. "Mortal men" had become divine-like. They were both "rich in flocks" and they were also able "to keep a watch on cases of law." They were equally able to take care of their animals and establish a moral world, a first ambiguity not fully explained since animals and the law are somehow connected. The gods, displeased by these human accomplishments, made the decision to alter the order of the world and its hierarchy. The gods decided to deprive human beings of their "golden" being. People had become silver. Their lives could not be compared to their ancestors. They had other responsibilities. The nature of reality had changed. Far from the apparent beneficence of a prior history in human civilization, not without its similarity to the garden of Eden as far as the spontaneous and abundant food available to them and without the desire, or the need, to kill animals for food, the second race of human beings "had only a short time to live, and this with much torment because of their folly, for they committed acts of ruinous hubris against one another and refused to worship the gods and offer the blessed ones sacrifice (*therapeuein*) on their holy altars, as is prescribed for men in their customs" (133–38).

Hesiod does not use the customary word for sacrifice, *thysia*, in this case, with the implications of animal slaughter. The omission and restraint is already an indication of his *interpretation* of the myth. The blessed gods are describes as "undying" (immortal) at the same time as the brute fact of death for the sacrificial animal is described as *therapeia*—the same word Plato will repeatedly use in the *Euthyphro*. Hesiod emphasizes how sacrifice as a form of *therapeia* is a "service" to the gods instead of being, as in the past, the definition of the human relationship with each other and their world. The gods are therefore responsible for the actual situation. The human world is characterized by the vague *hubris* (though the "against one another" suggests conflict and violence, as in the situation prior to the flood in Genesis 6) and by the reluctance to worship the gods most especially in the ritual of sacrifice. The refusal to worship or offer animal sacrifice is not so much a mere affirmation of secularism or atheism, if such a consciousness can be imagined in the ancient world, but rather the sense of *theology* now being too archaic, its conception of the gods/human/animal relationship inadequate to a Greek consciousness. Girard did not consider the passage as it reflects his interpretation of a sacrificial outlet: without sacrifice, he argues, violence is ubiquitous. Sacrifice is instituted to deflect the violence of the community toward a "scapegoat." *Works and Days* seems to support Girard's theory: without a sacrificial outlet, violence ensues.

Hesiod disagrees. All the reasons for Girard's theory being suspect are to follow, with one decisive event as important as any in a myth to preoccupy us almost completely: the meeting at Mekone and the consequences of Prometheus's act of defiance as narrated by Hesiod in the *Theogony*. Hesiod is both mythic and allegorical. He is already reflecting and writing on several levels of meaning—for one, on the meaning of *therapeia* as a service refused to the gods and instead oriented to the well-being of others. The events about to unfold in Hesiod's *Theogony* surrounding the relationship between human beings and the gods reach a decisive moment when, at a place called Mekone, the poet does concern himself with an urgent meeting so as to settle a dispute—or at least come to an understanding, some necessary agreement. Rather, the focus turns on Prometheus and a decision that will be commemorated across the history of Greece and be represented in the transitions between literary accounts, from Hesiod's poetry, to the theatrical representation in Aeschylus' *Prometheus Bound* and, finally, in a parable told by the sophist Protagoras in the context of a discussion with Socrates. What will the Sophist represent in his myth?

Protagoras will tell his audience how the need to learn respect for others and be knowledgeable about justice within the *polis* will be mandatory. Unless these all-important virtues are learned and followed, Zeus will impose the death penalty as a fitting punishment. The conjunction of animal sacrifice and the death penalty do not readily present themselves at first; other events have to take place, as in the transition between Cain's urban life and the terrestrial experience of the flood. Periods are chronological in history; in myth they overlap in meaning. The conjunction between animal sacrifice and the death penalty does not appear as a declaration; the poet knows what the meaning and consequence of impiety is, so does the tragic playwright. The poetry must devise other forms of expression for the reader to interpret what may be concealed in the very appearance of things, words, and expected meanings.

(And yet, despite the intervention of the poet, consciously writing an ancient myth with *his* interpretive logos, tradition seems to have agreed upon a consensus understanding.)

Responses can be reassessed.

> The myth of how Prometheus tricks Zeus at Mekone, told by Hesiod, centres around the division of an ox into two parts, on the one hand, bones and fat, and on the other, meat, hide, and the stomach. At this one event, usually considered to have led up to the institution of animal sacrifice, Prometheus hid the bare bones of the slaughtered ox in the glistening, obviously appetizing fat, and it is the sight of these bones instead of the meat which causes Zeus' anger.[7]

Two points, to start, will be central to my argument: one, at no time does Prometheus "trick" or deceive Zeus; two, more importantly, the events at Mekone (contrary to what is "*usually considered*") do not lead to the institution of animal sacrifice; a completely opposite reading can be suggested. One other commentator writes, "The story begins with a feast held at Mecone and attended by men and gods."[8] The reason for the meeting at Mekone has nothing to do with a feast, a banquet, or any celebration at all. The gathering of human beings and gods has one purpose and one purpose only: the ritual of animal sacrifice as a religious observance has become an issue of concern and calls for a discussion.

The *poesis* of the Greek is a *making*. *Poetizing* creates a human world. Hesiod does not mimic. He does not inherit a mythic conception; the poet does not compose without at the same time making necessary alterations. He composes as an interpreter, making his poetry wholly rational. These are not editorial intrusions; the poet cannot be considered as one who transmits tradition, but rather the human being who gives readers the opportunity (the imperative) of interpreting what has been handed down. His intervention is, also, timeless. He communicates to the reader of today just as readily as his contemporaries. A reading of Hesiod's *Theogony* will allow us not so much to trace the *genesis of the gods*. The genealogy, as a whole, is a superficial representation of a traditional reality. Hesiod is primarily interested in the depiction of one scene, when human beings meet the gods at a place called Mekone and, during a

7. Ekroth, "Bare Bones," 15.

8. Sommerstein, "Hesiod and Tragedy," 279.

historical transition in their relationship, are supported in their endeavor by Prometheus. The poet's urgent message to interpret is already a mark of philosophy.

> The mythical themes, episodes, and figures that he retains, and sometimes touches up, fit together in the course of his account as the combined parts of a unified message whose global significance and rich complexity it is the poet's purpose to transmit. In the work of Hesiod, then, we have to recognize what may be described as a learned mythology richly and subtly elaborated that possesses all the finesse and rigor of a philosophical system while at the same time remaining totally committed to the language and mode of thought peculiar to myth.[9]

Heath concludes with one estimate of the role of Hesiod as a "didactic" poet. If the *Theogony* is in fact *didaktikos* and therefore "able to teach," it does so first and foremost in terms of making it obvious what his intentions are as a poet who uses, necessarily, handed-down traditions of mythic thought. "Hesiod was presumably conscious of the role poets played in transmitting traditions in early Greek society, and doubtless he would be happy to think of his moral exhortations as having beneficial effects on his audiences."[10] Didactic, then, might not be the most appropriate description. *Morality* is much too narrow as a category.

(This has been the limit of an almost unanimous reading: once the myths in Genesis and Hesiod are released from their moral obligations, their *metaphysical* meanings are better able to be examined.)

Hesiod is much less interested in moral exhortations than in metaphysical foundations of thought and being. If Hesiod the poet is a "teacher," he provides two invaluable lessons—one in relation to himself, the other in relation to the reader. The poet interprets and transform the material he inherits according to principles that are not, merely, imitative; and, consequently, he gives the reader the mandate of interpreting his text and revealing what it may present, perhaps for the first time. A poet has to believe in his *words* being *spectacular*. Other meanings begin to appear once they are no longer heard; words are interpreted beyond what can be *seen*.

The presence of Prometheus in different *genres*, of writing, of thought, indicates how the historical transitions beginning with Hesiod's

9. Vernant, *Myth and Society*, 217. See the last chapter "The Reason of Myth."

10. Heath, "Hesiod's Didactic Poetry," 262–63.

poetry cannot be *constrained*; his character requires thought to be expressed at the very heart of humanity's voice, the voice of the mythic poet's singing, the voices of the characters on stage, alone or in the unison of the Chorus, and the voice of the philosopher in dialogue with himself and others *in writing*. If, as a classicist tells us, "philology notes that 'pharmakon,' the regular Greek word for drug, is cognate with words meaning 'sing,'"[11] Hesiod the poet may be presenting his origin of the gods and a unique appearance by human beings as a *remedy* from an intolerable condition of being. Soteriology or the twin impetus of salvation and healing are both intended to overcome an enfeebled state. The original may have been a lullaby to put everyone to sleep. The poet's words alert us to a world. The poet inaugurates a metaphysical consciousness that will move, historically, from myth to tragedy to philosophy and always with one deliberate and consistent preoccupation—the determination of human beings to make themselves independent of the demands of the gods and the past history of tradition.

Hesiod has been defined as the poet who *creates* the origin of the gods, as if he put into place an entire metaphysical worldview. Some are tempted to *blame* him. But once Hesiod's writing is interpreted to be much more wily than previously considered and astute enough to prepare his readers for a suspicious relation to his world (Hesiod is by no means gullible, and there is also no deception here) another version appears that runs counter to prevailing conceptions as to Hesiod's poetry no less than the meaning of Prometheus's acts. One suspicion has been noted: to simply assume that Hesiod is constrained by the limits of myth (that is, the stories he *inherited*) does not consider him sufficiently perceptive or creative to be able to prepare for another kind of thinking. It is already philosophical insofar as the poet presents his material to be interpreted. Parenthetically, the concern here is not to decide on an argument for or against multiple authorship—as suggested by Lamberton,[12] or, less so, if any of Hesiod's work is "authentic." The interest in history, as such, is peripheral. The individual poet, for my argument, is not the issue; just as the authors of Genesis are less significant than what we have in front of us to read. A name, an original text, subsequent editorializing may all be of interest to philologists. Not here. The only preoccupation is

11. Burn, *World of Hesiod*, 45.

12. Lamberton, *Hesiod*.

a reading and interpretation of the work in order to understand what it *reveals* from (and through) the human imagination.

In his *An Introduction to Early Greek Philosophy*, John Robinson opens uniquely with the poetry of Hesiod and, not only does he distinguish him from Homer, he also places him at the origins of philosophical thought.

> It is only in Hesiod's *Works and Days* that man occupies the center of the stage, and even here Hesiod's concern is entirely different from Homer's. He is concerned with man as such, in his relations to the social order, to the gods, and to the necessities of life. With such questions the Greek philosophers, too, were concerned, and the answers which they gave to them were deeply colored by their reading of Hesiod. If we start at the beginning, we must start with Hesiod.[13]

Hesiod's poetry presents us with both philosophical thought and, consequently, the pursuit of what the Greeks called *sophia*. Jaeger believes "Hesiod's theogony was a sophizesthai in mythical form."[14]

The beginning in Hesiod's *Theogony*, however, has been exposed to a number of misleading interpretations; stated more forcefully, beginning from the events in Mekone and the decisions made by Prometheus, his motivations and the intended consequences of his acts have been misunderstood. A defense allows for a different interpretation of his acts. When two traditions are considered together and placed side by side (what can be called Judeo-Greek thought), a *parakletic* hermeneutics comes up with a completely different argument and a necessary defense against all the false accusations brought against these ancient *characters*. Accusations have too often been made; they are followed by judgments and verdicts and punishments. Dissenting voices have not bee usually heard.

The consensus has led to one narrow conclusion. The poet and, later, the playwright Aeschylus, are both taken at their word. Prometheus is described by Hesiod as "devious"[15]—to isolate this one word from the poem as a start. Are readers going to be impressionable? Commentators have been unanimous in defining Prometheus, and in his relationship to the gods, as a "trickster." Is it really his intention, as we shall see, to trick or deceive Zeus? His acts can be rethought from this hesitation, "*which seems to imply*," Rutherford adds, "Prometheus' attempt to improve the

13. Robinson, *Introduction to Greek Philosophy*, 3.

14. Jaeger, *Early Christianity and Greek Paideia*, 47.

15. Hesiod, *Theogony*, 521.

human condition by arranging that man get the better part of sacrifice."[16] *Seems*, indeed. This is but the first impression that will be rethought at the appropriate time. A beginning is important here as it will be elsewhere. A limiting consensus has been as obvious in relation to Prometheus as in the episodes of Genesis examined before. Does Hesiod define the truth of Prometheus? Or does he make it possible for the reader to reevaluate a judgment made about him? Do the words of the poet, while confirming an ancient *prejudice*, take over the material and, in the writing of his account, completely transform our impression of the truth and reality of what Prometheus actually does and stands for? Before a characteristic or an act can be attributed to Prometheus at *Mekone*, preliminary examinations are necessary, just as they were with *Nachash* in Genesis.

One noticeable consequence can be witnessed by commentators, in relation to Hesiod and, once more, by recalling Genesis: those who disobey the gods and rebel against their demands are pronounced guilty without so much as a consideration of their motives or the intended outcome of their actions. "Sin" or *hamartia*, however the "fault," "flaw," or "miss" is understood, remains a ready judgment. Condemnation usually follows. More often than not, it is a judgment with a punishment; it is usually severe and perpetual. A rethinking of Prometheus and what he represents for humanity can be undertaken and at the place where human beings and the gods were involved in a prearranged meeting and a "negotiation" that has challenged readers and commentators alike. The first impression of the scene makes it enigmatic. The poet has given us a sense of his elusive meaning, in effect emulating Prometheus himself, not as a form of *deception*. On the contrary, the *truth* of the matter was intended for the commemoration of the act as well as the attitude of a different humanity in the past that refused to worship the gods by sacrificing animals. Prometheus initiates nothing less than a foundational act that will have far-reaching consequences. One intriguing suggestion can be entertained. Edwards writes,

> We may be sure that changes in alphabet and orthography took place during the earliest period of the text's transmissions, but there is no satisfactory means of determining what more radical alterations may have been introduced in the editing of the poems (for example, by the substitution of more readily intelligible expressions for unfamiliar forms of dialect origin), or to what extent an early written text may have been

16. Rutherford, "Hesiod and the Literary Traditions of the Near East."

> influenced by a parallel oral one maintained by rhapsodes, which might perhaps be equally liable to expansion and interpolation.[17]

The revolutionary nature of Hesiod's philosophical position (quite apart from the specificity of his language) may have had antecedents in the oral presentation of one, perhaps more, rhapsode. Hesiod may be commenting on a rare memory of a tradition that has already recognized animal sacrifice as a problem. Poets have already insinuated themselves into a confrontation with the concepts of *theology*. Myth, theology, society; they are inseparable in Hesiod's poems and constitutes a far-reaching reflection on the nature of metaphysical beliefs and their foundations for a historical order of being.

Hesiod's description of the event, which amounts to no more than an allusion and avoids providing any details at all, is at once allegorical and social. Myth has been undermined, at least for its consistent and unwavering transmission. A critical consciousness has become aware of itself. The conception of the gods (as they have been handed down by a conservative tradition) has suddenly become questionable. If, then, the date of Hesiod's composition can be narrowed down even as late as the early seventh century, the Greek mind has already begun to *analyze* the nature of the myths and, far from merely inheriting an oral tradition, the act of writing begins to make the analytic critique systematic and permanent. Despite the interesting conjecture, ultimately the source of the poem (whether from an individual named Hesiod or from a later edition or, perhaps, even an interpolation) cannot determine the reading of the text. Once a prior humanity, as Hesiod told us in his "ages" section, did not sacrifice to the gods, that insight has *historical consequences*. Once sacrifice is relinquished, it makes possible to rethink the nature of piety and, more absolutely, the very nature of human existence—as will be witnessed, for example, in the poetry of Orpheus and the philosophy of Pythagoras, to name but two individuals and "schools" of thought, just as the unique prophet Malachi was unequivocal in his Jewish world.

The "negotiation" at Mekone (that began as a *dispute*) as rendered in Hesiod's *Theogony* does not sufficiently represent the extent of the human beings as they make an appeal to the gods—a judicial appeal and an attempt to abolish an inheritance from the primordial past. The possibility of a new history has already been imagined. The humans are not, at this point, simply arguing the law: they are making an appeal to the gods to

17. Edwards, *Language of Hesiod*, 13.

completely reorganize all relationships in the world, that is, the triadic relationship of gods, humans, and animals. Human beings are far from compliant; they may not have a historical record of the past, nor an oral memory handed down to them to verify their suspicions. But Hesiod, a human accomplice and in no way complicit with the gods, tells us elsewhere and in a different myth that cannot be read independently of each other that in the past human beings were not subordinate to the gods. In the section in *Works and Days* on "the ages of man," let us remind ourselves once again that there was a time when human beings "refused to worship the gods and offer the blessed ones sacrifice on their holy altars, as is prescribed for men in their customs." In the present, there is, then, an emulation of their ancestors as the courageous human beings who, as self-defining, refused to acknowledge the supposed superiority of the gods.

Hesiod opens, for us, the one singular scene in the *Theogony*: "For when the gods and mortal men fell to disputing (*ekrinonto*)[18] at Mekone, Prometheus, acting in a spirit of kindness, divided and dished up a great ox, deceiving the mind of Zeus" (535–37). One sentence; and yet every single element has repercussions, almost to the point of being inestimable, with the complications only beginning as the events continue toward a well-known end—the punishment of Prometheus by Zeus, the lawmaker. The scene is sparse and economical. If reading can be self-deceptive, it can also be inattentive. Hesiod demands as much hermeneutic attention as possible. *Paraklesis* will here be all-important. The poem is going to reveal its comprehensive argument as long as every single element is pursued, without fail, individually and in relation—and to what is "forethought" and anticipated. Four themes will frame the interpretation, even when they are incomplete and the poet expects the reader to *work*, filling in gaps, reading between the lines: one, the nature of the dispute (and "negotiation") between the human beings and the gods; two, the reason for the presence of Prometheus as an *advocate* in the meeting; three, the "division" of the slaughtered ox that, by all appearances, is supposed to be about portions, meat served at a table and a shared meal; four, the one word that everyone has agreed is both pertinent and accurate—*deception*. One is tempted to call this a universal *misinterpretation*, like the supposed deception of Eve by the "serpent." Hesiod is taken at his word, carelessly. The poet is not a reporter of facts; the truth of a

18. The translation of *ekrinonto* in the *Theogony* by Lombardo is "negotiating."

scene, especially when a "crime" will be committed, is not immediately disclosed.

Before any of the elements of the poem are examined, the poet has some advice for the reader that cannot be taken for granted or forgotten: it may be the single most important confession by the poet who, relaying an ancient story while also being inspired by the Muses, warns the reader. The inspiration of the Muses implies many kinds of creativity. "We know how to tell numerous lies which seem to be truthful, but whenever we wish we know how to utter the full truth" (29–31). In a poem that deals with a world-altering confrontation between human beings and the gods, with Prometheus acting on behalf of humanity and during one *last sacrifice*, the reader has been given notice: *self-deception* is possible. The *reader* may be deceived by appearances and the traditional meaning of words, forgetting the meeting at Mekone because paying too much attention to the culinary skills of Prometheus as he handles meat, fat, and bones, as if he was preparing as meal. The chef might be concerned with presentation, and dexterity is being watched; so is the poet and the use of his words, his overall composition. Appearances are tricky, as are truth and lies when they are placed side by side, one on top of the other in a temporary disguise.

F. Carter Philip points out that the verb *krino* may have a legal meaning, referring to a dispute and in need of a settlement; and while it "*does not have to have* legal connotations,"[19] it implies the need to come to a decision. Legal or not, there is a confrontation, and a *division*, first of all, between human beings and gods. Vernant believes so; the scene involving Prometheus is done "in the presence of gods and men, in order to distinguish between them (*ekrinonto*)."[20] Jenny Strauss Clay makes the same argument. What it was that was being distinguished," she notes, was "what is a god and what is a mortal."[21] All these are pertinent; the divine/mortal distinction is an issue just as the legal argument being presented by human beings at Mekone is crucial. Girard adds an important point, though noticeably, he does not here mention Prometheus at all. "*Crisis, crime, criteria, critique*, all share a common root in the Greek verb *krino*,

19. Philips, "Narrative Compression," 292, my emphasis.

20. Vernant, *Myth and Society in Ancient Greece*, 186. Chapter 8, "The Myth of Prometheus in Hesiod," will be the subject of a few more comments.

21. Strauss Clay, *Hesiod's Cosmos*, 101.

which means not only to judge, distinguish, differentiate, but also to accuse and condemn a victim."[22]

A resolution between the two meanings does not seem possible, unless both are unified into one argument: the division (and now, let us recall the "Golden Age") is also a legal matter. Human beings are attempting to change laws. The gods, with the upper hand, reject any proposal that is suggested or offered. Hesiod does not tell us what the negotiation is specifically about: but if we recall the unknown nature of the origin of sacrifice (instituted when the race of silver men was created in *Works and Days*—and here it might be appropriate to stress once again that the poem is written by a farmer like Adam and his son Cain) then it can only be the recollection of a past time that the human beings are invoking during the first moments of the meeting.

Human beings have lived with an intolerable situation since the beginning of their lives. They have been raised by their parents, emulated them and others, and learned to perpetuate the order of the world. They have created communities of like-minded people; they have shared their lives with domesticated animals who have provided them both with essential relationships—of caring and of mutual benefits. They have lived with animals, attended to their births, reared them to maturity, and protected them from predators and from the wild. Domestic animals have provided innumerable benefits. They have endured difficult labor with the perseverance of the ox and the generosity of other animals (goats for example, who have made it possible to turn milk into cheese) who have provided wool and warmth from the elements. Despite this enduring relationship of care and mutual benefit, each serving the other and with human beings appreciating the service of animals (indeed, human life would be much harder physically without them and unthinkable *emotionally*) the gods have forced them to live an intolerable contradiction. They could only put up with it for so long. The negotiation at Mekone, then, could not be more exact: human beings appealed to the gods that one particular necessity imposed on them was no longer sustainable.

Human beings have been forced to carry out an observance that could be abolished. Their relationship to the gods has been predicated on a ritual to be observed as part of their subservience to their demands—one without any sense except obedience, and on the most serious matter of life and death. The gods have demanded that animals be sacrificed

22. Girard, *Scapegoat*, 22.

as a form of worship to them even though they could not, as was obvious to all, either participate in the ritual or take advantage of the meat to eat; apparently, the ascending smoke, a final by-product of the entire ritual, was a sufficient sign of human worship and subservience. Animal sacrifice has had but one purpose: human beings were forced to kill and eat the very animals that provided them with companionship, help them with work both in the fields and in the city, and with food that was not created from the natural world from the ground, plants, and trees. The poets have long recognized how the world may be transformed by the imagination; all mimetic impositions can be rejected and replaced with a new creation. Before turning to the details of the events at Mekone, one argument has to be presented and in contradistinction to commentators who misinterpret Hesiod as well as the acts of Prometheus.

The dispute and negotiation at Mekone begins everything. The poet does not write for the gods; poetic words are for human ears and eyes only. Human language emerges from out of the inspired psyche of the poet who both creates and interprets and so reveals a truth to human beings. Hesiod does not inherit the realities of the past; he uses them for his own purposes and ends—in part to create a reality that has been known before, in a distant past, and remaining to be recollected from out of the imagination more archaeologically inclined than the present of time and history. Hesiod the poet takes his readers from their present to an *imaginable* time; the future can be created by a restoration. He may have enigmatic messages only given clarification by the assistance of Hermes, the hermeneutic translator, but the poet too has an individual language capable of being interpreted by human discernment and opaque for the obtuse gods. The enigma of language runs both ways. Human beings too have secrets and keep them well safeguarded from the natural curiosity of the gods who wonder, when insecure, jealous, uncertain, about the human sophistication to reflect on the nature of their existence; after all, they know how sudden divine successions can be.

Murder has so often been part of their generations.

The confrontation between human being and gods at Mekone is a decisive event in poetic history. The act by Prometheus, however, is not at all *deceptive*. The poet has made himself dynamic in the representation of Prometheus, taking what has been traditional and rewriting it with an altogether different interpretation. The "division" of the portion of meat reflects the division of human beings and the gods. Previously, there has been a proper measure (between humans and gods, reflected in the division of portions, what is *proper* to each), but at Mekone all previous arrangements have been suspended. The world has been put on hold. When the poet describes Prometheus dividing the portions, the act has to be interpreted as an *allegory*. The poet does not represent the mythic reality of the past; he has transformed it, hinting at a new time, a breach in historical continuity.

How the introduction is interpreted provides the impetus to the story. Human beings have now realized, fully and unequivocally, that the continued demand by the gods to be worshiped with sacrifice has turned them into killers and butchers; violence and slaughter has been defined as a religious ritual in order to make it legitimate. The meeting in Mekone represented the human attempt to disassociate themselves from their service to the gods and, at the same time, to transform the relationship of being in the world as a whole. Unlike the cynicism of the gods, wholly indifferent to human rationality now developing on its own, independently, and precisely to shift the place of the gods, human beings are conscious of themselves and their development and aware of their desire for freedom and self-sufficiency. The meeting of Mekone and the imposed decision by the gods, unilateral and without as much as considering the request of mortals, soon leads to Prometheus's defiant acts, as well as the consequences he is already conscious of and prepared to accept. After all, Prometheus has "forethought," can anticipate the future not, perhaps, because he has been favored with the gift of divination but for his ability to assess the past; only by analyzing the vicissitudes of the past does he have the ability to anticipate a future to come, for himself and for human beings.

Prometheus is not a tragic figure. Aeschylus's *Prometheus Bound* is not a tragedy.

Since the "negotiation" has failed and the gods have insisted on the relationship continuing according to a well-established tradition, Prometheus decides to act on the behalf of humanity. Just as human disobedience was necessary to initiate the social world in Genesis, Prometheus's rebellion will ultimately lead to a transformed human world. Prometheus's handiwork in a mythic kitchen had led to the unanimous belief in an act of trickery, deception, some scheme to dupe the gods. But to interpret Prometheus's act of manipulating the parts of the sacrificed animal (meat, bones, fat) as deceptive fails to recognize his intentions as irreverent and mocking. Prometheus is a supreme *ironist*. The mythic creatures who intervene and act in support of human beings against the authority of the gods are not deceitful; they have other intentions in mind.

Turning to the *Theogony* allows us to continue a *parakletic* hermeneutics for both the poem and Prometheus. All of his acts, "acting in a spirit of kindness," are done to *support* human beings, as a *therapeia* or service to them. We are not informed about the nature of the dispute, nor about the outcome of the negotiation—stalemate or settlement; but if Prometheus's act as he apparently sacrifices an ox can only be related to the nature of the dispute (*it seems*, in terms of the parts of the animal consumed, and perhaps the portions) then the description of the *deception* can now be completely rethought. The *Theogony* reads, "On the one side he put the flesh and the rich and the fat inner parts hidden under the skin, concealed in the paunch of the ox; on the other side he put the ox's white bones, arranging them well with skillful deception, concealed in the silvery fat" (538–42). The poet seems to tell us that Prometheus has been sly, deceptive, a trickster; no one can fault the reader for believing the description. Again, the consensus is overwhelming. Juries have made a decision and handed over a verdict. Prometheus hides, conceals, arranges, and deceives. The description of the scene, its reality (as it appears) in no way reveals Prometheus's consciousness or his intentions. Hesiod has been extremely careful to arrange his own language and, most especially, the difference between his precise *words* and what can only be read by an act of interpretation that notices the "deception" somewhere else. Words too can be made to appear; the division of the animal is analogous to the representation of words. Beneath appearances are other intended meanings. Readers, however, have ignored the difference between Hesiod's lines and Zeus's words.

Everyone believes Zeus. They believe what *he says* to Prometheus. "Then the Father of Gods and of Men addressed him as follows: 'Son of Iapetos lord surpassing others in glory, ah my good fellow, how very unfairly you make the division!' Thus did Zeus, whose plans are unfailing, chidlingly speak. And Prometheus, the clever deviser, made him answer, gently smiling the while and mindful of skillful deception" (543–48). Again, there are two different elements here: one, the sense of Prometheus being filled with glory and good while also being a "deviser" and "deceiver." One wonders, however, if he has been wrongly *identified.* He has been picked out as one among others, or even many, a mere "type." "Prometheus is more clearly a culture-hero of the trickster type, by whose philanthropic trickery the actual, the advantageous division of sacrifice as established."[23] This one interpretation, often repeated, can be questioned and revised. Prometheus does not provide human beings with the advantage of the better portions of meat. The scene at Mekone is about the abolition of animal sacrifice, an argument that requires several different commentaries as the poem continues. To return to an often-made description: the association of Prometheus to a "trickster figure" had been made by Burkert by tracing its relation to the Babylonian epic *Aratrahasis*. "Further threads lead from cunning Arathrasis to the Promethean myth. But these are less specific when set in the context of the very common trickster figure."[24] Vernant, literally, calls him every name in the book. In "The Myth of Prometheus in Hesiod,"[25] the name-calling is too much: the denigration of Prometheus's character is all too familiar and include his "guile," "cunning intelligence," "skill in trickery," "cunning foresight," and "deception." Wirshbo defines the original event as "the banquet scene at Mekone"[26] while also calling Prometheus a "prankster." Beall writes that "when gods and men originally divided, Prometheus divided an ox, cheating the mind of Zeus. He cunningly disguised the meat to look like the skin, the bones like the meat."[27] The innumerable and consistent observations, if any advancement is to be made on the interpretation of at least this one passage if not the *Theogony* on the whole, require a reconsideration of the entire *sequence* of meanings.

> When the Greeks wondered why the gods in sacrifices received the worse part and man himself ate the better, they explained it by the act of Prometheus, or whoever else may have figured in the story of the successful deception of Zeus. Zeus himself was clearly the dupe who when he was offered the choice between the two piles of meat chose that which had a thin layer of fat on its top but consisted underneath entirely of bones. The theft of the fire, which Prometheus accomplished next, was another deception of Zeus.[28]

23. Lombardo, "Notes," in his translation of *Theogony*, 98.

24. Burkert, *Orientalizing Revolution*, 106.

25. Vernant, "The Myth of Prometheus in Hesiod," is in chapter 8, 183–201, of *Myth and Society in Ancient Greece*, 196. Unfortunately, considerations of length make it impossible to more completely respond to Vernant. To do so, it would also be necessary to provide a detailed commentary on "At Man's Table: Hesiod's Foundation Myth of Sacrifice," chapter 2 of *The Cuisine of Sacrifice among the Greeks*. My one main argument: Prometheus certainly did not invent sacrifice.

26. Wirshbo, "The Mekone Scene."

27. Beall, "Hesiod's Prometheus."

28. Solmsen, *Hesiod and Aeschylus*, 48.

It is clearly impossible to make Zeus in any way the "dupe" in the entire sequence of events. He knows precisely what Prometheus is up to. The whole scene is organized by Prometheus for maximum *effect*; not one is in any way related to a deception. On the contrary, nothing could be stated with more clarity—if, on the part of Hesiod, with more irony and created by him with all his linguistic sophistication. He is acerbic. As long as the reader remains captivated by the spectacle of the sacrifice and the ritual, the truth of the matter will remain elusive and *covered up*, precisely like the mixture of meat and fat and bones. There is no cover-up and no deception. Prometheus reenacts the sacrificial scene in order to make a mockery of the entire ritual and to present the gods with an ironic message. Given what Solmsen tells us about Hesiod and the "division" of the meat, a comment has to be made on its "distribution." As a poet, Hesiod is here at his most provocative. First, a few comments on the sense of commensality are necessary, then the observation (an *impossible* one), that Prometheus *invented* sacrifice. He did no such thing; nothing could be further from the truth.

In a footnote to his translation of Plato's *Minos*, Pangle draws our attention to the relation between the Greek "distributing" (*dianeimai*) and the law (*nomos*).[29] Although the sense of equity is in relation to ownership of the land, the consequences are no less important for the maintenance of domestic animals and for their use as sacrificial victims. Hesiod has no interest whatsoever in representing the idea of equality in the distribution of *meat*. His argument is more all-encompassing. The law created by Zeus following this act of rebellion on the part of human beings and Prometheus leads, directly and in the detail provided by Aeschylus in *Prometheus Bound*, to a most peculiar death penalty that is a macabre *inversion* of the sacrificial ritual. The imperative of eating sacrificial meat will be foremost in the mind of Zeus as the devises the punishment for Prometheus.

"Hierarchy is instituted and demonstrated in the distribution of meat,"[30] as Burkert tells us. The vertical division is applicable on earth as it is on Mount Olympus. Prometheus acted with a particular end in mind; or, to be more precise, Hesiod the poet created the scene so as to completely overturn the sacrificial ritual since it confirmed, within the *polis*, a hierarchy of power and privilege and undermine the ideal of the

29. Plato, *Minos*, 60.

30. Burkert, "Sacrificial Violence," 439.

demos. The problem of meat-eating is not merely a detail; it raises several interrelated conflicts at the heart of the mythic, tragic, and philosophical reconsideration of the animal sacrifice.

This will not be the last time meat-eating becomes much more than dietary.

Eating meat is a metaphysical act.

West reminds us that "in Hesiod the theft of fire followed its withdrawal by Zeus in response to the trick that Prometheus played on him at Mekone over the division of meat."[31] One fact has been overlooked. Zeus deprived the human beings of fire because of their refusal to sacrifice, that is, kill and *roast* animals on behalf of the gods. At this point one assumption can be rethought. "Let us recall to mind the main line of the story. *In the beginning* gods and men live together, sitting down to table at the same feasts. But Prometheus is given the responsibility of allotting to each group its own share of food. He plans to exploit the opportunity offered him to hoodwink Zeus and defraud him to the advantage of the humans."[32] They add, "Sacrifice is therefore a ritual that stages and confirms the separation between gods and humans." Far more important than a separation (and that means hierarchy) between gods and humans are the social separations, the ones, for example, highlighted by Detienne.

There are no indications whatsoever that human beings and gods ever ate together. No concern with portions has been shown; nor is Prometheus given the responsibility of serving equitably. (These are assumptions nowhere demonstrable in Hesiod.) Finally, the one point of stressing some "fraud" being committed is not reflective of the scene. Instead, it is Detienne himself who, in relation to the Orphic sect, reveals the truth of the matter.

> Orphism is a movement of religious protest that defines itself by an attitude of refusal, refusal of the whole politicoreligious system organized around the Olympian gods and the distance that separates them from men. . . . To change one's diet is to throw into doubt the relationship between gods, men, and beasts upon which the whole politicoreligious system of the city rests.[33]

There is no sacrificial culture without a corresponding social arrangement of privilege, of hierarchy, and more important than all of them, the

31. West, "Prometheus Trilogy," 365.

32. Detienne and Vernant, *Cunning Intelligence*, 125, my emphasis.

33. Detienne, *Dionysos Slain*, 70.

politicoreligious system that includes the irreducibility of the law. One further argument by Hénaff cannot be sustained. "It is through sacrifice that meat consumption, *which is essential for life*, enters into the system of relations between humans and gods."[34] As is made abundantly and repeatedly clear by all subsequent traditions of thought, in both Judaism and Greece and, eventually, in the rise of Christianity, once the relationship between the divine and human beings is mediated by the slaughter of animals, a fundamental dilemma in religious worship has been introduced and remains irreconcilable. There is no more pressing dilemma in the ancient world than the tradition of animal sacrifice—and for reasons that are not (as I am arguing) strictly limited to the slaughter of animals. The conjunction between animal sacrifice and the death penalty as it developed in Genesis 1–9 can also be witnessed in the Greek world and in the presence of Prometheus in poetic myth, tragedy, and philosophy. The dynamic of historical thought is unmistakable. Greek myth, tragedy, and philosophy are to be read as a conjunction.

All traditional arguments have been suspended. Any assumption about a "deception" on the part of Prometheus is simply not possible given what we know of his act and Zeus's response. One other argument made by the "Paris school" is, also, placed into doubt—unless we actually believe Aeschylus when he writes that Prometheus invented sacrifice as a "murky craft." At this point Aeschylus will soon have to be introduced, for his role as a tragic writer and for his depiction of Prometheus's punishment. The specific punishment he suffers, as a *complete inversion* of sacrifice, could not be more indicative of the metaphysical foundations of the Greek world and the separation between gods, human beings, and animals.

Detienne writes, "By the invention of sacrifice, Prometheus assures passage from the communal repasts of gods and men in the Golden Age to the meat diet; in the other, by bringing fire and inventing the various techniques, Prometheus wrests humanity from savagery and bestiality."[35] This "explanation" raises doubts; it seems more like a modern projection. Modern consciousness seems unable to enter myth. Unless its *philosophical logos* is noticed, myth is misunderstood. *Prometheus did not invent sacrifice*. The gods invented sacrifice (after the creation of the Silver race) to create a division between human beings and themselves.

34. Hénaff, *Price of Truth*, 190, 191, my emphasis.

35. Detienne, *Dionysos Slain*, 57.

Far from human beings moving away from "savagery" and "bestiality"—as if the Golden Age was, then, "barbaric," a term with precise meaning in the Greek world—meat-eating confirmed their willingness to accept a new hierarchy and the vertical supremacy of gods, humans, animals. Vidal-Naquet writes, "Prometheus, who furnished fire for cooking and introduced sacrifice, was also responsible for the break with the gods and with wild beasts."[36] One more commentator agrees. "Hesiod emphasizes Prometheus' role as the *inventor* of sacrifice, a key institution that dominates Greek religion and public life."[37] The classical interpretation does not persuade.

Prometheus did not create, invent, or otherwise begin the practice of animal sacrifice. On the contrary, not only did Prometheus not "help" human beings establish the ritual, he explicitly acted so as to ridicule the gods and their need of slaughtered animals. Prometheus exposes the violation of nature from a former time because human beings are first compelled to develop a pastoral relationship with animals only to then slaughter them in a religious ritual. The logic of sacrifice in Hesiod can be rethought if we are to recognize the explicit relationship between animal sacrifice, Promethean disobedience, and the death penalty—in his case particularly poignant since it did not end in death but in a ceaseless torture whereby an eagle ate his liver—that is the organ used by haruspices to *read* its lines for divinatory purposes. In order to properly understand Prometheus as a literary creation by Hesiod and its reinterpretation by the tragedy in Aeschylus's *Prometheus Bound*, one traditional definition, virtually repeated by everyone, should be abandoned. Nothing is more improbable than Prometheus inventing sacrifice. A whole tradition of thought has misunderstood Prometheus just as they have mischaracterized the role of *Nachash* in Genesis 1–3. These intersections in the Judeo-Greek world now require a reinterpretation—a reappraisal of the *record* and how the accusations, judgments, and judicial findings must now be reexamined in light of the evidence that, until now, has been ignored. If Hesiod is indeed at the "beginning of Greek philosophy,"[38] as others previously mentioned also believe, then a decisive history has its intimations if not its origin (for Jews and Greeks alike) in myths that are intended to lead, self-consciously, to a completely different order of thought. Once

36. Vidal-Naquet, *Black Hunter*, 288.

37. Dougherty, *Prometheus*, 6. She later adds, "Hesiod explains that Prometheus helped mankind establish the institution of sacrifice" (15, my emphasis).

38. Diller, "Hesiod und die Anfänge der griechischen philosophie."

we see Hesiod as an incomparable poet of civilization, his presentation of Prometheus was intended as a rethinking of handed-down tradition. The "serpent," *Chavah*, Cain, and Prometheus are interrelated as representatives of the reason in myth.

Rowe calls Hesiod a "proto-philosopher," with some qualifications. "Hesiod predates the rise of philosophy," Rowe tells us, "and his influence clearly helped to shape the theories of its earliest representatives; but we should not therefore assume too easily that he 'comes before them' in all respects."[39] The significant argument is not to merely point out some precedence between poetry and philosophical *concepts*. Hesiod presents us with the emergence of an exegetical imperative; his poems spur on the hermeneutic responsibility of the reader and, in many ways, are invitations to establish a relationship with the meanings of the poet. In the *Theogony*, Hesiod presents himself as a poet of the myths of the past and simultaneously as someone who provides the reader with the opportunity for an entirely other interpretation.

The consensus view that Prometheus "invented" sacrifice has been rejected. As Plato made clear in the *Critias* as a *philosophical* response to the misinterpretation of foundational myths, poets like Hesiod were not, simply, representing the ancient world they had inherited orally from tradition. "Gods distributed the whole earth and between them in larger and smaller shares and then established shrines and sacrifices for themselves."[40] The composition of Hesiod's poetry is already an interpretation of what he has inherited. So now we are in a better position to turn to the significant scene in *Theogony* and then to see how Aeschylus in *Prometheus Bound* supplements it. Not only does Prometheus not invent sacrifice, he attempts to do precisely the opposite—that is, abolish it and (along with the human beings who are intent on renegotiating their subservient position) create a new social order. Once the incident at Mekone is interpreted from the standpoint of the abolition of animal sacrifice as a religious ritual, then Zeus's punishment of taking fire from human beings can be seen as a *vengeful* act. Why does he take away fire from human beings? If they have now refused to carry out sacrifices, when fire is necessary to render the slaughtered animal edible, then they will have no access to fire for any reason at all—not for light, not for warmth, not for any purpose. The vengeance of Zeus will have one other consequence.

39. Rowe, "Archaic Thought in Hesiod," 135.

40. Plato, *Critias*, 113c.

Prometheus is not a so-called "trickster figure," since his decisive act of covering up a bone with fat and then giving it to Zeus was hardly done as an act of deception. Surely Prometheus, he who has forethought and a discerning intelligence, was not delusional about Zeus's abilities. The act of giving Zeus unsavory fat and bones was an act of supreme rebellion, and with *hilarious mischief* in no way apprehensive about his punishment. Prometheus was irreverent, without respect for the pretensions of supposedly all-powerful gods and who could get a laugh at their expense. The Prometheus of the *Theogony* no less than the Aeschylus play can in no way be implicated in the creation of sacrifice.

The gods are oblivious to the imagination and *feelings* of the poet; the gods could never understand the intolerable imposition on a shepherd who took care of his flock and then, at an appointed time (some festival to revere and worship the gods) had to butcher animals he had cared for and talked to, tended and shared his life with. The gods could never understand the contradiction between a sacrificial society and a pastoral one. They live in a lofty abode on Mount Olympus and cannot appreciate what it means to live on the earth, close to the ground, amid nature. Sacrifice and pastoralism have always been incommensurable. Human beings, however, make an equally stunning claim that is, again, completely lost on the gods. The gods react out of ignorance; they are perplexed at first, then outraged, finally as dismissive as Zeus in Plato's *Symposium* when the protohuman rebelled against their supremacy. Once Prometheus, the courageous being who has forethought (that is, can see an anticipate the future) acts on behalf of human beings by *ridiculing* the gods, then Zeus can be expected to respond typically. Zeus exercises his power to inflict punishment. Hesiod himself becomes so preoccupied with the relationship between Prometheus and the gods that, at least for a time, the humans are forgotten. However, we cannot ever ignore that Prometheus's every act is done for human beings, as generosity, kindness, a *gift that he does not expect to be returned*. Prometheus exemplifies a poetic concept with far-reaching consequences. Hesiod transforms the idea of *charis*, understood as an act of gift-giving as reciprocity (what the Romans will call *do ut des*, "I give so you may give"), into an act of generosity. Prometheus does not expect a return. Eventually, the free act done for another will be called *grace*.

There are now two remaining issues to deal with; they have to be analyzed separately and in order. First of all, when the confrontation between Prometheus and Zeus has led to a *declaration* through an act, the god has but one response. The punishment fits the "crime," as Hesiod now tells us in the *Theogony*.

> "Son of Iapetos, you who surpass all others in planning, ah my good fellow, you ever are mindful in skillful deception!" Thus in his wrath Zeus, whose plans are unfailing, spoke. And he never forgot the act of deception but thereafter no longer gave to the ash trees the strength of weariless fire, which is boon for mortal men who dwell on the earth. (559–64)

Zeus does not punish Prometheus—or does so only indirectly. Zeus punishes human beings in order to deprive of them of the fire they need to live. Nothing in the relationship between Prometheus and Zeus at Mekone led to the punishment. If the decision by Zeus and his counsel is to be understood, it must be in relation to the original dispute—that is, when human beings told the gods they no longer wanted to sacrifice animals.

Human beings had begun to rethink the meaning of traditional theology.

Can the political be anticipated in the separation between the polis and religion?

The gods deprived human beings of fire as an act of resentment; if they demanded to end the ritual of animal sacrifice as form of subservience to the gods, then they would be left with no fire at all and therefore be forced to return to a state of nature and without warmth for the cold, light to counteract darkness, and for its ability to forge metal. The bizarre paradox of the punishment also involves returning human beings to a prior state of creation. Human beings have *recollected*, mythically if not in memory, a past time when they did not sacrifice animals, as in the time during the Golden Age. Zeus punishes them by returning them to an in-between time, a liminal history where aspects of culture were lacking. Without fire, human beings are thrown back to a primordial time when fire did not heat their homes, light the darkness, cook, or cauterize wounds—to name but four uses.

The refusal to continue the ritual of animal sacrifice led, directly, to a particular form of punishment. The consequence of the episode at Mekone is *only beginning*. Prometheus now acts, and again in the service of the human beings he cares for. He steals the fire from the gods. "But the goodly son of Iapetos deceived him by thievery, stealing the strength of weariless fire, that far-shining brightness, caught in a fennel stalk's hollow—a deed that pierced to the heart Zeus the Thunderer on High, stirring his spirit to anger, when he beheld among men the far-shining brightness of fire" (565–71). At this point, any interpretation can go in two directions: to the creation of woman and all the repercussions her existence will have for mortal men (and the overlaps between Pandora and *Chavah*) or, more pertinent for the argument to come, the grave punishment suffered by Prometheus.

(If pursued completely in a different direction, from our beginning, the study would have necessarily gone toward not the conjunction between animal sacrifice as a religious ritual and the death penalty as a judicial law, but in the consequences of women and their representation of desire, sexuality, and child-bearing—in other words, life. *Chavah* and Pandora are the Judeo-Greek figures at the origin of this one consequence that, here, cannot be pursued.)[41]

"Thus to deceive Zeus's mind is impossible to get around it, for not even the son of Iapetos, crafty Prometheus, avoided his deep wrath, but he in spite of his shrewdness suffers under the compulsion great inescapable bondage" (613–16). This is now the most appropriate place to leave Hesiod's *Theogony* and, with Prometheus's punishment, which is more specific than the vague "bondage," lead to Aeschylus's tragedy in *Prometheus Bound* and make the attempt to recognize (and argue for) the specific punishment suffered by Prometheus and how it is a *response to Mekone*. Prometheus is exposed, fully, to the law. He is judged, pronounced guilty, and condemned to the death penalty—one, however, with a particular end. It never finishes. Prometheus does not die. A world has now entered into dialogue: the mytho-poetic has led to tragedy, with all the consequences of both the work of the playwright as well as its theatrical representation for human beings to watch, listen, and most especially, interpret.

"In tragedy, the city must both recognize itself and bring itself into question. In other words, tragedy involves both order and disorder. The tragic author displaces the political order, turns it upside down, sometimes does away with it altogether. The presentation or staging (in the literal sense) of the evidence depends upon these shifts."[42] Aeschylus stages a problem for the audience to reflect on, think about, and perhaps

41. For the beginning of any such discussion, see the chapter by Bremmer, "Pandora and the Creation of Eve."

42. Vernant and Vidal-Naquet, *Myth and Tragedy*. See esp., Vidal-Naquet's chapter 12, "Aeschylus, Past and Present," 264.

resolve within themselves. At the same time, at another level, they are given the task of interpreting the meaning of the play. Several elements have to come to the forefront; just as the animal in Genesis can be taken for granted and overlooked, so too the animal in the tragedy soon becomes as important as any of the other characters, whatever their identity or function, whether a messenger-god like Hermes or like the Chorus of Oceanids.

> It is a single aspect that shall be considered here, the question why tragedy is called τραγοδια—a word which seems to *impose the animal on the development of high human civilisation*, the primitive and grotesque on sublime literary creations. If we seek an explanation of the word, we cannot avoid going back to earlier strata, to the religious basis of tragedy and indeed to Greek cult in general.[43]

While my concerns are not, precisely, with "the religious basis of tragedy," it is the connection between religion and the animal that is the main concern. One insight into the *Prometheus Bound* comes to us by way of Cicero: "Let Aeschylus come forward, not merely a poet but a Pythagorean as well, for we are told he was; how does Prometheus in Aeschylus' play bear the pain he suffers for the theft of Lemnos!"[44]

This is a remarkable testimony: if Aeschylus is a Pythagorean, then we have to consider whether, philosophically, he interpreted the myth quite differently than the majority of his contemporaries and, in fact, "rewrote" the play to conform to a non-sacrificial philosophy, one that also did not include meat-eating in his diet. Aeschylus the Pythagorean stages a decisive transformation in Greek consciousness and, consequently, in its history. Once the human beings and Prometheus declared to the gods that the animal would no longer be slaughtered in the context of a religious ritual (and as the first indication of a new future where meat-eating would come to an end, as envisioned by Ovid) Zeus's punishment would be a definitive response.

It is no accident that "the tragedian omits the Mekone episode (Th. 535–64), in which Prometheus divides the sacrificial meat deceitfully, trying to dupe Zeus."[45]

The tragic writer does not need to include it; everyone in the audience is more than aware of the reason why they are now looking at

43. Burkert, "Greek Tragedy and Sacrificial Ritual," 88, my emphasis.

44. Cicero, *Tusculan Disputations*, 171.

45. Munteanu, *Tragic Pathos*, 166.

Prometheus chained to a rock and soon to endure a much more fitting punishment than "bondage." Whether we can actually call Prometheus "the scapegoat (*pharmakos*) of Zeus"[46] is, for us, beside the point. Unfortunately, the philosopher of the scapegoat, René Girard, did not ever consider the circumstances of Prometheus in myth, tragedy, or philosophy, mentioning him only in passing. He writes, "Prometheus is the sacrificial victim who is chained and cannibalized over and over again (the eagle perpetually eats his liver) in a repetition of the sacrificial ritual."[47] Girard makes two arguable statements here: one, Prometheus cannot be *cannibalized* by an eagle; two, his punishment is not a "repetition" of the sacrificial ritual but, when properly interpreted, its *inversion*. This precedence is established in Aeschylus; and it will reach its culmination much later, as we shall see.

The play requires one reading: what is the relationship between the practice of animal sacrifice that has been called into question and, essentially, repudiated as a cultural ritual, and the institution of a penalty here approximating, in all its mythic/tragic manifestation, an execution? Allen gives us an intimation of the meaning of the punishment. It will have to be supplemented with other, more detailed observations.

> Prometheus' punishment generates an entire drama based on his penal situation. The play in effect parses the mechanism of authority. It reminds us that obtaining physical control over someone designated as a wrongdoer is by no means the whole story of punishment. Looked at closely, any punishment is not a *single final moment of execution* but, and more important, an *unfolding drama about the attempt to establish a final moment as authoritative*.[48]

For Prometheus's experience and for everyone who watches or reads, the execution is inseparable from the final, authoritative moment of the meaning of the punishment as decreed by Zeus. The "execution" is a commentary on the animal sacrifice the human beings have repudiated and that Prometheus conspired with them to end. The attempt to abolish animal sacrifice leads to the origin of the death penalty. What remains to be interpreted is the meaning of the punishment and how it confirms my interpretation and reveals Zeus's judicial rationality, one that the Chorus

46. McLelland, *Prometheus Rebound*, 19.

47. Girard, *Evolution and Conversion*, 53.

48. Allen, *World of Prometheus*, 33–34.

points out is "his justice is a thing he keeps by his own standards"[49] and "a thing done by a tyrant's private laws" (403).

The capital punishments suffered by Prometheus bring the entire episode at Mekone, interpreted by Zeus as an illegal act, first by the human refusal to sacrifice, then by Prometheus's many acts of disobedience, to a conclusion. First, Hesiod in the *Theogony:*

> And in fast bondage he bound Prometheus, the devious planner, whipping the painful bindings over a column at midpoint, and against him sent a long-winged eagle to feed on his liver, which was immortal; but whatever this long-winged bird ate during the day grew during the night again to perfection. (521–26)

Apollodorus confirms the punishment. "An eagle swooped down upon him daily and ate his liver, which grew back during the night."[50] Only with Aeschylus, however, do we get a much more full sense of the punishment in addition to the importance of his liver being devoured. In *Prometheus Bound*, Aeschylus adds, "Then Zeus' winged hound, the eagle red, shall tear great shreds of flesh from you, a feaster coming unbidden, every day: your liver bloodied to blackness will be his repast" (1022–25). The eagle, then, is analogous to a "hound," the animal who first makes his presence in this Greek tragedy and who will, noticeably, reappear during two other momentous events later in history.

The birds flying overhead and the dogs roaming around the foot of the cross during the crucifixion of Jesus will be conspicuous by their presence and much more for their meaning.

The form of the punishment was devised by Zeus, ingeniously, to reflect the "crime." Prometheus aided and abetted human beings in repudiating the ritual of animal sacrifice and raising, for the first time, the possibility of abolishing the ritual. Zeus's response was absolute and consistent with a divine response, one that inverted the order of the world (as it was, seemingly, created by the gods) and imposed a capital punishment on Prometheus that would involve an animal, a "winged hound," eating his flesh and liver. There could be no more fitting punishment for Prometheus, the one who aided human beings in bringing animal sacrifice to an end, than being picked at by a bird—an animal, not accidentally related to ornithomancy[51] or divination by "reading" the flight of birds.

49. Aeschylus, *Prometheus Bound*, 188–89.

50. Apollodours, *Library*, 32.

51. As mentioned by Bonnechere in "Divination."

Beside the consumption of his flesh, it is also significant that his liver is also being devoured, for in antiquity the liver was read by a *mantis* who inspected it for signs—and whether the future would be propitious.[52] Prometheus's ability as a diviner is nullified by Zeus in the method of his punishment. The Chorus of Oceanids in *Prometheus Bound* is, finally, the collective voice telling the audience of the *polis* and the individual reader how there is only one way to avoid divine displeasure.

"May I never dallying be slow to give my worship at the sacrificial feasts" (529–31).

The resolution could not be more final. If human beings are to avoid the most gruesome punishment of all, they are required to continue the animal sacrifice as a ritual they have inherited from the past, precisely the advice given by the Athenian in Plato's *Laws*.

The presence of Prometheus in the myth of *Theogony* and in the tragedy of *Prometheus Bound* have allowed us to trace a persistent problem; and though we cannot judge myth and tragedy to be ignorant or unaware of the consequences of human beings initiating a dialogue with the gods in order to fundamentally alter their relations, it will take the full-fledged consciousness of the philosopher to make a certain history explicit and analyzable. The execution of Socrates by the Athenian state forces his student Plato to embark on a corpus of writing that, for all its diversity and intricacy of drama and argument, presents a *case* to the democratic readers of his dialogues so as to comprehensively represent Socrates. If the philosopher did not ultimately choose to defend himself in a court of law made up of his "peers," Plato turned to a series of compositions that, when read together, could present an argument not simply for Socrates's innocence, but for how the origin of the death penalty and the institution of animal sacrifice could not easily be separated.

52. Collins, "Mapping the Entrails."

Chapter 4

The Execution of Socrates

No defense of Socrates the condemned man and philosopher can be adequate to the testimony of his existence as he approaches his death, not unless the final confrontation that has been essential to the whole of his existence becomes our fundamental concern: the argument for "the abolition of this law,"[1] as Socrates says to his friends Crito—the one that makes judgment and execution binding, the public opinion of the many leading to the death of the one. A *parakletic* hermeneutics could make the case that *all* of Plato's writings are consecrated to a defense of Socrates; the defense of the philosophical *life* becomes all the more urgent and inseparable from the death sentence handed down in the court of law. By reading Plato's defense of Socrates as a confrontation with the laws of the state, most especially considering the "crimes which deserve the death penalty,"[2] the philosopher's preeminent reflection of the nature of wisdom has to necessarily lead him to this one, ultimate question. By themselves, the historical events or Plato's defense will not be able to give us a complete impression of Socrates's motivations before and after his trial, the time in prison waiting for his death sentence to take place, and the secondhand description of the moments leading up to drinking the poisoned concoction. To attempt a partial reconstruction of Plato's writings as they have been consecrated to the existence of Socrates the citizen and philosopher has to be, admittedly, partial and incomplete. There will be many interlocutors: among the most important will be the voice

1. Plato, *Crito*, 50b.
2. Plato, *Laws*, 778d.

of "the Laws" in *Crito*, the speech of Protagoras and the presence, once again, of Prometheus. One beginning, to recall the poet Hesiod, prepares our reading.

In the *Lysis*, Socrates says, "I think we ought to follow the path which we turned along before, and look at the question according to the precepts of the poets, who are, so to speak, our fathers and guides in wisdom."[3] The suggestion to "follow the path" of the poets holds: if Hesiod prepared a method for reading his poetic composition in the *Theogony*, with Prometheus representing how meanings of the *logos* are concealed within myth, then one of the most important responsibilities of the reader will be to remember how Socrates devoted himself to writing lyric poetry ("adapting Aesop's fables and a prelude to Apollo"),[4] while waiting for his death sentence to be carried out. The apparent anomaly is, for Socrates, perfectly consistent as an illustration. After all, Aesop was executed by being thrown from the promontory high above the precinct of Delphi, the sacred place represented by the temple to Apollo (the god of healing) and for its inscription for everyone to know themselves by examining their lives. Plato makes a philosophical argument: the examination can be carried out by reading—both "between the lines" and beyond how we would like to see ourselves—and by carefully *thinking with* others, in sequence and so to consider how moments in the life of Socrates were exemplary. The capital charges are well known. The philosopher, from the beginning of his vocation, was bound to reconsider the nature of religious belief and expressions of piety—in Athens represented by sacrificial ritual—as well as "corrupting" his students. Being called to reflect on the most sacred beliefs of the city and the individuals entrusted with their continuity (the young) could have serious consequences, as Socrates knew long before his arrest. He was not prophetic or a diviner. Socrates was more than aware of the inevitable.

Nearing the end of the *Gorgias* and prior to turning, once again in a Platonic dialogue, to one of the meanings of Prometheus, Socrates says, "I shall have no defence to offer in a court of law."[5] Socrates was never interested in an *apologia*. As Nicias, one of his interlocutors knows, someone who has an authentic conversation with Socrates involves "giving an account of his present life-style, and of the ways he has spent his

3. Plato, *Lysis*, 213e–214a.

4. Plato, *Phaedo*, 60d.

5. Plato, *Gorgias*, 521.

life in the past," in other words, being "cross-examined by Socrates."[6] This could never be a judicial undertaking. A longer reference on philosophy and the law will be necessary. For now, before bringing up Prometheus in the context of another myth, Socrates says,

> That is the situation in which I am sure that I shall find myself if I come before a court of law. I shall not be able to point to any pleasures that I have provided for my judges, the only kind of service and good turn that they recognize; indeed I see nothing to envy in those who survey or those who receive such services. And if it is alleged against me either that I am the ruin of younger people by reducing them to doubt or that I insult their elders by bitter criticism in public or in private no defence will avail me, whether true or not, the truth being simply that in all that I say I am guided by what is right and that my actions are in the interest of those who are sitting in judgment of me. So presumably I shall have no alternative but to submit to my fate, whatever it may be.[7]

The words attributed to Socrates as he anticipates his inevitable trial are reminiscent of Prometheus in Aeschylus. But like Prometheus, he does not accept "fate," as if it was a supernatural event ordained by the gods. Socrates too is characterized by "forethought." To say, as Prometheus does, that "I have known all before, all that shall be, and clearly known,"[8] is for Socrates no more, and no less, than the ability to understand the nature of consequences in the world. He is an effrontery to the law and its limits. That much is certain; what remains to be examined are the specific laws he broke.

The first and most important capital charge against him is due to his irreverent conception of Athenian religion and his belief, instead, in gods "of his own invention instead of the gods recognized by the state."[9] The charge of impiety, and of Socrates believing in his own gods, remains vague and without specific details. His belief, his faith, his conviction, can be made much more explicit. Beginning with the long discussion on the nature of piety in the *Euthyphro*, on the day before his trial, shows Socrates at his most rational. Referring to one of his accusers, Socrates says that "he claims I'm a manufacturer of gods, and he says this is why he's prosecuted me, that I create new gods and don't recognize the old

6. Plato, *Laches*, 188a–b.

7. Plato, *Gorgias*, 522.

8. Aeschylus, *Prometheus Bound*, 100–101.

9. Plato, *Apology*, 24c.

ones."[10] A reading of the dialogue leads to one, much more precise conclusion than not believing in the gods of tradition: Socrates puts into doubt the entire human relationship to the gods as expressed in both *sacrifice* and prayer. Once the philosopher dares to introduce doubt and skepticism into the piety of the *polis*, then its metaphysical foundations are no longer stable. The world-order of gods, humans, and animals and their proper relationship cannot be maintained as before. The dialogues written to commemorate the final period of Socrates's life are historically discreet; the days or weeks are relatively short as they begin with a private conversation in the *Euthyphro* and culminate, with a report after the fact in the *Phaedo*, with his execution. The death penalty (lawful, according to the state) has never been more convenient for his accusers and for the individual jurors who pronounced him guilty. The death penalty as it is carried out begins Plato's writing and its totality as it devotes itself to Socrates the philosopher. Socrates is executed by the state for one reason: he dared to rethink the meaning of *therapeia* or "service" to the gods and, instead of the exemplary show of piety in animal sacrifice, transformed it into a therapeutic speech dedicated, as Apollo prescribed, to the well-being (the health) of others and the city as a whole.

The testimony in the *Phaedo* is one beginning, along with the other eye-witnesses of the event of Socrates's death. The historical transmission has obviously been successful in preserving a record of a series of incidents in the city of Athens in 399 BCE. Despite the details of Socrates's life as it approaches its end, however, Plato has a recurring preoccupation. Other writings, on the law and justice (and their difference), for example, are an attempt to understand the metaphysical foundations of a social reality and how Socrates thought and spoke so as to first undermine and then reconceive an alternative.

The cave and the republic: the philosopher has no more intense confrontation—between the deception of shadows and the illumination of a transformed reality. Still, poetic metaphors are suggestive; but they can hardly be sufficient for conceptual thought or the rigors of philosophy. Wisdom, as a word alone, may be evocative but empty of meaning unless capable of being thought, and lived. The *agon* cannot simply be initiated in the present. It must involve two simultaneous adversaries: an immediate one (since traditional authority has made him culpable for a crime against the state) and perhaps a more important one because it requires

10. Plato, *Euthyphro*, 3a.

a fundamental return to a distant, archaic past. The cave and the republic are not isolated. Both of them are sustained by opposing conceptions—the cave by distant myths, the republic by a poetic imagination no longer reliant on the Muses for inspiration. The absolute law, represented by the death penalty, does not ultimately concern Socrates—as an individual. Rather, the philosopher who has eluded the prison and the illusions of the cave, and all its pretensions to the truth despite its appearance, has the responsibility of becoming a *mythic poet* and therefore attempt to repeat, with a difference, the consequences of an origin that has become binding.

To recall the previous discussion of Socrates's anticipation of his trial in the *Gorgias*, Plato returns to the same thought in the *Republic* and, specifically, in the allegory of the cave, discusses the situation of the philosopher who returns to the cave to edify the citizens of the city.

> Do you think it at all surprising that anyone coming to the evils of human life from the contemplation of the divine behaves awkwardly and appears very ridiculous while his eyes are still dazzled and before he is sufficiently adjusted to the darkness around him, if he is compelled to contend in court or some other place about the shadows of justice or the objects of which they are shadows, and to carry through the contest about these in the way these things are understood by those who have never seen Justice itself?[11]

Plato's place in time urges him to return to a primordial time, to origins—real and imagined, historical and speculative—so as to uncover how the present has been determined. Who has defined the parameters of the real? Only by reflecting on Socrates's metaphysical principles did Plato give himself the obligation of fulfilling one decisive aspect of his teacher's philosophy; and so, the dialogues leading to his death were preparations, a historical introduction to a much more all-encompassing problem: if, as the *Euthyphro* and subsequent dialogues argue, Socrates was charged, tried, and executed due to his philosophical opposition to the one foundational ritual of piety and how it sustained the politico-religious order of the city of Athens, then his argument for the irrelevance of animal sacrifice led, directly, to his judicial execution.[12] The *therapeia* once used

11. Plato, *Republic*, 517d.

12. Among the few who make the charges, the trial, and the execution directly related to Socrates's separation of himself as a citizen from the religious practice of animal sacrifice, see Burnyeat in "The Impiety of Socrates." See also Connor's "The Other 399: Religion and the Trial of Socrates." Lännström's title is the most suggestive. "A Religious Revolution? How Socrates' Theology Undermined the Practice of Sacrifice."

to refer to the "service" provided to the gods in the form of animal sacrifice was transformed by Socrates into a form of speech dedicated to the well-being of others.

Plato's sustained reflection on the death of the philosopher led him to return, on several occasions, to origins—of the world, humanity, and how piety and the laws were binding and reciprocal. In the end, Plato may have had only a sense of their relation, vague, a presentiment or intimation; but in examining several works, including the *Laws*, he often discusses the institution of animal sacrifice and the judicial death penalty as simultaneous creations. Brutal violence, precise methods of killing, the death of animals and human beings; a conjunction between the sacred and the judicial was now evident if still partially obscured. When Plato begins to write as a witness to the death of Socrates, he does not limit himself to being a historian precisely because, as Socrates's pupil, as a philosopher, the superficial appearances of reality (as in the cave of the *Republic*) force one to move toward a different sight, a different perception, a different vision. Only with a complicated reconstruction of origins does Plato believe that a series of historical events in the life and death of a philosopher will reveal a previously neglected tradition, one obscured by the order of the city and now illuminated for the first time. Socrates did not believe in the gods of the city. The wisdom of the poets he earlier recognized had to be *emulated*. We are forced to contemplate an ultimate irony: not only does Plato *not* condemn the poets, despite what is claimed in the *Republic* about their *imitative flaws*. He has to mimic them in spirit in order to return to the origins of a reconceived world so as to make it possible to reimagine the future. To anticipate such a world, it was first necessary to return to origins and reinterpret, from the ground up, how the world had developed then and how it could be transformed in the present. In the *Laws*, he gave his last testimony.

> There was a time when we didn't dare eat beef, and the sacrifices offered to the gods were not animals, but cakes and meal soaked in honey and other "pure" offerings like that. People kept off meat on the grounds that it was an act of impiety to eat it, or to pollute the altars of the gods with blood. So at that time men lived a sort of "Orphic" life, keeping exclusively to inanimate food and entirely abstaining from eating the flesh of animals.[13]

13. Plato, *Laws*, 782c.

There was a time when human beings did not eat animals. The decision was not, however, merely dietary and in relation to avoiding meat consumption. No one ate meat at the same time as they did not sacrifice animals. In essence, and in a passage in the *Laws* repeated from the earlier *Republic*, Plato confronts his readers with a historical fact about the nature of human life as it has been organized within the *polis*. It was not, as so easily presumed, a natural order. The execution of Socrates initiates, for Plato, a rethinking of the conception of human life and how it has been developed, in history, from its beginning. Animal sacrifice and the death penalty, as observed in the city of Athens at the time of Socrates's execution, lead Plato to return, as far back as he possibly could in order to remind all his readers that, if a past was wholly different than the present, then another future completely different than the present could also be created.

Plato takes us to Socrates's jail cell early one morning, there to initiate two conversations, an all-too-human one with his friend Crito, and another, much more revealing one with the embodiment of "the Laws." For the first time, and much more evident than in the trial scene of the *Apology*, the laws will speak and thereby betray both themselves and the city of Athens. The laws themselves must speak, make declarations, and assert their authority. "It's certainly beyond the masses to know the right course, Euthyphro," Socrates tells his friend on the eve of his trial and in relation to the charge of homicide he is bringing against his father, "I mean, I really don't think it's an action to be taken by the man in the street, but only by somebody already far advanced along the path of wisdom."[14] The deliberation requires wisdom precisely because homicide is a *capital crime*. There is, then, only one crucial question for Socrates: can wisdom and the death penalty coexist in the city? Or stated otherwise, can the wisdom of philosophy allow for the law (ancient and revered because of it) to carry out death sentences on human beings whether they are citizens, foreigners, or slaves? Several interrelated writings will be consulted and interpreted before a response can be given on the abolition of the death penalty as consistent with philosophical wisdom. Ultimately, if the pertinence of philosophy is to sustain the dignity of human life and not simply be some mere interest, for example, a *theory* of knowledge, then no philosophical argument deserves more of our attention. Once we turn to the speech of "the Laws" in the *Crito*, one repeated confrontation will

14. Plato, *Euthyphro*, 4ab.

become evident: the state lawfully executing Socrates or the philosopher "destroying" the laws and, ultimately, the state. The laws, however, admit that if their legitimacy depends on divine edict (by none other than Zeus, as we will see) even the slightest doubt about the existence of any of the gods threatens the entire edifice of society, that is, the metaphysical structure of the gods above sustaining everything below, including the cultic ritual most demonstrating the piety of the city.

Entering Socrates's jail cell as he waits for his execution to take place allows us to turn not to his friend's plea for him to agree to escape, but for his apparent identification with the consciousness of "the Laws" and how they argue for their absolute legitimacy.

In the *Crito*, there are two dialogues—or, rather, two declarations: Socrates as he speaks to his friend Crito, and "the Laws" as they insist on putting the philosopher in his place. Once the monologue of "the Laws" are heard and understood, then Plato can then begin his repeated return to the primordial past, on the one hand, and a future possibility on the other. The Laws may be self-assertive and absolutely confident in their continued existence; they have lived since time immemorial and have been secure. Once their origins are traced, however (as, for example, in the *Protagoras*) then their legitimacy suddenly begins to be put into doubt.

The Laws may be self-possessed, assured of their legitimacy, speaking with vanity to Socrates about their status. They cannot be denied, however, the validity of their perceptions and how they present their arguments (as a support of the trial and the "correct verdict") by accusing Socrates of *destroying* the laws. The Laws are generalizing: when they refer to laws as a whole, they are forgetting Socrates's argument, the reason he places himself, as a philosopher, between a judgment and its act. His ethical argument has to be considered in relation to justice; his ethical conclusions have judicial consequences. "So one ought not to return an injustice or an injury to any person, whatever the provocation" (49c). The idea of the "return" is Socrates's argument against any pretensions in the legitimacy of retributive justice. One point needs to be stressed: Socrates and the Laws are inimical to each other. Roslyn Weiss writes, "The disassociation of Socrates and his views from the views expressed by the Laws in their speech makes possible the full restoration to the Socrates of the Crito the radical independence of mind that characterizes the Socrates of the Apology."[15] The reference to the speech of the *Apology* is not necessary,

15. Weiss, *Socrates Dissatisfied*, 161.

however, despite Richard Kraut's assertion: "The evidence of the Apology forces the responsible reader to adopt a certain interpretive policy toward the Crito."[16] Socrates's speech in a court of law does not necessarily need to be consulted. Only in the *Crito* does Socrates make his arguments against the death penalty implicit.

The Laws are in effect presenting a counterargument. They will, to the best of their ability, defend themselves. Before Socrates engages in a mock conversation with the Laws, he has one statement to make to his friend. "I am afraid, Crito, that these are the concerns of the ordinary public, who think nothing of putting people to death, and would bring them back to life if they could, with equal indifference to reason" (48c). There is (there can be, in the current state of things) no difference between the people of the city and the Laws as far as reason is concerned. The death penalty, Socrates states, is irrational. *Reasons* and motives, rationalization and self-justification, however, are more than in evidence. They are all committed to the defense of the city and its laws.

The Laws present Socrates with their argument and defense. It is a cross-examination. "Can you deny that by this act which you are contemplating you intend, so far as you have the power, to destroy (*apolesai*) us, the Laws and the whole State as well. Do you imagine that a city can continue to exist and not be turned upside down, if the legal judgments which are pronounced in it have no force but are nullified and destroyed by private persons?" (50a–b). The first reference to the "abolition of this law" has to be repeated. The Laws believe Socrates is making the attempt to nullify the force of the judgment and to prevent it from being carried out. Socrates stands between the judgment and the act, the guilty verdict and the death penalty. Charges, according to the Laws, have been added. Socrates is also being accused of attempted murder and, at the same time, "nullifying" (abolishing) the penalty for such a crime. According to the Laws, he has made himself divine—or, at least, as he claimed during his trial, in the service of the divine and in particular the god of law and healing, Apollo. No wonder the Laws are incensed by Socrates. They continue their cross-examination: "Answer our questions: after all, you are accustomed to the method of question and answer. Come now, what charge do you bring against us and the State, that you are trying to destroy us?" (50d). Socrates does not respond to this specific question; he has no charge to bring against the state, except the one that is not *directly* stated on the legitimacy of carrying out the death penalty. Plato simply

16. Kraut, *Socrates and the State*, 12.

allows the Laws to state their case and make the conflict obvious to the reader. "So, that if we try to put you to death in the belief that it is just to do so, you on your part will try your hardest to destroy your country and us its Laws in returns?" (51a). The issue has been announced: it is a conflict between the legitimacy of the death penalty and the attempt to abolish the execution of the law. As the Laws finally recognize, this is the reason why Socrates's teaching was considered a criminal act: he has been teaching his students to reflect on the legitimacy of the law as it has been handed down by generations and maintained as authoritative by the polis. "For any destroyer of laws might very well be supposed to have a destructive influence upon young and foolish human beings" (53bc). The corruption of the young has been more precisely defined. Socrates has led them to reconsider the legitimacy of the laws as currently enacted in the city. If the philosopher has, at the same time, turned himself and necessarily into a historian, then he has no choice but to return to the past and analyze how it has been determined (from its *beginnings*) and how it has been developed. Socrates is an overwhelming danger to the city since one of the lessons he imparts to his students is to reflect on the nature of the laws and, as its most privileged power (its decisions to decide on matters of judicial life and death) to continue to reflect on its change. His is a perpetual obligation of the thinker. Leo Strauss believes "the law of the city may be foolish and hence harmful or bad. Therefore the justice that consists in giving everyone what is due to him [as the laws believe they have fulfilled dutifully] may be bad. If justice is to remain good, we must conceive of it as essentially independent of law."[17]

Always retaining the prior argument on the composition of Hesiod's poetry in our interpretation of the Prometheus myth, a brief turn from the dialogue with the Laws in the Crito to another related dialogue pertaining to the idea of justice allows us to once again notice a distinction. A few Platonic texts can now be recalled in support of Socrates's *foundational argument* in the *Euthyphro* repudiating animal sacrifice as a pious and holy act and the consequences (once the cultic ritual has been abolished) for the laws of the state and the justice system. Let us note, as an initial comment on justice—particularly relevant for Socrates as he is confronted with the inviolability of the law as socially and historically constituted and yet knows it has a serious flaw that, in principle, invalidates it. The shadows of justice and his *eidos* of the law are incompatible.

17. Strauss, *Natural Right and History*, 146.

Since Socrates has stated that the justice in a court of law is entirely made of "shadows," all other arguments (in the *Crito*) are to be interpreted from this one perspective. Other dialogues are no less clear. Again, we now have the obligation to specify what is the nature of the *eidos* of the law. Unless it can made real, in the world, dedicated to human beings, then it has no validity at all and remains, simply, a metaphysical phantasmagoria, more empty than the word, more useless than the concept.

We can overlook Crito's frantic worry about the fate of his friend and his single-minded desire to do what is both expedient and easy, that is, pay the appropriate people with customary and traditional bribes so Socrates can make a quick escape and save his life. In the argument to follow, Socrates brings in the authority of the Laws of Athens as interlocutors. In their first statement (when defending themselves to preserve their existence) they ask Socrates if, by the act of running away and rejecting the verdict, he intends to "destroy" the laws. In other words, the Laws are accusing Socrates of a peculiar crime; he is being accused of murdering the Laws. This one source of anxiety on the part of the Law, who are afraid of being *abolished*, returns (with the exact same language), in the *Minos*.

In attempting to answer "What is law?" we have, once again, a reference to "lawlessness" as being something that "destroys" (*apollus*i)[18] the city—as previously, *kills* it. But when Socrates asks his unnamed interlocutor, "Didn't we declare law to the official opinion (*dogma*) of the city?" (314d), then the law is founded upon a state belief—hardly a respected word in the lexicon of Socrates's philosophy. Once the law has been associated with the truth, then an immediate problem arises when laws are considered differently in different places—for example, in Carthage, where they practice human sacrifice as both legal and pious. The interrelationship of the legal and the pious is not one among others. The dialogue has unequivocally stated how the laws and the politico-religious institutions of the state are inseparable. Once again, it is Strauss who argues, "The *Minos* leads up to the view that a bad law is not a law."[19] Socrates becomes even more provocative (and subtly so) when in his dialogue he begins to inquire about various capacities of expertise and knowledge regarding different skills necessary for the well-ordered human world. In quick succession and almost to lead his unaware partner

18. Plato, *Minos*, 314d.

19. Strauss, "On the Minos," 79.

in dialogue, Socrates uses the example of the individual most capable of pasturing a herd of sheep and a herd of cows. He asks a final question: "And whose laws are best for the souls of humans?" (318a). It is answered immediately by "the king." The three interrelated examples, from the first one, do not lead to the individual who is best to look after the souls of animals because, on the contrary, in some cases these animals will be led to slaughter in the context of a politico-religious festival requiring sacrifice. If the individual taking care of a herd of animals cannot possibly be concerned with the care of the animal's soul (as analogous to the king who takes care of the herd of human beings) then the king who makes laws does not do so to take care of the soul of his "subjects."

Socrates leads his argument to its conclusion: by first of all equating "the many" with being "impious," he can now say, "For there is nothing more impious that this, nothing more guarded against, than to err in speech and deed regarding the gods" (318e). There is, however, a consequence to this impiety: if one makes a grave error in judgment and perception on the nature of the gods as the foundations of society, including its religious practice, then what occurs as a consequence is the complete misunderstanding of the human/animal relationship.

The end of the *Minos* is remarkable for, one, accusing the many of having ignorant and, worse of all, impious opinions about the gods; these opinions have had all manner of pejorative influences on the city. Socrates now introduces Hesiod once again and claims "poets wield great power over opinion."[20] Does Socrates mean the poets sustain the opinions of the city? Or, rather, are the writings of Hesiod, for example, in a conflict with the opinions of the city and intended to be a constant reminder of an altogether different worldview? If so, then Strauss's conclusion that a bad law cannot be considered a law at all is consistent with Socrates's belief. Strauss is succinct as well as consistent. He has responded to this one exigency in different texts: "Socrates did not think that there could be an unqualified duty to obey the laws."[21]

Socrates's argument to his friend is subtle and restrained, only announcing the intent and purpose at one specific juncture (the *only one*) where he explicitly mentions the death penalty. But if we follow the conversation with his friend as a preparation for the speech of "the Laws," once his ethics are absolute that "we ought not to repay wrong with

20. Plato, *Minos*, 320e.

21. Strauss, *Studies in Platonic Political Philosophy*, 66.

wrong or do harm to any man," his declaration cannot be limited to the action of a private individual. The ethical maxim has consequences for the law insofar as it entirely repudiates the law of retributive justice; if lawful retribution has been repudiated, then one law in particular must also be abolished.

When interpreters of *Crito* turn to the dialogue and assess Socrates's position, Crito remains (despite his deficiencies) an important if passive interlocutor. Crito is not at all a philosopher; he is practical, only concerned with the immediate situation and a problem to be solved by escape. Socrates has other, more important thoughts to consider: "The possibility that the law itself may be at fault and require to be tested by the appropriate standard, namely the Idea of the law."[22] However, once we refer the law to the "Idea," to the *monoeides* of the philosophical categories of the true, the good, and the beautiful, the specific problem (and the one most urgent for Socrates not individually but as a philosopher) can only be recognized by one *specific* law. The *Crito* has only once mentioned the practice of executing the judicially guilty; it has repeatedly argued for the ethical prohibition against retributive justice. The law is not only "at fault." Its premises are misguided, for reasons that Plato then reveals in many other associated writings. There is only one argument in the *Crito*: the death penalty should be abolished. To sustain the argument, other declarations by Socrates have to be consulted. When R. E. Allen, for example, writes that "Socrates died, not because of what he did, but because he was the kind of man he was,"[23] the defense of his *character* is understandable but insufficient. Considering the nature of his *daimonion*, Socrates has to be understood from what he *did not do*, most especially when commanded by the state.

The specific aspects of the trial have been examined by many, both for his *apologia* and for Socrates's affirmation of a philosophy that could not be reconciled to the ideals of the polis—however much he *appears* to submit to its laws. For the sake of the argument here, there is one (and only one) statement by Socrates that in the context of our discussion now becomes all-important. During a series of events that were threatening the stability and certainly the democracy of the polis, Socrates was *ordered* by the oligarchy, as he tells everyone, "to go fetch Leon of Salamis

22. Guardini, *Death of Socrates*, 82.

23. Allen, *Socrates and Legal Obligation*, 29.

from his home for *execution*."[24] Socrates refused. Why? Were his reasons limited to an act of disobedience and a philosophical response to the illegitimacy of oligarchic power? Or was his refusal inseparable from his opposition to the death penalty? Once we listen to his response immediately after his declaration, then the affirmation of Socrates giving "all my attention to avoiding anything unjust or unholy" (32d) is both a defense of his conception of justice and how it is sustained by his conception of the holy.

Both the law and the holy are independent of the polis.

The singularity of Socrates is shown in his ability to reconceive the holy against all human pretensions of representing the divine, the sacred, and the Laws within the political order of the polis. Although we cannot at the moment testify on Socrates's behalf and the separation between governmental law and the holy, we also cannot avoid (at the very least) a question: Is Socrates's idea of the *holy* specifically directed at a belief making him independent of any governmental order, or is the holy in any way implicated with the carrying out of a judicial sentence leading to death incompatible with his idea of being a philosopher? My response now has to attend to several other dialogues that are related to Hesiod and to the idea, like the wise poet, of reinterpreting myth.

Plato has simultaneous *agons* occurring in his dialogues: on the one hand, comparing the philosopher to the traditions of the city, on the other, reflecting on himself as he participates in the ongoing unfolding of a culture that is now in relation to (and some distance from) the mythopoetic imagination of his predecessors. Myths are so interwoven with philosophy, as a kind of prerequisite for Plato's dialogues and speeches in the present, that they need to be recollected, relied upon, to sense how reality is both supported and at a considerable distance from its origins. Since the figure of Prometheus has been so essential in the history of Greek thought, Plato had no choice but to turn to him at moments when he needed his readers to already have a context for his discussion and then prepare for an interpretation. Philosophy has to partly define itself by its commentaries on poetic thought, with Plato's readers intimately familiar with their meanings, at least as they had been inherited.

"No Greek author could write without being in the shadow of poets."[25] That much Plato would concede; and he would more than likely

24. Plato, *Apology*, 32c, my emphasis.

25. Adamson, *Classical Philosophy*, 197.

comment on the metaphor of the *shadow* here. Scholarship has led to one important conclusion: "There is a significant and distinctive place for Hesiod in Plato's project of presenting philosophy."[26] In the first of the dialogues to preoccupy us because of the figure of Prometheus, the sophist Protagoras gives us one long-lasting impression. Before turning to the most significant parts, a genealogy can be imagined—one necessarily in relation to another; for if "the *Theogony* may owe something to a body of Orphic poems,"[27] then the well-known remnants of Orphism in Plato also come through Hesiod's poetry. The genealogy has been set: the Orphic poems that, since the introduction, have been present as a source of an anti-sacrificial ethos, are now carried through to Hesiod's poetry and, finally, in Plato's ability to recombine their ideas for the future. How does he do this? The philosopher must set himself the task of the individual who can reconceive the possibility of the future by first returning to the past. Doing so begins the philosophical need of a recollection of the knowledge of tradition, one that (unlike the truth of mathematics, for example) is not nearly as self-evident.

In Plato's *Protagoras*, the character of the same name and Socrates engage in a conversation on whether virtue can be taught; education seems to be primary, as long as other preoccupations are anticipated—none for us more important than the presence of Prometheus once he intervenes to support the recently created human beings and to question the law of the death penalty instituted by Zeus. In order to provide a demonstration of his belief, Protagoras (given the choice by his audience) does not use a reasoned argument but instead tells a story, a *muthos*, one assumes rendered as non-poetic speech so as to avoid being mistaken for a performer and entertainer. Protagoras is a sophist, not a rhapsode. He does not want to be mistaken for someone who, like Ion, can be accused by Socrates of turning their "art" and making "right and proper for you to dress up and look as grand as you can."[28] Protagoras soon makes one truth explicit: those who read poetry superficially are bound to completely lose its meaning. While it has often been observed that "Plato's account remains the first and indeed the only Greek attempt to articulate consciously and with clarity the central fact of poetry's control

26. Van Noorden, *Playing Hesiod*, 89.

27. De Romilly, *Short History of Greek Literature*, 25.

28. Plato, *Ion*, 530b.

over Greek culture,"[29] Havelock also adds that Hesiod preceded him—anticipates the critical rationality of philosophy—by alluding to the "hidden depths" of his words. Interpreting the poet as conservative is a misunderstanding, as Protagoras insists on revealing. One of the Sophist's remarks has long-lasting consequences for the act of reading, of understanding, of interpretation. The "ancient quarrel"[30] of poetry and philosophy is no longer as clear-cut once the thinker reimagines the mythic past.

Protagoras begins with a distant past, a "once upon a time" so remote it could only be recollected by a myth, one his listeners are of course familiar with. The renowned sophist immediately makes himself politically astute when he tells his listeners, identifying with Socrates, that being a teacher and attracting young, impressionable students in foreign cities can arouse "no small resentment and various forms of hostility"[31] The comment is more than personal; he states a truth about the present and an equally important element of any poetry, any writing, any thought.

"Personally I hold that the Sophist's art is an ancient one, but that those who put their hand to it in former times, fearing the odium which it brings, adopted a disguise and worked undercover. Some used poetry as a screen, for instance Homer and Hesiod" (316d).

Protagoras shows himself to be a wily commentator who is aware of the intentions, and compositional techniques, of a poet such as Hesiod. The regard Plato has for poets, at least in the *Republic*, seems completely at odds with Protagoras here, who presents the poets as fully aware of the effect of their writing and, far from being imitative, are presenting innovations of thought that could be understood to be a threat to the integrity of the city. Here we are at the origins of Leo Strauss and the conception of a certain kind of writing (a "disguise," "undercover," and a "screen") to avoid being persecuted. The Sophist has learned from the poets to disguise his words.

The poet is presented as a thinker who, due to his awareness of the conservative nature of the polis, must veil, disguise, and provide a "screen" for his words. Now we can recall the interpretation of Hesiod's *Theogony* and present the poet as someone who simultaneously writes poetry based on the myths of the past and provides a commentary on its meaning, on its truth as he *interprets* it. Or, more provocative still: has

29. Havelock, *Preface to Plato*, 97.

30. Plato, *Republic*, 607b.

31. Plato, *Protagoras*, 316d.

Plato in part learned to write from Hesiod "between the lines"? Was it the writer of the *Theogony* and the origin of the gods who, representing the mockery of Prometheus and therefore his own irreverence, managed to convey meanings behind a screen. "Persecution," Leo Strauss writes, "gives rise to a peculiar technique of writing, and therewith to a peculiar type of literature, in which the truth about all crucial things is presented exclusively between the lines."[32]

Protagoras, the Sophist, seems to confirm our previous argument. Gullibility is no way to read him; what he *writes* is not at all what he *means*. Those seeking the pleasure of the aesthetic will not experience Hesiod's metaphysics or his commentary on present necessities of thought. Is this the real reason for Plato's rejection of the poet? The beauty of the lyrics and the rhapsode's voice force the listener to be passive and simply listen, for his personal enjoyment, rather than attend to the disguised and veiled meaning everyone must interpret. Protagoras preplans his story and tells it "undercover," relaying an ancient myth so as to provide an illustration of the present. Ironically, it is the Sophist who, in recalling a version of the origin (emulating and commenting and interpreting the poetry of Hesiod) tells the reader what is necessary if the truth is to be recognized. The individuals unworthy of Plato's philosophy and ideal city, the poet and the Sophist, here are exemplary for their ability to think.

Not for the last time, Plato will return to a primordial past so as to provide a commentary on the present. Protagoras has prepared the reader for a certain kind of discernment. In a succession of dialogues, origins will be recollected from myths and given prominence as explanations for the present. The truth of his story will only be evident when sufficient attention has been given to his purpose and method.

When the time came for human beings to be created, the gods took two elements, earth and fire, and together formed their being—though their essence, their particular nature, remained undetermined and left to Prometheus and Epimetheus to "equip" them as well as given them "powers," that is, their respective abilities. The gods, of course, preceded them. For some reason, Epimetheus was extremely eager to have the opportunity to give to animals and to human beings what was proper to their existence. If there was ever a time to invoke "sibling rivalry," here it might be pertinent. Hesiod's autobiography is embedded and concealed beneath the myth. The real-life brother he resents for being good for

32. Strauss, *Persecution and the Art of Writing*, 25. For a recent development of the thesis, see Melzer's *Philosophy Between the Lines*.

nothing is given the identity of the hapless Epimetheus. He attempted, it seems and to the best of his ability, to spread their particular excellence and make animals and human beings equal—or, at least, equitable, ensuring that each would not become extinct and had the means to survive. Epimetheus made a fateful decision: he was more concerned with the survival of the species than with any one individual member. After this initial preoccupation with the species as a whole, he attended to their bodies, both in terms of their features and in their immediate environment, including the food they would eat.

The essentials are important in the myth by Protagoras as they were in the garden of Eden. Mortal creatures were in the world, embodied, and in need of sustenance. One decision betrays a complete lack of wisdom. Or, better yet, Protagoras fully realizes how the myth he is now recounting was handed down to him and he can contemplate an alternative, as a criticism; the telling is inseparable from his interpretation. When Epimetheus ordered the food to be eaten (i.e., grass, fruit, roots) he also included a carnivorous world of the hunted, killed, and devoured. "Now Epimetheus was not a particularly clever person" (321b), Protagoras tells us. In the initial distribution of characteristics, animals were given what was appropriate to each species but in so doing he completely neglected human beings. Epimetheus "did not know what to do with them" (321c) until Prometheus came to inspect the work and quickly realized a serious omission had been made. Human beings had nothing to allow them to live in the world of nature. Since they would soon emerge into the world, Prometheus needed to give human beings a "means of salvation (*soterian to anthropo*)" (321c), some ability for them to be able to take care of themselves. To do so he stole from Hephaestus and Athena the gifts of skill in the arts as well as fire, including the knowledge that allowed them to preserve their life if at the exclusion of "political wisdom." Like Aeschylus, Plato does not allude to or mention the episode in the *Theogony*.

The fundamental disagreement between human beings and the gods he reserved for the myth of Aristophanes in the *Symposium*.

Details are omitted. The necessary insertions must be filled in by the listener. The story is incomplete without the participation of the listener—no different (exactly the same) as when Hesiod needed a reader. Protagoras does not mention the episode at Mekone. There was no necessity to do so.

Everyone was familiar with the story.

Human beings could *survive*; but they would not be able to understand themselves as a community led by principles, with values, virtues, and the emphasis on *aretē* or excellence. Prometheus's decision to steal what was not in his possession to distribute later led to his "trial" and punishment. In myth, tragedy, and in the parable told by a philosopher, Prometheus must stand trial for his actions though no reader can ever become knowledgeable about the details and the process—much less any "due process" inherent in the law. Aeschylus was unequivocal. Zeus acted with sovereignty and power. The law is ordained by a god; the law is inseparable from its origins. *All laws are divine.* Only this accounts for their legitimacy.

The consequences of Prometheus's theft of divine abilities could not be nullified or reversed; human beings, from then on, would make use of these skills to create a human world no longer determined solely by nature. They acknowledged piety, the particular *bind* of establishing a relationship with the gods as well as some of the most important aspects of culture, language. Even so, in the beginning they were still vulnerable to the threats from nature, wild animals, for example. They made the decision to congregate, live in communities, build cities—as Cain did after his expulsion from the land; but still they could not ensure their safety, since they lacked the proper political skill. Finally, when it seemed no other alternative would save humanity, Zeus sent his messenger Hermes to give human beings necessary qualities: he gave them the ability to respect each other, create bonds of friendship, and above all lead their lives according to principles of justice. Hermes, with similarities to the Greek *angelos* or messenger, taught human beings a divine lesson. Since everyone was to receive these gifts (respect for all and justice) from Zeus himself, he instructed Hermes to make one point clear.

"You must lay it down as my law that if anyone is incapable of acquiring his share of these two virtues he shall be put to death as a plague to the city" (322c).

As a consequence of everyone receiving two virtues, respect and justice, Zeus issues an accompanying law. He imposes the death penalty on anyone who is unable to learn two cardinal virtues. Should human beings be unable to be respectful and just (that is, *fail* to act) they will be put to death according to Zeus's law.

In Aeschylus's drama, Zeus's law seemed imposed and arbitrary. In this case there is a choice: be just, learn to be virtuous, or to be executed. Justice and the death penalty are interdependent. As soon as Protagoras has finished with his *muthos*, he once again resumes his dialogue with Socrates and then makes the claim that "a man cannot be without some share in justice, or he would not be human" (323c). A human being is so by virtue of his sense of justice, one that is not essential, as it were, but taught. The sense of justice can only be acquired in the context of teaching and learning. If so, if justice can be taught, then when a "wrongdoer" does in fact commit an act of injustice—one of his examples is "irreligion" (*asebeia*)—then he is punished not for the sake of the crime since, as he says, it cannot be undone. Impiety is the most fundamental example of a lawbreaker; and so we are once again reminded of Socrates's charge of impiety (and worse) actually inventing a new religion based on his reinterpretation of the meaning of Apollo the healer, the *soteria* previously referred to as a necessary condition of being. Once Socrates has been found guilty of impiety, the death penalty ensures that all previous stability, social order, and civic ritual, will be restored and preserved.

> In punishing wrongdoers, no one concentrates on the fact that a man has done wrong in the past, or punishes him on that account, unless taking blind vengeance like a beast. No, punishment is not inflicted by a rational man for the sake of the crime that has been committed (after all, one cannot undo what is past), but for the sake of the future, to prevent either the same man or, by spectacle of his punishment, someone else, from doing wrong again. But to hold such a view amounts to holding that virtue can be instilled by education; at all events the punishment inflicted as a deterrent. (324a–c)

First of all differentiating the human from "blind vengeance like a beast," the death penalty is not, the argument runs, for the sake of justice or retribution; it is supposed to act as a deterrent, the reason the death penalty was usually carried out publicly and as a *spectacle*. The sight of the execution had to instill a combination of terror and prudence. The public spectacle of the death penalty is supposed to be a deterrent. Returning then to Zeus's initial law, the death penalty has not been created and imposed on a perpetrator for the sake of the crime; rather, the one found guilty and executed is but an example for someone else who may, in the future, contemplate a similar capital crime.

Once we turn to Prometheus's initial act of providing gifts for human beings, the consequences of his acts (which were clearly known to him) were irrelevant to him. For when we learn in Aeschylus that Prometheus acted out of love for human beings and would sacrifice his life for them, then the death penalty became a moot point. The complexity of his punishment was but an attempt on the part of Zeus to come to terms with the baffling act—in the mockery in the *Theogony* and the disobedience in tragic drama no less than in philosophy. Once again we witness (in this case, through no fault of their own) the abilities given to animals by Epimetheus and how it provoked Prometheus to act. Animals were given some natural endowments intended for human beings. Once they were bereft of anything, including how to use fire, humans were left destitute if not for Prometheus's involvement. Protagoras did indeed recount a myth from the distant past and a parable with contemporary relevance—or, to be more precise, Plato invented a dialogue with the name of a sophist so as to comment, once again, on the nature of justice, law, punishment and, most especially, the death penalty. Prometheus's punishment was not a deterrent at all; on the contrary, anyone witnessing, on stage or in writing, his act, had to be assume the tacit possibility of a similar obligation in the future. Prometheus remains the individual who was willing to accept even the harshest penalty of all as long as he could impart the greatest gift of all: it was not the technical skills of a god (making *things*, like Hephaestus) but rather creating ideas tending toward that most important of human attributes, the *sophia* capable of infinitely contributing to the excellence of a human being. The philosopher who questions the concept of piety and holiness (as Socrates did in the *Euthyphro*) must suffer the ultimate judicial penalty; and once the impiety of Socrates is proclaimed to be essential to his teaching and involves the rejection of animal sacrifice and the expected reciprocity of prayer, he guilty verdict was a matter of necessity. Zeus, apparently, created the virtue as well as the punishment, death, for not living up to its standard. The philosopher shows himself to have exceeded the *political conception* of the divine by providing one fundamental argument: the idea of the holy exceeds the demands of political authority no less than the conception of the divine used instrumentally by the state.

The speech by Protagoras is one more complement to the meanings of the mythic and poetic past and, most especially, the presence of Prometheus, who comes on the scene and intervenes at the most necessary moments in the history of human beings as they first learn, self-consciously, to define themselves. The single most important affirmation by Protagoras was on the nature of poetic expression; the words were a screen, a cover-up for a disguised meaning that had to be found only with careful inquiry.

There is no myth without interpretation; there is no myth without a logos.

Once Hesiod knows himself to be a reflective and not merely aesthetic poet, then the whole tradition has become open to reinterpretation. The foundation of the death penalty by Zeus was a feeble attempt to intimidate inquirers from finding an alternative to all the traditional truths told about the past and that now served to maintain a stable and recognizable reality. This is the reason the state (through the figure of Zeus) creates the death penalty. As a deterrent, it intimidates those who are capable of reinterpreting traditions and, by doing so, transforming the idea of reality and the truth. Suddenly, the writer in ancient Greece has achieved a profound purpose. Aesop the fabulist, Hesiod the poet, Aeschylus the playwright, Plato the philosopher: all of them are now to be understood comprehensively and united by one common purpose. They cannot be reduced to the aesthetic. All of them are to be understood as metaphysicians who confront the entire history of their people and, at their particular historical juncture, provide a continuous and much-needed reassessment of an ontological reality on the way to being imagined, created, and developed. The contribution toward the future can only begin, always, by a return and recollection. It is not, in this version, anything like the *anamnesis* of the slave-boy of the *Meno*. The philosophical knowledge and wisdom of the philosopher can now be more precisely defined: at the same time as he recollects the mythic past, he reinterprets and, in so doing, alters the nature of reality and the human beings who, for far too long, were dependent for their self-conception on an archaic and no longer adequate conception of being. Plato's argument in the *Republic* can no longer be defended. Poetry does not dedicate itself to "pleasure and imitation" (607c) as its guiding principles. Once the purpose of Hesiod's poetry has been recollected from out of the profound composition of the *Theogony*, his poetry is neither merely mimetic nor aesthetically pleasing. Hesiod re-presents the metaphysical foundations of the polis in order to rethink their legitimacy, their authority, and their continuity.

One other dialogue again takes up the problem of crime and punishment and the death penalty. Earlier, an allusion was made to the *Gorgias* where the discussion became all the more poignant when considered in relation to Socrates's death and as a consequence of a judicial accusation. Plato represents Socrates as someone fully anticipating what will occur based on his teachings since he does not offer *pleasure* or what is best (as presumed by the many) but like the diagnosis of a problem and its painful remedy—cautery is his example—it is resisted despite its cure. Or, to use another example: he is not like the *rhapsode* who gives his listeners pleasure in music, song, and poetry, but demands *work* to be interpreted and understood. The *Gorgias* is a dialogue aimed at readers beyond the initial jury; there are other tribunals, other courts, beside the one in the Areopagus. The many references to Socrates addressing his "defense" in a court of law never change; they simply point out the same reality. His remedy will be judged to be *poisonous* to the continuity of the polis, unsavory, causing nothing but aversion. "I shall be like a doctor brought before a tribunal of children at the suit of a confectioner" (521). Not surprisingly does Socrates use a medicinal example; for the philosopher has always been, above all, someone who devoted himself to the health of the psyche of every single individual no less than the polis—the very reason the allegory of the cave does not ultimately diagnose the prisoners as mere slaves to their perceptions (their view of reality) but as actually sick, mentally ill, and in need of a *cure*.

> That is the situation in which I am sure that I shall find myself I come before a court of law. I shall not be able to point to any pleasures that I have provided for my judges, the only kind of service and good turn that they recognize; indeed I see nothing to envy in those who purvey or those who receive such services. And if it is alleged against me either that I am the ruin of younger people by reducing them to doubt or that I insult their elders by bitter criticism in public or in private no defence will avail me, whether true or not, the truth being simply that in all that I say I am guided by what is right and that my actions are in the interest of those who are sitting in judgment of me. So presumably I shall have no alternative but to submit to my fate, whatever it may be. (522)

Socrates repeats the same words uttered by Prometheus in Aeschylus's "tragedy." The philosopher who fully expects to face the death penalty is not a tragic figure; and just as Prometheus said he will bear "the destiny fate has given me,"[33] neither submits to fate, destiny, much less the tragic since they are supremely conscious of their decisions and its consequences. Tragedy is not the proper category for understanding his decision.

The culmination of the *Gorgias* is one more complementary dialogue to the whole of Plato's defense of Socrates, most especially in outlining how the charges against him correspond to the nature of his teachings and how "service" (the *therapeia* traditionally given to the gods) has been

33. Aeschylus, *Prometheus Bound*, 104.

now rededicated only to the *health* of human beings. This is the *soteria* provided by Prometheus in the *Protagoras*. He transforms the order of the polis. Psychotherapeutic philosophy has replaced the custom of relating to the gods in a relationship of reciprocity. Once Socrates completely transform the nature of piety and holiness, he was inevitably going to be prosecuted and either banished or executed; for him to choose the death penalty rather than accept being banished to some safe and hospitable city was one final testament of his teaching and of the philosopher who was single-mindedly dedicated to the well-being of others. Apollo demanded no less from him. Socrates therefore initiates the first religious revolution in antiquity and with two simultaneous affirmations: the *examined* life of human beings will lead them to rethink their nature as well as their place in any given society—including the very institutions and laws that sustain its continuity: animal sacrifice and the death penalty. Once Socrates undermined the nature of the gods as presently conceived, all other consequences (on the primacy of the law) were put into doubt and became open to being, literally, rewritten.

Socrates's dialogue with his friend Euthyphro the day prior to his trial can be completed by the dialogue in *Gorgias* as it now moves to yet another consideration of the meaning of Prometheus in Greek culture as a whole and, specifically, as the figure who exposes the machinations of Athenian law. We should be aware, at this juncture, of Annas's important reminder. One last emphasis is not superfluous: "Taking the myths to be Plato's lapses from rational thinking encourages passively uncritical readings of them."[34] Plato adopts myth so as to show how the poet, Hesiod in our case, is dynamically active in the writing and interpretation of his material. From everything we have gathered from Hesiod's poetry and Plato's relationship to him, surely we can no longer hold the traditional and erroneous view of Greek poetic myths as somehow, in whole or in part, to be simply rejected and overcome by the sophistication of philosophical thought. One wonders if Plato was writing with his own "screen" in the *Republic* when he apparently accused the poets of mere "pleasure (*edonen poietike*) and imitation (*mimesis*)" (607c). Hesiod was less concerned with either pleasure or imitation than the metaphysical reinterpretation of traditional myths. Once Prometheus appears, once again, in a dialogue by Plato it allows us to recognize the importance of this pivotal figure for the self-understanding of the Greek world. Every

34. Annas, "Plato's Myths of Judgment," 120.

reappearance of Prometheus is simultaneously an insistent repetition and a further interpretation of his fundamental *meaning* as conceived by the poet, the playwright, and the philosopher.

By telling his interlocutor Callicles a "story," a *muthos*, he will show him a representative idea. It will need to be interpreted with care. Plato reaches one conclusion—though it might not be as obvious as it seems. Like the primordial story in the *Protagoras* (including the appearance of Prometheus and Zeus) the *Gorgias* also includes a story, a myth, on *postmortem judgment*. The story told by Socrates leads to a remarkable detail once again related to Prometheus. Although Socrates's belief in life after death cannot be pursued here, one preoccupation (*the only one that matters*) will focus on the death penalty. Life after death is entirely speculative and, more to the point, existentially irrelevant. The death penalty, however, is a historical practice determined by gods, kings, and laws that the philosopher denounces. The entire quote is necessary, beginning again with "there was a time." Plato often has to return to a prior age in order to explain how the present has been created. Here, prior to the long quote, one comment is necessary: the death penalty has now been extended from the limits of existence toward a *postmortem* infinite, as if the religiopolitical authorities at some point made a decision to control the heavens above, the earth in the middle, and Hades below. The death penalty, enacted once in time, could be extended infinitely and thus make punishment eternal. Plato therefore returns to "there was a time," again during the age of Cronus, to remind his readers.

> Now there was in the time of Cronus a law concerning mankind which has remained in force among the gods from that time to this. The law ordains that, when his time comes to die, a man who has lived a righteous and pure life shall depart to the isles of the blessed and there remain in complete felicity, free from sorrow, but that the man whose life has been wicked and godless shall be imprisoned in the place of retribution and judgment, which is called Tartarus.
>
> In the time of Cronus and in the early days of Zeus men were tried during their life-time by living judges on the very day on which they were fated to die. This led to perversion of justice, so Pluto and the overseers of the isles of the blessed came to Zeus and complained that men were arriving at both destinations contrary to their deserts. Then Zeus said: "I will put an end to this. The cause of this miscarriage of justice is that men, being tried in their life-time are tried in their clothes. Many whose souls are wicked are dressed in the trappings of physical beauty and high birth and riches, and when their trial takes

> place they are supported by a crowd of witnesses, who come to testify to the righteousness of their lives. This causes confusion to the judges, who are also hampered by being clothed themselves, so that the soul's vision is clouded by the physical veil of eyes and ears and the rest of the body, and their own venture as well as the accused's constitutes an obstacle between them. Our first task, then," said Zeus, "is to take from men the foreknowledge of the hour of their death which they at present enjoy. I have charged Prometheus to bring this to an end."[35]

Whether Zeus, the lawmaker (the inventor of the death penalty) fully understands the consequences of his new edict cannot at all be certain. He has demonstrated very little indication of any wisdom at all. Once again Prometheus, the Titan with the gift of foresight, emerges from out of the profound meaning of myths to take away any knowledge of the moment of a human being's death. At the same time as Zeus instructs Prometheus to take away the knowledge of death at a specified time, he must also necessarily abolish the death penalty and the appointed hour of execution. It is only fitting that Plato (in defense of Socrates) would make the defiant Titan who acted in the *service* of human beings, for their welfare, be the very one who announces the impossibility of any executions. Whether he simultaneously also abolishes the belief in life after death and postmortem judgment is a question that is hardly tangential to the problem at hand but, for our argument, for the time being omitted. Did Socrates believe in life after death? Or, when referring to judgment day in the court of law during his trial, was it merely a conversation held only for the jurors? Too often Prometheus has been seen as the individual who *gives* a thing or ability to human beings. The *Gorgias* presents us with a perhaps more important "gift" than the knowledge of a *techne* useful for life—as in the *Philebus* when a certain kind of thinking "was a gift of the gods to mankind, hurled from heaven along with the brightest of fire, thanks to some Prometheus."[36]

More important than any gift from Prometheus is his involvement, in two different Platonic dialogues, on both the creation of the death penalty and the abolition of human beings knowing, ahead of time (with foresight), the hour of their death. The consequences of Zeus's instruction and Prometheus's incomparable act has one consequence nowhere announced and yet remarkable in its necessary effects. If all human beings must not know "the hour of their death," then no court of law may

35. Plato, *Gorgias*, 523.

36. Plato, *Philebus*, 16c.

condemn a human being to the death penalty. The very being who, in myth and tragedy, suffered the punishment of a perverse death sentence has now (in philosophy) become representative of the abolition of the death penalty. The *hope* he had earlier given human beings has now become irrelevant. The hope, for example, of the condemned awaiting to be executed has been nullified and stricken from human experience; the one about to be executed no longer hopes for a reversal of the judgment or, perhaps, forgiveness, mercy, or clemency. The death penalty and the hope for a pardon have both been eradicated. Human life has been restored; it can no longer be taken by a judicial act.

The return to two primordial myths has allowed us to argue for the abolition of the death penalty in Plato's writings; he has mounted a defense much more formidable than the one evident during the trial of Socrates in the *Apology*.

One final examination of the interpretation of a myth by Plato completes, for my purpose, how previous allusions to the creation of the death penalty and its abolition are essential in his overall defense of Socrates. The temptation is too hard to resist; so, for the last time, one other primordial myth will be mentioned, in this case to remind ourselves how often Plato depended for his thinking on confronting the past. Critias begins his history of the war between Athens and Atlantis with the same words as Protagoras in his myth of origins: "Once upon a time the gods divided up the whole Earth between them according to its regions"[37] Prior to any discussion of the war, however, Critias tells us about the nature of the gods and how they established a certain order to the world. They were creators; they had a vision in mind of the world they wanted to create for themselves. Once we learn that the gods were primordial and consequently influenced human life, they "established shrines and sacrifices for themselves" (113c), an origin, as usual, without any corresponding reason. We know, at one time, there was a difference; but how the events developed and for what reason the reader is never told. This marks one fundamental difference between the biblical world and the history of the Greeks. For some reason not at all explained, the mythic element does not reveal itself except indirectly, gods created a *human necessity*: piety and worship and most especially the ritual Socrates determined to be antithetical to human responsibility. Once Plato's discussion is emphasized for its comprehensiveness and as wholly dedicated

37. Plato, *Critias*, 109b.

to the defense of Socrates, the turn to the mythic past is done to expose its arbitrariness; there is no necessity in the rituals practiced in the city, whether those are in relation to the service of the gods in the form of animal sacrifice or in the reaffirmation of power over life or death in the execution of individuals found guilty of capital crimes.

Once the brief description of the origin of piety is addressed and the physical features of the country are exactly described, Critias then connects the religious foundations of the country with its political/legal order.

"Their arrangement for the distribution of authority and office were as follows. Each of the ten kings had absolute power, in his region and city, over persons and in general over laws, and could punish or execute at will" (119c).

Once the social order of the country and the gods' initial division of the earth is exactly the same, it appears as though the *imitation* of the gods resulted in the human world. The twin pillars of social order have been established by kingly rule as the emulation of the divine: the religious slaughter of animals and the judicial execution of human beings consecrate reality as divine. If so, Plato makes the reader aware of a fundamental Socratic teaching: the world of human beings is predicated on an earlier, more primordial and, one assumes, wiser order. But this is precisely where Socrates disagrees; his reason leads him to being "impious." He cannot accept the assumption; more strenuously, if the conception of the gods is entirely "ignorant" (based on preconceptions) then the responsibility of the philosopher becomes to, first of all, make everyone aware of the gods as a *conception* without an accompanying ontological reality and, second, revise both the ideas about the gods and the human life they determine from beginning to end. When we now take into consideration the nature of "absolute power," "laws," and all kinds of judicial punishments including the death penalty (again, all based on the gods) what Socrates proposes is nothing less than an absolute rethinking of *everything*. This is the reason why Nussbaum, in her reading of the *Protagoras*, calls Socrates "the new Prometheus."[38] He does not, as in Hesiod's myth or in the *Symposium*, challenge the gods directly. Instead, and what amounts to also proclaiming the gods to be both a conception and, effectively, nothing more than shadows, Socrates confronts the gods insofar as they are *beliefs* with all-pervasive social consequences. The order

38. Nussbaum, *Fragility of Goodness*, 93.

created by the gods, in the *Critias*, involves both animal sacrifice and the death penalty; they are presented as natural outcomes. Socrates may have been charged with impiety; the charge was nothing more than a pretext, turning his philosophy into a divine crime.

In his "once upon a time," Critias makes the worship of the gods and the laws of the city imitations, one predicated on the other. The absolute power of life and death demonstrated with every religious ritual of sacrifice is imitated in the enactment of justice and, as its highest expression, the death penalty. The description of the sacrifice carried out by the ten kings of the country of Atlantis could not be more elaborate. The power of the ten kings was, somehow, guaranteed "by the injunctions of Poseidon, enshrined in the law and engraved by the first kings on an orichalc pillar in the temple of Poseidon" (119d). God, kings, the law: the binding relationship was made secure by a meeting at the temple of Poseidon every five or six years, with accompanying pledges and one ceremony in particular that consecrated their contract. The description in its entirety is called for:

> There were in the temple of Poseidon bulls roaming at large. The ten kings, after praying to the god that they might secure a sacrifice that would please him, entered alone by themselves and started a hunt for a bull, using clubs and nooses but no metal weapon; and when they caught him they cut his throat over the top of the pillar so that the blood flowed over the inscription. And on the pillar there was engraved, in addition to the laws, an oath invoking awful curses on those who disobeyed it. When they had finished the ritual of sacrifice and were consecrating the limbs of the bull, they mixed a bowl of wine and dropped in a clot of blood for each of them, before cleansing the pillar and burning the rest of the blood. After this they drew wine from the bowl in golden cups, poured a libation over the fire and swore an oath to give judgment in accordance with the laws written on the pillar, to punish any past offenses, never knowingly in future to transgress what was written, and finally neither to give nor obey orders unless they were in accordance with the laws of their fathers. (119e–120ab)

In returning to this one primordial myth, Plato has now made his most compelling argument of all for the conjunction of animal sacrifice and the creation of the law. At this point in their history, the mutual collaboration between the ten kings is maintained by a sacrificial ritual supported by Poseidon and the other gods. At an undefined later time and prior to their war with Athens, however, Zeus became dissatisfied with them and how they had begun to alter traditions for the worse. Although *Critias* ends before the conflict, it was Zeus (so the story goes) who manipulated events to unfold as they did. Whatever the outcome, the story was instructive for its relations to the "once upon a time" of *Protagoras* and the related myth in the *Gorgias.* We must imagine Socrates, who listened to the story, responding. When reflecting on gods, laws, and human beings, Socrates the philosopher insists on returning to the past of tradition—preserved not so much in memory but in an oral inheritance—and to make it possible to revise everything that has been said and written about the gods and, therefore, at least make it possible to revise the whole of human life both individually and socially. The examined life must be comprehensive.

Chapter 5

The Abolition of the Death Penalty in the Gospel of John[1]

The gospel accounts of Jesus may begin differently, with a genealogy, nativity stories, and the *logos*, with John uniquely recognizing "in the beginning was the Word," but they are unanimous in leading the reader toward the end of his life as a condemned criminal who suffers the most shameful and degrading punishment under Roman law. According to the gospel accounts, Jesus has been denounced by some individuals within the hierarchy of the Jerusalem leadership (with Caiaphas, as the high priest, making a final and persuasive argument to a chosen assembly) and sentenced to death by the politico-religious state of the Romans who had sole jurisdiction in all capital cases. For a reason never sufficiently explained, the Gospel of John presents Caiaphas as the one individual who believes Jesus needs to be put to death. To the assembly he says, "You do not understand that it is better for you to have one man die for the people than to have the whole nation destroyed" (John 11:50). *You do not understand.* The words stand out. John represents the high priest as being uniquely aware of the meaning of Jesus and the circumstances of his life and ministry. His compelling arguments must have been successful. "So from that day on they planned to put him to death" (John 11:53). The

1. A version of this essay was presented at the annual conference of the Semiotic Society of America at Berea College, Kentucky, on October 5, 2018. I would like to express my gratitude to Gilad Elbom for his invitation to participate in the panel on *Theological Alternatives* and most especially for our many conversations. In addition to Gilad, I would like to extend my thanks to my co-panelists, Fredrick J. Long and Gila Safran-Naveh.

intention to kill Jesus, however, has been omnipresent; the references to persecution, apprehension, arrest, and being killed are many.

At the same time, John the Baptist is instrumental in the beginning of the gospels for being someone who confesses, witnesses, and testifies on behalf of Jesus. He does so without fail, and *pro bono*, and with one detail often overlooked: interpreted from the standpoint of an association with two animals, Jesus can be witnessed as a sacrificial lamb (John 1:29) and a dove of the spirit (John 1:32), two animals that can represent Jesus in two different, incommensurable ways: on the one hand, as spirit, on the other, as sacrificial. As for John the Baptist, he will be killed by edict, sentenced to death during a banquet at one of Herod's royal palaces. The strange conjunction of food and an execution will be anticipatory, preparing for the creation of the Eucharist during the Last Supper where no dead or sacrificed animal will be present.

Although the four gospels are sufficiently conscious of Jesus' persecution by the political and religious authorities of Jerusalem throughout his ministry and, in the case of Luke, immediate danger to his life once he begins to speak with authority—certain people in the synagogue of Nazareth want to throw him off a cliff (Luke 5:29), a punishment sometimes substituted for stoning to death—the Gospel of John continually refers to the law and often repeats examples of judgment, condemnation, testimony and, above all, the role of the witness, the *martyr* who has been anticipated as the Christians who will be put to death for their beliefs and (above all) for their refusal to simply follow one supreme order by the Roman magistrates to interrogate them: to perform a sacrifice in the name of the emperor and share a meal together with others. The imperative of killing an animal and eating together as a politico-religious institution must be maintained in order to support the *status quo*.

"The courtroom metaphor is characteristic of John's Gospel. The motif of a trial runs through the whole of this Gospel."[2] The trial is, however, prepared with extrajudicial events and the almost constant presence of opponents, in many cases who interfere with Jesus' ministry by cross-examining him and who are (after John 4, and numerous times) intent on killing him. Jesus has so divided the many factions of the Jewish leadership—priests, scribes, Pharisees, Sadducees, and the individuals with the most authority such as the Herodians—that some now were "seeking all the more to kill him" (John 5:18). The threat of death is virtually constant

2. Baukham, *Jesus and the Eyewitnesses*, 116.

and relentless. But if we are to understand Jesus, within himself, in the presence of his consciousness in addition to his words and acts, he has no concern for himself or his safety. He continues to *work* on the Sabbath, for example. Despite the fragility of his human condition and the experience of terror, without parallel, in the garden of Gethsemane as he anticipates his death, Jesus' life is exemplary by virtue of what it represents and reveals. The presence of Jesus in the world can only be imagined as a *revelation*, a disclosure of a previously inconceivable truth and reality.

> I will proclaim what has been hidden since the foundation of the world. (Matt 3:35)

This one tremendous claim, written first in the Letter to the Romans with the emphasis of revelations being a mystery (16:25) and repeated in Colossians (1:26), represents Jesus, in self-conception, as the *logos* who, with the fullness of wisdom and prior to creation itself, reveals an unprecedented truth to the world. The revelations of Jesus are manifested so as to fundamentally alter what has been, until him, inconceivable, in human consciousness and in the truth of the world to come within all future history. During his ministry, Jesus will bring about the end of two conceptions of reality intimately related and sustaining the world of antiquity: animal sacrifice and the death penalty. The Gospel of John presents the event known as the "cleansing of the temple" beginning at 2:13 and thus much earlier than all the other evangelists, and for a specific reason: his public ministry in the city of Jerusalem begins with an unprecedented act against the sacrificial cultures that are shared by Jews and Romans alike, both sustaining their traditions (and supreme laws—one dedicated to YHWH, the other to the emperor) in and through sacrifice.

Prior to any one example of his confrontation with the law, the essence of his revelations must be described, however approximate and incomplete they must appear; despite the sophistication of ideas on the revelations of Jesus, they must remain open and capable of further elaboration. First, and always keeping in mind the power of Jesus' *parousia* in the present, as a presence, the origin must take us to the Gospel of John and the *logos*. The reader has a singular responsibility, the "need to rediscover the meaning of the words and figures employed in the New Testament, a task entrusted to the exegete first of all."[3] While "the word is the only possible means of revelation,"[4] we cannot be prepared to allow the

3. Léon-Dufour, *Life and Death in the New Testament*, xxvi.

4. Achtemeier, *Introduction to the New Hermeneutic*, 96. He adds, "The new

logos to remain linguistic, uttered or written, not unless it has the same dynamic as the creation emanating from "then God said" of Genesis 1:3. By "revealing itself in that which is its revelation, its Word,"[5] Michel Henry draws attention to the presence of Jesus as language and meaning to be understood from out of himself, his words, and his gestures. "Revelation takes place in a long process of events, experiences, and interpretation,"[6] with the latter crucial for any hermeneutics that affirms how our interpretation allows us "to unfold the *possibility of being* indicated by the text."[7] The revelations of Jesus are ontological; they are to be perceived and internalized, by the spirit, in order to become real, the true, in the spirit and in the world. "Christ's word brings out the meaning not only of our personal existence but also the meaning of all human existence. Thenceforth there is not the correcting in detail of our view of the world but of *re-orienting all being*."[8] While Bultmann is partly correct when he writes that revelation is "the experience in which one is raptured from the things of every day life and one's own limitations,"[9] the "limitations" cannot be simply acknowledged to be individual. Only by recognizing how the revelations of Jesus are intended to be world-transformative (as a comprehensive and still unimaginable totality) will it then be possible to individually assess the consequences of his teaching; we remain called to a responsibility too demanding, of ourselves, to ever be closed. They are far from being complete; history has been slow, gradual, while the revelations from the past remain in effect as a calling, for a future. Jean-Luc Marion perhaps comes closest of all to understanding the profound consequences of Jesus' revelations. "Christ exercises a hermeneutic on the world and its wisdom. But he accomplishes it only because of an entirely different characteristic: its radical newness, its unsurpassable innovation. . . . *His revelation introduced realities and phenomena into the world that*

hermeneutic must provide the existential questions that will allow the text to function as what it is, i.e., as a linguistic response to, and illumination of, existence" (98). See also his "How Adequate Is the New Hermeneutic?" and *The New Hermeneutic*.

5. Henry, *I Am the Truth*, 92.

6. Schillebeckx, *Interim Report on the Books of Jesus and Christ*, 12.

7. Ricoeur, *Hermeneutics and the Human Sciences*, 56, my emphasis.

8. Latourelle, *Finding Jesus through the Gospels*, x. He adds that Jesus "deciphers the human condition in all dimensions and accomplishes it *beyond all that was foreseen*" (xi, my emphasis).

9. Bultmann, *What Is Theology?*, 88.

never had been seen or known before him."[10] The affirmations are decisive: what remains is a hermeneutic reading adequate to at least representing *one* of Jesus' revelations, one that cannot simply defend *him*, but everyone who has been so condemned; and none can be more important than an extreme incident of life and death and when a human being is threatened with the death penalty as a consequence of a capital crime. All conceptions of life (*bios* or *zoe*) must be elevated beyond existence and the presumption of the law as an institution. A foundational revelation must be the affirmation of life—without qualifications. While segments of the Platonic corpus were each brought together to provide intimation of a rethinking of myth and as a simultaneous defense of Socrates, the Gospel of John is as explicit as possible in presenting an actual case—as the defendant, the prosecutors, and the *parakletic* defense is presented. For the first time in antiquity, Jesus represents an unequivocal position. He does not only have to consider an individual case. Jesus will *write* a law that will be set as a precedent for all future capital cases.

One incident in particular in the Gospel of John has proven to be a dilemma for commentators, one without solution or resolution. Turning to many different interpretations allows a reader to witness how much conflict this *pericope* has created. It has been ignored and discounted. The desires of *censors* and would-be editors have been evident; some make the most astonishing claims—and even more shocking decisions; taking liberties is an understatement, and all for the wrong reasons. We remain oblivious to the revelations of Jesus unless they, always and simultaneously, turn reflectively back to our consciousness (as a calling) to respond firmly to *our* limitations and most especially *our* judgments. A hermeneutic of revelations would expose even our unconscious to analysis and therefore make merely cognitive judgments no longer possible. The woman caught in adultery in John 7:53—8:11 has presented rather severe, almost insurmountable challenges to readers—whatever their discipline or disposition. The beginning on the Mount of Olives the night before, in the place where Jesus will be arrested, is hardly coincidental. Theology no less than history has been confronted with a decision; it has not always been made despite the urgency—as a matter of someone on the verge of being executed, by stoning no less, a danger he will experience from the beginning of his ministry in Nazareth in the Gospel of Luke.

10. Marion, *The Visible and the Revealed*, 71, my emphasis.

On two different occasions before the scene previously described with Caiaphas, Jesus is exposed to the danger of being stoned to death—that is, killed lawfully according to Jewish justice or simply punished by a gathering of people who cannot suppress their anger and murderous intent; from the perspective of pious Jews, their response is in keeping with their ancestral laws extending to Genesis and reiterated in the torah. First, when Jesus makes one of the most consequential sayings of his entire ministry and uniquely represented in the Gospel of John with "Before Abraham was, I am," a saying his listeners could not possibly understand from out of his consciousness, their response was visceral: "So they picked up stones to throw at him" (John 8:59). Second, when Jesus equates himself with God, "The Father and I are one," again their response is reflective of their immediate reaction to kill him. "The Jews took up stones again to stone him" (John 10:31). Being stoned to death, one method of capital punishment, follows from the one incident that will concern us. The severity of the punishment leading to death must also be understood as the collective action of a "jury" who, by law or custom, has been given the justification for their acts. The permissible action will soon be *outlawed*—that is, consigned outside the power of the law.

His response to all the threats against his life and as a fundamental expression of his teaching could not be more comprehensive. "I am the way and the truth and the life" (John 14:6). Jesus embodies the simultaneity of this conceptual trinity precisely at the location—Golgotha, the place of the skulls, where the flesh of the condemned was stripped from the body by birds and dogs—where *life* will make death irrelevant since it (life) cannot be reduced to the body and where the absolute fixity of the nails in the cross—steel and wood, earth and nature—are merely materials of the world. The moments of the crucifixion are not intended (by Jesus, as opposed to the Romans) as a *spectacle*, as the idolatry of the justice system and its law. Jesus, as represented most faithfully by the Gospel of John in relation to death, leads everyone back into the life of Jesus in order to reflect on the revelations uttered by him and, in the one and only moment when he *writes*, into the ground, *into Adam*, as an unprecedented inscription. The one and only time Jesus writes cannot be sufficiently stressed. "It has often been said that the Bible can be used to support either side of any argument. . . . A conspicuous example, coming readily to mind, is capital punishment."[11] Jesus is far from the uncertainty

11. Cochrane, *Jesus of Nazareth in Word and Deed*, 34.

and ambivalence of either/or. His presence, words, and writing will be interpreted as *absolute*. A position, parenthetically, can be supported by any argument; no more consequential effect can be imagined than when accusations are made and a trial ensues, with the innocent and the guilty sometimes suffering *because* of the law.

The history of John 7:53—8:11 and the case of the woman caught in adultery has been judged by commentators to be a textual problem and more than likely added by a later writer (presumably, a follower of John) and has therefore allowed many to completely ignore it as somehow *inauthentic*. Such an evaluation, made by historians who are intent on discovering facts with proof and evidence or by theologians who assume the responsibility of reflecting on Scripture, has thereby neglected to pursue what has (for a good reason) *remained* in the Gospel of John. Its omission would be a devastating loss. The meaning of the entire episode has suffered from a too-strict interpretation that has effectively ignored what may be one of Jesus' most important teachings. *May* is too prudent. If *salvation* is one of Jesus' sacred responsibilities, no greater accomplishment can be imagined than saving a life within creation. The idea of salvation inherent in *soteria* has nothing metaphysical or other-worldly about it; saving a life, from death (from the law prescribing death as a judgment) occurs in the world or nowhere at all. The one who proclaims himself to be the way and the truth and the life cannot in any way and under any condition relativize such an affirmation—most especially life.

His revelations enter history from out of Jesus alone, from his *exousia*, his "authority" and, more importantly, his singular *resource*. They have no other origin. Jesus remains a problem most especially for historians and theologians who insist on *reducing* him to his time and place—a belief that is simply inconsistent with everything we know, and can imagine, about Jesus the man. Hengel writes, "Jesus stood outside any discernible teaching of Judaism."[12] The statement has nothing to do with separating him, only, from Judaism; it means Jesus cannot be understood within the limits of *any* context.[13] Far from understanding him from his historical or cultural place in first-century Judaea, there have been unique calls to regard him as someone who is, according to von Balthasar, "the absolutely singular." His presence "does not result from a combination or synthesis of Jewish and Hellenistic expectations. *It is incapable of*

12. Hengel, *Charismatic Leader*, 49.

13. As I argued in *Jesus, the Unprecedented Human Being*.

being expected."[14] Whether the prophets such as Isaiah could anticipate him remains an open-ended question; returning Jesus to his anticipation by the prophets is a theological *decision*. A historical understanding of Jesus cannot but fail to adequately represent him. There are many who insist on confining Jesus to the certain limits of time and place. Horsley believes that the gospels can only be understood "against the historical background of its origin and reference."[15] Historians may be comfortable with their extremely limited assumptions. One writer has no misgiving. Breech provocatively writes that "there is absolutely no basis for assuming that Jesus shared the cosmological, mythological, or religious ideas of his contemporaries."[16] Stauffert makes an equally important affirmation. "Jesus is much less a child of his time and of his people than has hitherto been widely thought." Indeed, stressing his uniqueness allows him to further add that Jesus is "without parallel—in history, not only the history of Palestine."[17]

Before examining the near-consensus view that the text of 7:53—8:11 in John's gospel is not part of the original, an emphasis on its importance in the history of Christianity should be emphasized. Given how often the entire section is ignored (most especially in *complete* commentaries devoted to John's gospel) the issue is noticeable. At the appropriate time we will have to ask ourselves why, if inauthentic, the passage was first included and then retained despite all the theological hand-wringing most especially by church fathers who had to deal with the difficult topic of adultery, that is, desire, sex, and marital infidelity. The woman caught in adultery is a precedent case; all commentaries are decisive for all future orthodoxy and binding. Ambrose, Augustine, and Jerome all devoted thought to this problem; given *their* particular historical context and the development of church doctrine as it pertained to sexual morality and

14. Balthasar, "Jesus, the Absolutely Singular," 124, my emphasis.

15. Horsley, *Liberation of Christmas*, 18–19. Similar observations are countless. Jesus "must be understood as a Jewish figure teaching and acting within Judaism, or we will misunderstand what he was about." Borg, "Seeing Jesus," 8. Jesus was a "first-century AD Galilean Jew, a man firmly situated in time and space." Vermes, *Jesus the Jew*, 16. "Jesus was a man of his time." Lindars, *Jesus Son of Man*, 1. "Jesus was fully conditioned by the culture and thought-world of his time." Collins, "The Origin of the Designation of Jesus as 'Son of Man,'" 407. "Jesus belongs firmly in the world of first-century Judaism." Wright, *Who Was Jesus?*, 39.

16. Breech, *Silence of Jesus*, 218. He adds, "Jesus might be more complex and original than commonly supposed."

17. Stauffer, *Jesus and His Story*, 11, 125.

questions of virginity and marriage, church fathers were only able to interpret John within the limits of their present. History limits *us*, not Jesus. While early Christian commentators were all too preoccupied with the problem of forgiving a woman who had committed adultery and therefore worried their theological decision condoned such an act, they were completely unaware of the reason the gospel writer included the incident. Sexual morality was not the issue, sexual licentiousness or the dread of permissiveness less so. The sexuality of the case may be enticing; it is, unfortunately, sensationalistic enough to distract readers from the much more serious issue.

Adultery was not at all Jesus' concern when he was confronted with a woman who was, apparently, found in the act by more than two witnesses (as was necessary by law for her to be prosecuted) and in danger of being stoned to death as prescribed by Mosaic law. While it is factually true that no one could be "convicted and executed on the evidence of incompetent witnesses,"[18] as stipulated by law, during the entire incident Jesus is not restrained by the limits of the law. Beyond all particulars of the events, what must be foremost in the minds of the readers is Jesus' *consciousness* at the time. As soon as the reader is distracted by the limits of theological considerations and his identity—as, for example, the son of God or the Messiah—then his presence during the incident will remain partly obscured.

The so-called crime of the woman was not, ultimately, the issue, at least not for Jesus. She had sex with a man who was not her husband. Much more serious and indicative of Jesus' relationship to the entire incident was the legitimacy of the death penalty—for *any crime*. Keith tells us that the section in John "was one of the most spoken, read, remembered, and transmitted stories about Jesus in the early Church, deserving its reputation as one of the most popular stories in the gospels."[19] So Keith concludes his study. If true, then a reason must be found. "This section about the Adulteress was probably the most read single section in the whole history of the Church."[20] The descriptive flourish can hardly be avoided. "This little periscope is one of the great jewels of Christian scripture."[21] And yet, strangely, many modern commentators avoid it completely, and

18. Derrett, *Law in the New Testament*, 183.

19. Keith, *Pericope Adultarae*, 260.

20. Gregory, *Canon and Text of the New Testament*, 514.

21. Borchert, *John 1–11*, 369.

for reasons that sometimes are not even explained. The omission is serious, most especially in a context when Jesus himself writes something unknown but not unfathomable in the ground. *Where* he writes (the ground) has not been considered. *He writes on the body of Adam.* The consequences of such an act are as inconceivable for the witnesses as the "cleansing of the temple."

The most strenuous objection comes from bibliophiles and philologists. According to all the most sophisticated research on the history of gospel *manuscripts*, the passage occurs first in the fifth century in the Codex Bezae,[22] though clearly, the story of the woman caught in adultery was well known before and was the object of intense theological preoccupation. The beginning of John 8:1–11 has been the subject of controversial arguments, with the consensus tipped in favor of the entire section not at all part of the original gospel. C. K. Barrett writes, "It is certain that the narrative is not an original part of the gospel."[23] R. H. Lightfoot reserves his commentary on the section until the very last part of his substantial commentary, as if making it nothing more than a footnote.[24] Without taking into consideration another part of the gospel that is denied its central role as the all-important conclusion (chapter 21) the section in John dealing with the woman and the death penalty has been much too neglected. The particular crime, adultery, is not significant—and this without minimizing the group of men who are intent on stoning her to death, a particularly grievous form of capital punishment since no one individual can feel his individual participation and responsibility. For Jesus, there is only one *absolute* question: is *anyone* justified in carrying out the death penalty. Farley defines the section in John as an "insertion."[25] Wells believes the section is an "interpolation."[26] He further adds that "both Catholic and Protestant commentators admit that it breaks the sequence of the narrative in which it occurs. It was presumably inserted from some apocryphal source by a late editor who thought it too good to

22. Ridderbos, *Gospel of John*.

23. Barrett, *Gospel according to John*, 589.

24. Lightfoot, *St. John's Gospel*.

25. Farley, *Gospel of John*.

26. Reading only a few hundred volumes will make it apparent that quite a few scholars take extreme liberties not only with the Gospel of John, but equally with others. One scholar (here unnamed) would like to delete the entire incident of the temple cleansing in Mark and, therefore, in the other three gospels. A slippery slope? More like a *bona fide* cliff.

miss."[27] "Too good to miss" sounds nothing more than salacious; and the argument that it "breaks the sequence" does not recognize what is surely obvious to a careful reader and its place in the *whole* of the gospel, most especially when Jesus is exposed to threats of death and, finally, his own execution. Why are scholars so intent on excluding this one tremendous example of Jesus' teaching? Is it to provide some defense of their support for the death penalty and therefore to justify the repeated justification of the most extreme form of punishment in the Torah?

Another interpretation is both possible and necessary; but let us nonetheless read more arguments. Some need to point out that the passage "is not found in the earliest and most reliable Greek manuscripts."[28] Others write that "one can only regret that the manuscript evidence for this periscope is weak."[29] In a remarkable judgment made by the four co-authors of their commentary on the Gospel of John, they write that "the story of the adulterous woman should not be given the same authority as scripture."[30]

Anyone who does not feel the most extreme hesitation with such a claim (whether they are Christian or atheist) is then perfectly comfortable with anyone in our own time deciding what part of Scripture should have authority. Their main argument, attested virtually unanimously, is the passage being a later addition. It was not included in the earliest manuscripts. Needless to say, when such pronouncements are made, a reader should pause, and in such a case for a considerable period of reflection, further reading, and a reconsideration of the motivations, first of all, of sustaining such a belief and for its *consequences*. The collective of the Jesus Seminar is even more astonishing. "The Fellows of the Jesus Seminar have decided to recognize its independent status and reclassify it as a fragment of a lost gospel."[31] If ever the Greek *hubris* could be applied to New Testament scholars, this is the time. The members of the seminar can decide, recognize, and reclassify all they want; they will be unable, thankfully, to *do* anything to the gospels. Others mention it and avoid the problem altogether—even with a title such as *The Riddles of*

27. Wells, *The Jesus of the Early Christians*, 15. Highlighting the assumptions, if only briefly, is necessary. Wells believes it was "inserted" (one) by a "late editor" (two) who took it "from some apocryphal source" (three).

28. Kanagaraj, *John*, 87.

29. Sloyan, *John*, 97.

30. Barton et al., *John*, 176.

31. Funk, *Acts of Jesus*, 397.

the Fourth Gospel.[32] No less an authority than Bultmann has not a word on it despite the massive tome he devoted to John's gospel. Referring to John 7:53—8:11, as well as other passages, Bultmann writes, "Problems of textual criticism significant for the exposition of the Gospel of John are to be found relatively seldom. . . . In contrast to this there are reasons for doubting whether the Gospel itself has found entrance into the ecclesiastical tradition in the form intended by the author."[33] In his "interpretation" of John, "the *Pericope Adulterae* . . . is omitted as being no part of the original text of this Gospel."[34] Finally, in a collection of essays called *Authenticating the Activities of Jesus*, a look at the extensive index of biblical citations shows nothing from John 7:52—8:20.[35] One would think that the only description of Jesus writing would require, at the very least, some speculation, more so because of the context. But the *pericope* does not stand alone; it has never been isolated from the rest of the gospel.

A few references in the Gospel of John prior to more fully examining the experience of Jesus as he defends the woman from a capital charge gives us some sense of its importance in John's gospel and, with sufficient time, in the whole of Jesus' teaching. This may have to be repeated. I also have no difficulty in confessing that this is not a scholarly problem. When Jesus, on the cross, says, "Father, forgive them; for they do not know what they are doing" (Luke 23:34), this pronouncement cannot be understood within the limits of a particular time and certainly not in relation to Jesus' personal experience. Unless his words are heard in relation to every single individual who has ever been condemned in the world, then we are no closer to hearing, interpreting, and understanding the universal implications of his words, which is one of the reasons to read the gospels as a *body*.

One of the recurring words in the beginning of the Gospel of John is both *witness* and *testimony*. However much we may notice the profound theological foundations of John's writing and its relationship to the *logos* first articulated by God in the very act of creation in Genesis, the figure of Jesus and his meaning, as a human being, is first announced with "what has come into being in him was life" (John 1:3–4). *Zoe*. Irreducible life; and from that moment when he comes into the world to defend it, John

32. Anderson, *Riddles of the Fourth Gospel*.

33. Bultmann, *Gospel of John*, 10.

34. Dodd, *Interpretation of the Fourth Gospel*, 346.

35. Chilton and Evans, *Authenticating the Activities of Jesus*.

the Baptist announces how his own life, in addition to the ritual of baptism, will be dedicated to a preparation.

"He came as a witness to testify" (John 1:7).

He is a living *martyr*. In retrospect, the gospel interprets the life and death of John the Baptist as a martyr who will, before his own execution (not incidentally, at a banquet where his head will be on display on a platter) testify to the life of Jesus without any reference to a future trial. The martyr does not defend himself; there is no *apologia* possible in the mind of the one who is a witness. All words are only a prelude to giving himself up for an idea; or rather, ideas that intersect, with their own significance for the future. When John the Baptist and Jesus first meet, he is announced in terms of two animals, a lamb and a bird; while it would be theologically understandable to simply refer to the paschal lamb and the dove of the spirit, the animals are significant on their own because they are, also, representative of how the presence of animals will be inseparable from the life, thoughts, acts, and words of Jesus. Not for a moment can it be forgotten that the Gospel of John has the scene of the "cleansing of the temple" near the beginning of Jesus' ministry, one emphasis different from the Synoptic accounts. Before any allegorical association of Jesus the man with a sheep or a dove, it is the flesh and life of the animal in the temple precinct that he saves, individually, while at the same time making the single most important revelation of his ministry prior to the last days of his life. The cleansing of the temple is the announcement of the abolition of animal sacrifice, the first of a two-part revelation intended to affirm the inviolability of life against both religious and judicial laws.

John's entire gospel, from beginning to end, is concerned with Jesus' relationship to the law—a word to be understood well beyond the restricted sense of the regulations of Torah law. If Jesus is going to reveal, in his being, the sacredness of life, then one of the limits of the world will be exposed in the way the law has been ordered. This is the reason for Jesus invoking the name (and his invention) of the idea of the Paraclete, someone who acts for the defense and as an *ad-vocatus*, someone who has been *called* to speak. Whatever the conclusion of commentators, and without an extensive analysis requiring a reading of every single instance of Jesus' acts (on the Sabbath, for example) two examples will suffice—most especially the second for an argument requiring emphasis.

In the first example in the Gospel of John, we are taken to one of the feasts in Jerusalem. Jesus is walking among the afflicted who congregate around the pool of Bethesda waiting for a miracle to cure them. When he cures a man who had suffered from an infirmity for thirty-eight years and is now able to walk, John describes how a group of pious and devout people according to tradition, approached him and, because it was the Sabbath, told him it was "unlawful" (John 5:10) for him to carry his mat with him. Once Jesus is identified as the *perpetrator*—as the one who has committed a crime, a *capital* one—the verdict is swift. Despite John's description of "the Jews," which has been such a source of controversy, there is little doubt that *some* of the more lawful in the Jewish leadership would have accused Jesus of a crime. Others, who have been omitted, are without a doubt sufficiently conscious of their rabbinical responsibilities to consider the readings of someone who has been acknowledged as a *teacher*.

When John writes that "the Jews starting persecuting Jesus" (John 5:16), the reader cannot forget how the Jewish leadership as a whole, made up of many different groups, each with their own responsibilities and in some cases completely different beliefs—for example, the Pharisees and the Sadducees on the question of life after death—related to Jesus differently, some with hatred, others with understanding. One senses here an attempt to physically seize him, to stop him from doing anything on the Sabbath. The confrontation on the meaning of the law is now underway. Their first dialogue only seems to confirm Jesus' outrageous conception of himself as a direct representative (as a Son) of God. One act has broken the law; one affirmation has broken another. Jesus is clearly guilty of defiling the Sabbath and of blasphemy. "For this reason the Jews were seeking all the more to kill (*apoketeinai*) him" (John 5:18). *Apokteinō* has both the sense of killing a man and slaughtering an animal. The desire on the part of some people is already expressed; whoever they are, they want to kill him. He has been accused of serious crimes. Jesus has violated certain precepts and is culpable. From now on, the threat of death hangs over the whole of his remaining life. References to the law and the death penalty will be constant, both as preparations for his defense of the woman caught in adultery and, later, as the gospel reaches its conclusion with announcing Jesus to be *parakletic*—prefiguring himself as the one who defends others against persecutions, accusations, arrests, and the death penalty to be imposed on his followers in the future.

The threat of death hangs over Jesus virtually during the whole of his ministry. "He did not wish to go into Judea because the Jews were looking for an opportunity to kill him" (John 7:1). In this case, it appears as if the news has reached him from a specific source. It may now be pertinent to wonder if Jesus had supporters among "the Jews"—specifically within the leadership, and therefore individuals who were privy to delicate and secretive information—and who were willing to play the role of "double-agents." There has not been enough scholarship on the security forces of the region beside the obvious Romans and Herodians; but there are many indications in the gospels (and in Paul's letters) that make it obvious the region was rife with spies and collaborators, "agents" who were working undercover and reporting on activities carried out by groups. Jesus' constant movement was simultaneously part of his ministry and a pragmatic need to elude the authorities who were well aware of his teachings and activities and who clearly saw him as a threat. There were no doubt assassinations carried out on the orders of the proxy political leaders of the region—for example, by Herod Antipas—and, perhaps, by the religious leadership of Jerusalem who, at this time, were not legally able to carry out judicial death penalties. "We are not permitted to put anyone to death" (John 18:31), the individuals who denounced Jesus tell Pontius Pilate. It would be naïve to believe that the Jewish leadership followed Roman orders in matters of *their* national security. Although any such assassinations were carried out only in extreme cases and, as much as possible, with plausible explanations should the Romans be concerned enough to begin an investigation, the inability to carry out a death penalty by law allowed them to rely on extrajudicial killings. Jesus represented one such individual. Indeed, he was the most dangerous kind of man. "The world," Jesus said, "hates me because I testify (*martyro*) against it that its works are evil" (John 7:7). He has become the sole "witness," the only one who sees (whose perception has allowed him to expose everything being done) what is being done by those capable of acting with cynicism and impunity. "Challenges to Jesus in John 7 are typically cast in terms of the forensic process waged against Jesus."[36]

To those who are conspiring to kill him, and to the ones who listen to him teaching in the synagogues and are compelled by the mastery of his words—and, clearly, there is a division among the people—he asks them, "Why are you looking for an opportunity to kill me?" (John 7:19). He is addressing the individuals who are now in the crowd, who may have even infiltrated his group and are constantly watching him to find any reason whatsoever to arrest him. Are there assassins among them? If so, with so many individuals near him, carrying it out would be next to

36. Neyrey, *Gospel of John*, x.

impossible—unless, of course, brazen. "Judge with right judgment" (John 7:24), he tells everyone in the crowd, in this case referring to neglecting the law of the Sabbath but, in fact, representing his own rethinking of the Mosaic law as such. No one can possibly suspect what he means by "right judgment." As far as the desire to kill him, and this seems now to be known by the people of Jerusalem, no one can possibly contemplate what he means. To begin to understand Jesus as an unprecedented human being in no way determined by his time or place, it is necessary to imagine nothing less than his consciousness as determined by himself (and his relationship with God) and the idea of understanding "right judgment" specifically as it relates to killing another human being.

The commandment "thou shall not kill" is *absolute*.

In the context of Jesus' rethinking of the meaning of judgment, he has already thought to the end—that is, to the end of the death penalty and, ultimately and beyond all decisions by the politico-religious state, the end of all killing. The revelations he has given history to see and witness and then provide a testimony remains completely outside the limits of human perception unless we extend ourselves and our diminished humanity to his presence and then what he has accomplished. In this case, the abolition of animal sacrifice as the classical form of ritualistic piety leads, at the same time (and they have never been separated as individual practices) to the abolition of the death penalty as a judicially sanctioned law.

One notices a sudden shift as soon as the desire to kill Jesus becomes public knowledge. The temple leadership has changed its plans. An assassination can no longer be carried out. They must find other, legal means to stop him and his teaching. His influence is becoming too widespread and threatening to tradition. Therefore, "the chief priests and the Pharisees sent temple police to arrest him" (John 7:32). If Jesus is to be killed, it can no longer be carried out as an assassination. It must be judicially justified. It must be *legal*. The real confrontation has begun. Jesus has indeed come to fulfill the law; but it is a law no one remotely imagines. For anyone to see his conception of the law and the abolition of the death penalty, they would have to be reimagine themselves and the limits of their times and begin to properly see (with much more than the traditional theological imagination of priests or their interpretation of Scripture) what the *basileia* of God actually means.

The plans by the chief priests and Pharisees to arrest him have failed. The temple police sent to arrest him were so overwhelmed by his teaching that they were unable to lay hands on him. His words were especially remarkable. "Never has anyone spoken like this man" (John 7:46). The Pharisees now realize what must have been incredible to them—unbelievable but more and more probable. "Has any one of the authorities or of the Pharisees believed in him" (John 7:48)? His influence has potentially swayed even those in position of authority. He cannot be killed; he cannot be arrested. Those attempting to stop him are at a loss. The council meetings, perhaps now only conducted with a few individuals and only among the highest of the echelon, had to make other proposals. His influence, already widespread, could not be allowed to grow. The consequences could not be estimated. The leadership simply had no way to properly evaluate the teachings of Jesus and the meanings it had for the future. And so, precisely at this most delicate time for the Jewish leadership as they contemplate a way to stop him, the episode of the woman caught in adultery is presented by John. One of the most significant of all of Jesus' teachings is now to be revealed.

The interest in John 8 as an apparent "interpolation" is, at least, curious; for if the gospels are examined as a whole, it surely becomes apparent (as many have pointed out) that its composition as a whole has involved quite extensive "editorial tampering."[37] Or to make the comment less intrusive, the gospel writers of course relied on oral testimonies as well as texts as references. As writers, they made decisions. The compositions were creative; they were hardly copyists. But all we have, now, is the text. In the case of a possible editor in addition to the composition by John himself, they must have realized both the importance of the event in the life of Jesus and the necessity of including it in a gospel. The origin of the event as recollected may forever elude us; we must be, nevertheless, grateful for its inclusion, no different than in the individual decisions made by each gospel writer to include, alone, a moment or a saying in the life of Jesus nowhere else represented. It is unthinkable for scholars to give themselves the liberty of excision. By all means, turn to a reading of the gospels with dedication and commitment, whatever the motivations; but to exclude *anything* is unthinkable.

Despite the interest in pursuing scholarly research into the manuscript history of the passage, the purpose for the following reflections

37. Crossan, *In Parables*, 45. Among the many who comment on the general editorializing of the gospel writers, see Fredriksen, *From Jesus to Christ*; Perrin, *Jesus and the Language of the Kingdom*; Charlesworth, *Historical Jesus*; Dibelius, *From Tradition to Gospel*; Rhoads and Michie, *Mark as Story*; Hengel, *Studies in the Gospel of Mark*.

are neither to identify the origin of the passage nor any one (or more) authors—if indeed it is not John, a fact in itself that, in the end, does not matter; rather, the *story* is of utmost importance for revealing a belief held by Jesus that has not been sufficiently considered. The situation of the adulterous woman does not tell us what Jesus may have thought about sexual immorality. There is a much more crucial problem in the passage of John 8:1–11 than the reference to a woman's act of lust, sex, and/or love. That the story has been narrowly understood in relation to adultery has unfortunately led to a disavowal of the more important implications of Jesus' words and singular act. The event does not simply show Jesus to be defying, and opposing, Mosaic law, but one of its foundational statutes—that is, the death penalty and its universally observed law. Some who do comment are unable to recognize its judicial importance. It "teaches a lesson about love and compassion."[38] While thoughtful, this is far from being enough. Jesus does not appreciate the timidity of the ethical. The Gospel of John has sometimes been called the "spiritual" gospel.[39] Others, however, recognize John's testimony as, also, a legal document; or to be more emphatic, it is a juridical argument with several interconnected facets as it concerns the relationship between the continuity of the Mosaic law and Jesus' new interpretation of the law *as such*. Theological interpretations—based, for example, on grace and forgiveness—have overlooked an equally significant meaning in Jesus's acts and words related specifically to the repudiation of the law on the death penalty and, in particular, for inscribing on two different occasions an entirely new law; or, more precisely, calling for the abolition of the death penalty. F. F. Bruce points out that the preservation of the passages—"for which we should be thankful"—is also related to an important argument: "One reason for its being placed in the context in John may have been the idea that it served as an illustration of Jesus' words in 8:15, 'I judge no one.'"[40] The observation needs to be developed. In the context of an entire gospel many have recognized for its relationship to the law, Jesus' affirmation

38. Boyele and Dempsey, *Bible and Literature*.

39. See, e.g., Maahs, *The John You Never Knew*. The problem with focusing on the "spiritual," if one can call it such, leads to an omission that should not be ignored. If the gospel is going to be "decoded," how can one completely ignore John 8:1–11? In *The Spiritual Gospel*, Wiles devotes a chapter to "The Leading Ideas" and yet, in the section he names "Judgment" (79–81) he does not even mention the woman accused of adultery.

40. Bruce, *Gospel of John*, 413.

that he refrains from judging anyone, for any reason, has consequences that can only be noticed by reading, if not the whole of the Gospel of John, at least the sections most pertinent to the argument at hand. While his interpretation does not sufficiently draw on the scene, and from Jesus (from out of Jesus) Bruce at least tells us that we should be "thankful." Indeed, it is one of Jesus's most profound declarations and should also be read in conjunction with all of his pronouncements on the law, most especially the enigmatic relationship of abolition and fulfillment.

The theological difficulty can neither be ignored nor avoided; it can only be contextualized and heard (read) with two simultaneous meanings. When John tells us that "the law indeed was given through Moses; grace and truth came through Jesus Christ" (John 1:17), grace supersedes the law.[41] There can be no question of equality or symmetry between the two: the law (everywhere) has been instituted, grace is (uniquely) revealed. But the relationship between the law and grace is not an evident dichotomy; much less can it be reduced to two figures, Jesus and Moses. Jesus, who represents *logos* and life, opposes everyone who has created the very law making it judicially possible to carry out a death sentence. The *logos* and life *in Jesus* now begins to extend itself outward, from out of himself to others.

Jesus' relationship to Jewish law has been a source of much debate and opposing views; they range from perfectly obedient and observant of the Torah to completely rejecting it. The discrepancy of views are not so much an indication of contradictions in the gospel accounts; they are, rather, evidence of opposing views on Jesus' relationship to tradition. One notices momentary hesitations even if they are not always acknowledged or considered for their consequences. For example, when McDermott writes that "the closer one draws to the pre-Easter Jesus and his attitude toward the Law, the more apparent it becomes that his attitude is neither anti-Law nor anti-Jewish nor anti-tradition,"[42] the insistence is, if not withdrawn, surely reconsidered. On the next page he adds, "His sense of authorization found no parallels in the Judaism of his day." Others insist that "the story is not an attack on Moses or the law."[43] Arguments have

41. On the question of supersessionism, see esp. Klawans, *Purity, Sacrifice, and the Temple*. As I will argue, Jesus can no longer simply be interpreted as someone who engaged in a reinterpretation of Judaism. His intentions, for the world, were much more comprehensive.

42. McDermott, *Word Become Flesh*, 57.

43. Borchert, *John 1–11*, 376.

been made, and with justifiable appeals: "No traditional Jewish thinker could be opposed to capital punishment, since it is clearly mandated by scripture."[44] The argument, it seems, nullifies itself. Can Jesus be thought as a "traditional Jewish thinker"? On the issue of the blood for blood or *lex talionis* argument in Genesis 9:6, two authors are perhaps a little overconfident of their supporters. "*With most biblical commentators,* we take these words to be prescriptive, and not merely descriptive. In other words, God authorizes capital punishment as an appropriate response to murder."[45] While the appeal to a majority cannot in any way support their argument, the more objectionable assertion is their conviction in what "God authorizes."

I would not be so presumptuous in understanding the will of God when it makes the killing of another human being legitimate.

The act of murder, individually speaking, remains the one crime most referenced; in our case, of course, no murder was committed. On the contrary, we cannot exclude the feelings of love in the extramarital affair of the woman accused of adultery. If our position has been clear from the beginning, it is now time to turn to John and argue against the belief that "neither Jesus nor Paul rose up against capital punishment."[46] One has to make a strenuous objection. The Christian support of the death penalty is a *disgrace*. An argument may be necessary for those who allow themselves to forget that Jesus was crucified *lawfully* by the Romans (that is, according to their law) and as a consequence of a crime.

Jesus was sentenced to death as a criminal. Is the law, then, to be upheld, yes or no?

In John 8, after leaving the Mount of Olives, where he slept for the night, he makes his way to the temple early in the morning. "All the people came to him and he sat down and began to teach them" (John 8:2). He clearly has enough of a reputation for people to come to him and hear him speak. Hamerton-Kelly draws attention to others as they listen to Jesus and the "astonishment of the onlookers and hearers who ask about the source of all this teaching, indicating that it is *altogether*

44. Novak, "Can Capital Punishment Ever Be Justified in the Jewish Tradition?" Space does not allow for an interpretation, for example, of Gen 9:6; Exod 21:12–27; or Lev 24:21–22. "Clearly mandated" could serve as the beginning of a dialogue.

45. Beck and VanDrunen, "Biblical Foundations of the Law," 39, my emphasis.

46. Hauerwas, "Punishing Christians," 58. Hauerwas is paraphrasing Yoder's *The Christian and Capital Punishment*.

new and unparalleled in their experience."[47] The Jerusalem authorities are equally aware of his presence; they knew where and when to find him. "The scribes and the Pharisees brought a woman who had been caught in adultery; and making her stand before all them" (John 8:3), confront Jesus with a *case*. The scribes and Pharisees specifically bring a woman who has been caught in adultery to challenge Jesus on *teachings he has already made well known*. His relationship to some traditional observances are by now commonplace. He has also dared to reinterpret the laws considered most inviolable; but for the first and only time, a supreme law will be the issue. Although other laws Jesus disregarded if not rejected have been capital—i.e., those deemed blasphemous—the woman caught in adultery makes her death sentence by stoning an issue of incomparable importance. All prior arguments on the event being an "insertion" must ignore its structural relevance in relation to the whole of the gospel and, most especially, the numerous references (before and after) on Jesus being threatened with death. The emphasis can be repeated. Jesus was condemned by *Roman law*. He was lawfully killed. The theological significance of the crucifixion and the overwhelming power of the cross (then, and now) has sometimes allowed us to forget that Jesus was *executed*. Pontius Pilate sentenced him to death. One cannot look at the cross without at the same time seeing Roman law and punishment.

Jesus is condemned to death by a law.

One other assumption can easily be made, and it should be resisted: if we restrict the entire incident to an intra-Jewish issue (Jesus somehow stood only against the scribes and Pharisees), then we will be entirely unaware of fully understanding him. Many commentators have emphasized the relationship of Jesus to the Jerusalem leadership as one founded on specifically Jewish issues—the law, for example, on washing one's hands before eating, or in disregarding the Sabbath. In this case, however, any ethnic restrictions imposed on Jesus are misleading.

Revelations are universal or they are nothing at all.

If we take seriously, then, as we should, the definition of *all the people* who were listening to him, then there are certainly people present who are not Jews. The incident to unfold cannot simply be interpreted from the perspective of Jewish law. The scribes and Pharisees may themselves be solely preoccupied with listening to Jesus make a pronouncement regarding *their* laws. Jesus, however, speaks to *the law*, that is, the law as

47. Hamerton-Kelly, *Pre-existence, Wisdom, and the Son of Man*, 50, my emphasis.

it exists at the time and in every singular culture. The incident cannot be interpreted narrowly as Jesus's relationship to Judaism. Unless he is acknowledged, always and in every instance, addressing every listener universally, then we become vulnerable to imposing *our* limitations on *him*. That in itself may be a limitation to the spirit and the very definition of what he has defined as *unforgivable*: the spirit must not be blasphemed. When Jesus acts and speaks against the death penalty, he does so *universally*; when Jesus reflects on the death penalty and on its legality, and on its unquestioned practice, he will do so in the context of *every* law. "This is the diabolical strategy of evil: it takes the law, with which men fight against evil, into its regime and ensnares the man who obeys the law even more deeply in evil."[48]

The problem comes down to his listeners. In the temple, with both Jews and other people listening to his teachings, the death penalty (for Jesus) cannot be reduced to its Mosaic context and its scriptural validity much less its origin in God. The revelations, from out of himself—from that singular self-conception proclaimed with the stunning "Before Abraham was, I am" (John 8:58)—now makes Jesus anterior to all beginnings and therefore uniquely capable of inaugurating a new conception of being, of life, and of the spirit.

The woman has been brought before him. She has no doubt been insulted, roughed up, and publicly humiliated. She stands in front of him, accused, now fragile and awaiting a sentence. A defense is not possible. All that is required now is for the judgment to be passed and the death sentence by stoning to take place. "Teacher," a spokesman for the scribes and Pharisees says, "this woman was caught in the very act of committing adultery. Now in the law of Moses commanded us to stone such women. Now what do you say" (John 8:5)? For them, the case is simple. The law could not be more clear, the consequences of it being broken are precise. The leaders who confront Jesus are ultimately less interested in the guilty woman than in Jesus's response. At this point, we cannot be certain about the intentions of this particular group. The reader may easily, and mistakenly, assume they have come to Jesus to somehow entrap him. John tells us so. "They said this to test him, so that they might have some charge to bring against him" (John 8:6). According to John, the question posed to Jesus is agonistic, confrontational; in other words, it is not *rabbinic*, a perfectly natural question posed in the context of learned rabbis *debating*.

48. Moltmann, *Crucified God*, 293.

The sense of Pharisees simply being Jesus's enemies does not consider some of them as recognizing Jesus as someone who may not have the credential of a rabbi but is nevertheless more than intelligent enough to participate in a rabbinical debate. Let us not forget the incomparable image of the twelve-year-old Jesus in the temple of Jerusalem debating with the learned doctors. If he was already considered a sage at such a young age, one can only imagine the impression he makes on his interlocutors now. Strauss, however, argues that "in a community governed by divine laws it is strictly forbidden to subject these laws to genuine discussion, i.e., to critical examination."[49] Whether the argument can be maintained, in other words, whether the scribes and Pharisees were attempting to once again trap Jesus, or whether they were genuinely interested in a dialogue remains, for now, unanswered. This seems, at the very least, worth pursuing: given what we now know about some of the more influential leaders in Jerusalem even before the life of Jesus, and certainly after when we consider the rabbis of Yavneh post-70, the name of Hillel should be sufficient as a starting point for a renewed debate on the relationship between Jesus and some of the learned rabbis during his ministry.

The reader is left with a problem and must now consider two points: the far-from-obvious relationship between Jesus and the Jews (one individual, members of a group, all the various factions existing at the time) and the ultimate issue at hand on the validity of the death penalty as a law. One accused is identified; the other does not know (according to the scribes and Pharisees) he is also on trial. The real accused has been put in the position of being an expert in the law. They have called him a teacher; they identify him as a "lawyer" without the proper accreditation and, in fact, already guilty of being someone who does not study the law and put it into effect without prejudice but has the audacity to expose its most sacred statutes according to the Torah. Jesus has become the lawyer who presents a law as antiquarian and therefore no longer *legal*. Jesus represents a hermeneutics of *paraklesis*; he rewrites the law. Without here necessarily appealing to *natural law* as opposed to the law as it has been practiced in history (in Judaism and of *all other people*) only Jesus has come to the unique realization of the law from the past coming to an end.

49. Strauss, *Natural Right and History*, 85. One issue can only be mentioned here and serve for a discussion at a later time. If we read the text, there is no question of the Jewish delegation being hostile and with the intentions of exposing Jesus to a *crime*. In connection with this, see Bloch's *Natural Law and Human Dignity*. The word "dignity" will be all-important at the end of this chapter.

A law can be abolished. The death penalty can become a merely archaic reminder of the past.

Initially, and precisely in front of the very people who uphold the law, Jesus does not speak. He does not respond to their "What do you say?" Instead, and for the one and only time in the gospels, Jesus writes. "Jesus bent down and wrote (*egraphen*) with his finger on the ground (*gen*)" (John 8:6). While one cannot deny the ambiguity of *katagraphe* (it may be writing, with letters, or making an image) some refer to his act as "doodling on the pavement"[50] or "doodling on the ground."[51] What an odd word to use: many do so as a way to diminish the power of his act. No one seems to be able to imagine what he writes. He will write twice. The first time, he writes an insignia to represent the name of the woman on a tomb. Lindars writes, "There has been endless speculation about what he was writing as he doodled on the dusty pavement."[52] Before a "speculation" is presented about the second time Jesus writes in the ground, a comment is in order: by referring to Jesus's inscription in the ground as "doodling" (what people do, sometimes, when they are bored and distracted) commentators have decided to completely trivialize his act. Equally serious, they have neglected how Jesus writes into the *earth* created by God and the same earth used to create the first human being. Jesus is not doodling.

He is writing into the heart of the earth and Adam. Jesus writes into the ground, at the very place of *the birth* of Adam and his relationship with Eve, "the mother of all living."

"The one mention in the Gospels of his writing, when he 'bent down and wrote with his finger in the ground,' is of doubtful authenticity in the Greek manuscripts. Even if it is authentic, moreover, it does not report anything about just what it was that he wrote."[53] The "even if" is telling; and so is the uncertainty. No, we have no "report" on the words. Our hermeneutic imagination can hardly be limited by the words before us. The writer of the gospel knows what can be revealed from the tip of Jesus's finger *kerygmatically*. Paul's suggestion to the listeners of his letter to be attentive "to the revelation of the mystery" (Rom 16:25) and how it will be revealed to "all people" gives us an opportunity for an affirmation.

50. Martin, *Bringing the Gospel of John to Life*, 227.

51. Farley, *Gospel of John*, 148.

52. Lindars, *Gospel of John*, 310.

53. Pelikan, *Whose Bible Is It?*, 17.

Writing into the ground is a momentous event in the history of Jesus's life.

He writes his law directly into the creation of the world.

By writing letters into Adam, Jesus returns from the very place where he has always *conceived himself* to be—prior to "in the beginning." His revelation (as all four gospel writers testify in relation to the first) abolishes the pious ritual of animal sacrifice and the religious-legal institution of the death penalty. Only an advocate for the abolition of the death penalty has recognized the intimate relationship between animal sacrifice and the death penalty as it related to Jesus. "Jesus' death removed the need for the animal sacrifice required in the Old Testament. . . . Similarly, his death also removed the need for the human sacrifice of capital punishment. Because Jesus has righted the moral balance for all time, we no longer have to make sacrifices, either animal or human, to make things right."[54] Once Jesus writes it out into the ground for all to see and verify, the scribes and Pharisees immediately react. Jesus has simultaneously erased the law on the death penalty and inscribed his own law on the ground no one, among them, would see as simultaneously ground and dirt and sand and clay and all other elements making up the whole of Adam.

"Let anyone among you who is without sin be the first to throw a stone at her" (John 8:7). The accusers have now been given the chance to be executioners. They will have to carry out the death penalty, even as (perhaps) one or more of them realize how stoning a human being with innumerable accomplices first of all allows one to avoid touching the body of the accused. "And once again he bent down and wrote on the ground" (John 8:8). The second act is a repetition and a confirmation. The scribes and the Pharisees, apparently, had no choice but to leave. They no longer had a case. All arguments were off; all legal claims were moot. The second inscription nullifies the first. Jesus abolishes the death penalty at the same time as he removes the name of the woman from a funerary insignia.

Now alone with the woman, Jesus turns to her for the first time and asks her, "Has no one condemned you?" (John 8:10). When she answers him, talking for the first time, he also tells her, "Neither do I condemn you. Go your way, and from now on do not sin again" (John 8:11). When Jesus tells her to go free, the act cannot simply be understood as an individual

54. Hanks, *Against the Death Penalty*, 45.

judgment. The incident must be related to the entire Gospel of John and how Jesus is repeatedly exposed to the threat of death and, in particular, death by stoning. If Jesus is to be regarded as a revelation—as he said, of things hidden since the foundation of the world—then his words and acts are themselves indications of inconceivable ideas in history that, for the first time, become possible. Flood does emphasize the idea of "restorative justice" as opposed to punishment and even mentions Jesus's "new law,"[55] without, however, providing any sense of what such a law would include, despite his subtitle, expressing an all-important word. Better stated, "The teaching of Jesus is a 'new' revelation, not to be found in the Law. As such it supersedes the Law. The Law is subservient to the teaching Jesus brings and not vice versa."[56] The abolition of the death penalty before Jesus was inconceivable. For the first time in human history and from out of the revelations of Jesus himself, the death penalty was abolished prior to his execution.

On August 2, 2018, Pope Francis made one of the most significant decisions in the history of the Catholic Church. In a "New Revision of Number 2267 of the Catechism of the Catholic Church," Pope Francis made his decision based on the inviolability of the dignity of the human person "in the light of the Gospel" and urged everyone to oppose the institution of the death penalty and to work "with determination for its abolition worldwide."

55. Flood, *Healing the Gospel: A Radical Vision of Grace, Justice, and the Cross*, 16.
56. Pancaro, *Law in the Fourth Gospel*, 116.

Chapter 6

Roman Law and the Christians
Damnati ad Bestias

The revelations of Jesus, beginning with saving the life of the woman caught in adultery and arguing in her defense to prevent her accusers from stoning her to death as a judgment and execution according to the law, are singular moments of his phenomenological presence that disrupts any *parousia* as unfolding within mere time and epochal history. Jesus acted as an advocate, an *ad-vocatus* who spoke in her defense, arguing against a timeless law to preserve her life. Jesus elevates humanity to another possibility of being. The abolition of the death penalty as a previously inconceivable idea prior to his life and teaching is one act among the numerous interconnected moments that in many cases have remained, for those in his own time, elusive, enigmatic, and ungraspable—and today equally so in part because their recovery from out of the texts of the gospels and his sayings are concealed by history itself. In order to suspend certain judgments, and one in particular that is decisive for the future, the revelations as *an apocalyptic end* (in time) will be here interpreted from the meaning of *apokalypsis* as a disclosure, a manifestation, an appearance that will be intimately related to the martyr as a witness. The presumed and expected theology of any "end of days," so longed for, so yearned for as redemptive, is made irrelevant when Jesus, *as a historian*, anticipates the events to unfold for his followers and their inevitable confrontation with the Roman authorities and, in particular, after his own death and later during the reign of Nero.

The interpretation of revelations has been *ongoing*. The expectation of a redemptive end has rebounded, from the indeterminacy of a future, and held time and history in check. No movement forward is possible unless the end is nullified. Jesus was not, as has been so often claimed and with all the anticipation of someone in need of deliverance from the world, an eschatological prophet, a messiah who comes into the world to release one from the obligation of living a full and fulfilling life; he was fully aware of the meaning of history to realize what would happen to his followers after his death. They would be persecuted, arrested, and put to death; and yet none of them would actually *commit any crimes*. They were sentenced, first of all, for their "contumacy," more than any other reason for their refusal to comply with judicial orders to submit to one imperative: their well-known refusal to participate in the Roman religiopolitical system of sacrifice that made them repeatedly accused of *superstitio*; and much worse. "Denying the government's authority, contemptuous behavior, arrogance? Neither of these normally merited capital punishment."[1] On their own, no; there were other, more significant reasons for the judicial decisions. Christians were sentenced to death by Roman magistrates for three interrelated reasons: they refused to participate in animal sacrifice, make an "offering" in the name of the emperor, and *eat a meal* with others who were citizens and polytheists. Sacrifice, obeying imperial law, eating meat—with the latter, most especially, not usually considered in the analysis of the judicial experience of the martyr. Marta Sordi writes about the governors and judges who "had asked the Christians to make libations or to offer sacrifice to the image of the emperor. . . . If the Christians refused to comply, this transgression took on the meaning and character of *crimen maestatis*."[2] Two important points can be added. Christians were doubly subjected to the law and its representation of sacrifice: the "libation" involved pouring wine on the ground—for Christians, an intolerable act, symbolically horrifying—and two, eating sacrificial meat was profane to the extreme. There has not been sufficient attention paid to the confrontation between Christians and Romans on the irreconcilable difference between the sacrament of the Eucharist and the ritual sacrifice, internalizing the body of Christ and eating the meat of a slaughtered animal as a religious act. The martyrs, as witnesses, will represent an *apokalpytic* testimony. For all the attention and solicitude

1. Benko, *Pagan Rome and the Early Christians*, 10.

2. Sordi, *Christians and the Roman Empire*, 176–77.

shown to the Christians who were slaughtered in the Roman amphitheaters beginning in 64 CE during the reign of Nero, one perception has remained concealed by our preoccupations. *Our* hermeneutics has been self-serving, and in supposed conflicts that are matters of debate and polemics. For example, Daniel Boyarin writes, "Martyrdom as a discourse was shared and fought over between rabbinic Judaism and Christianity."[3] Once we define martyrdom as a "discourse" (however justified is its narrow analysis of a literary genre, the martyrology) we have excluded ourselves from understanding the *phenomenology* of the experience, for the martyr, the spectator, and above all for the judges who handed down the sentences of death. Finally, and this is where my preoccupations are focused: the condemnation of the Christians to the sentence of *damnati ad bestias* can only be understood, in its graphic, visceral horror, once the Roman magistrates are seen as politico-religious representatives of a sacrificial culture that, now, has begun to fully realize the metaphysical meaning of the Eucharist. Only by returning to the consciousness of Jesus as he approaches the experience defined as "the Passion" are we able to relate the interconnected events of his last days and, in order: one, his repeated warnings to his followers; two, the creation of the Eucharist during the Last Supper as a substitution for sacrifice; three, the presence of animals during and after his crucifixion. Jesus's repeated exhortation to his followers, the creation of the Eucharist as a substitute for animal sacrifice and meat-eating, and his crucifixion are all interrelated and, for reasons to be presented, one after another.

Before Jesus confronts his own personal history and the crucifixion (which, for us, has to be understood as *symmetrical*—in relation to the animals surrounding him at his birth and at his death, in the manger and on the cross) Jesus tells his followers to be prepared for a future ordeal. They too will have to be surrounded by animals, as he was during his birth in a *manger*—that is, a feeding-trough for *domestic* animals—and as he will be on the cross when surrounded by scavengers of dead meat, his body potentially carrion for birds and packs of hungry dogs. He does not use the word *martys*. The martyr is not yet a concept readily understood for his Jewish followers except in relation to the historical events of the Maccabees and their conflict with the last of the Hellenistic rulers of Jerusalem; nevertheless, in his conversation with his disciples, Jesus prepares them individually and his future followers for a difficult, in some cases

3. Boyarin, *Dying for God*, 114.

excruciating future. The revelations of a time to come are not intended to be eschatological in nature and have nothing to do with a metaphysical transformation of the world, either with the expectations of a coming messiah who will redeem the world or from an ultimate decision made by God. The revelations, when he speaks to his disciples and followers, repeatedly warns them about a confrontation between belief and the law; they will be intimately, personally related to the Christian martyr as a witness who will represent themselves while being supported, in presence, in thought, in speech, by the spirit of the Paraclete, the defender of the accused and the one who lives as an advocate and who speaks on behalf of those who will be accused, judged, and condemned to an atrocious death.

The Christian martyr soon comes into being. The men and women persecuted, arrested, and executed by the Roman state have been rightly called witnesses; their experiences (looked on by the many in Roman amphitheaters who screamed and urged them to be thrown *ad leones*) was watched as a spectacle. The Romans who were entertained by the sight of these executions could not have been aware at the time that they were all contributing to the revelations of Jesus. The spectacles of the Roman amphitheaters were entertainment for the bored and the unoccupied; and they were given food, free bread, along with the daily "entertainment." No spectator, except for a few Roman magistrates, could grasp the meaning of Christians being killed and *eaten* by wild animals. The Christian martyrs became witnesses to the revelations of Jesus and made them seen by others so as to take account of them and, for a few in a sudden epiphany, realize what the Christian condemned to death represented. The sentences of death and executions were logical to the extreme. The logic of the Roman justice system knew precisely what it was doing (what effect they were going to have) even if they could not fathom the metaphysical principles now defining an absolute reality. *History was coming to an end.* Jesus had warned his followers that this reality was inevitable. For all the aspirations of the Christians who were anticipating a messiah to deliver them from the world and to bring out about an apocalyptic eschatology, perhaps it dawned on a few minds that the *parousia* or "second coming" was here and now and fully *present* as never before. To make the teachings of Jesus perpetually and infinitely present, and with the sacrament of the Eucharist as exemplary, it is then necessary to make a further argument—one that is at once theologically relevant and also one that prepares us to enter the Roman amphitheater in order to understand the *metaphysical* implications of the Christians who will be "executed" by wild animals. Jesus did not prepare his disciples for an apocalyptic future. The revelations of his presence made all apocalyptic eschatology irrelevant. Before his death, he had prepared Christians for their future, in the here and now, as they would be subjected to the sentences of the Roman justice system.

In passages that have often been interpreted in the context of an apocalyptic expectation, once they are understood, instead, as preparations for their near-future when faced with the rigidity of Roman law, Jesus's sayings take on completely different meanings. His sayings are prophetic, but not in anticipating any "end of days." Taken together, the Synoptic Gospels all present one consistent vision. "When they bring you to trial and hand you over, do not worry beforehand about what you are to say; but say whatever is given you at that time, for it is not you who speak, but the Holy Spirit" (Mark 13:11). In the section of Mark's gospel usually called the "little apocalypse" and associated with Jesus's supposed announcement of the end of days, a far different interpretation can be reached once we understand his sayings as a warning to his followers about what will inevitably happen to them. "They will arrest and persecute you" (Luke 21:12), he told them. "You will be brought before kings and governors because of my name. This will give you the opportunity to testify. So make up your minds not to prepare your defense in advance; for I will give you words and a wisdom that one of your opponents will be able to withstand or contradict." All the gospel writers include these warnings in their teachings; when one considers the date of the compositions, beginning with Mark circa 70 CE, then his predictions have already come true. "They will hand you over to be tortured and will put you to death" (Matt 24:9). The brutality unleashed on Christians would soon be decisive in creating the witness to the revelations of Jesus. He knew what would happen. The expectations of a Christian eschatology misinterpreted what Jesus was saying: he knew that his revelations would need witnesses. Others had to be placed in the position of watching. The spectacles in the Roman amphitheater were the end of days he had proclaimed and the times that would lead to the formation of a new world. Jesus had prepared some of his future followers for their future, as accused, judged, and condemned. They would have no choice but to personally confront the magistrates of Roman law and be cross-examined as to their beliefs and to repudiate with one simple act: the offer of a sacrificial animal in the name of the emperor, thereby rejecting their belief in Jesus's accomplishment (represented by the creation of the Eucharist) and the return to a sacrificial culture. In order to return to the events of 64 CE during the reign of Nero and the martyrdoms of Christians in the Roman amphitheater, the meaning of their deaths (as witnesses) has to be placed in the context of Jesus's anti-sacrificial teaching. As all four gospels attest, one of the *foundational* acts of his ministry was to enter the temple precinct during the festival of Passover and overthrow the central act of piety for Jews *and* Romans—the slaughter of animals within the temple and as the highest expression of religious devotion. The public act, by itself, was finalized privately and with his disciples in the context of eating. There could not be a more interconnected series of events, in his life, that established his teaching while at the same time preparing all his followers for the future. The "cleansing of the temple," as the abolition of animal sacrifice, was followed by one of the most important of Jesus's *creations*. The origin of the Eucharist at the Last Supper was *the first* act replacing, absolutely, the ritual of animal sacrifice—one to involve the act of eating, ingesting, internalizing the body and blood of Christ instead of eating the butchered body of an animal. This is the point when the Christian and the ancient Greek, the Orphic and the Pythagorean, coincide. Theologians have been unwilling to stress one fundamental origin of an anti-sacrificial philosophy as well as the refusal to eat meat. Once again, Detienne's analysis allows us to stress the importance of the Christian aversion to eating meat as a consequence of a sacrificial culture. "If the diverse modalities of protest can be apprehended without derision in terms of cuisine, it is simply because the city as a whole identifies itself by the eating of meat—the flesh of a domestic animal cooked on fire—an act that coincides with the blood sacrifice and founds the dominant values of a world maintained midway between nature and the supernatural."[4] The creation of the Eucharist during the Last Supper can now be properly analyzed.

For the time being, and before all sacramental interpretations, one event above all draws us toward the day before the death of Jesus and the celebration of the Last Supper. As long as readers of the gospels continue to imagine "the Passover meal" as traditional and conforming to all its dietary necessities, with the slaughter and consumption of the Paschal lamb as central, they will remain bound by a historically determined understanding of Jesus and cannot properly imagine his consciousness or

4. Detienne, *Dionysos Slain*, ix.

experience at the table. The commensality of the Last Supper is absolutely unique. There is nothing traditional about the meal. All assumptions about a *dead animal* are only based on historical precedents; nothing, in any gospel writing, hints at a meal consistent with the tradition of Passover. The enormity of the night in Egypt that initiated the ritual as a commemoration of the event is foremost in the mind of Jesus as he prepares himself from a *new creation*; he takes his seat and recollects, prior to the ritual he creates, all the dead in Egypt during the night of death for firstborn and for the sheep whose blood was marked on the doors as a sign for death to pass by. The Last Supper is not a Passover meal. One traditional argument will be presented and rejected. Jesus did not identify with the commemoration of Passover or, much less, himself as a "lamb." "He saw himself as the *new passover lamb*," Pitre begins.

> Perhaps this is the one reason Jesus expected not only to be executed, but to be crucified, just as the lambs were crucified in the Jerusalem temple. The reason Jesus' identification with the lamb matter is that . . . the sacrifice of the Passover lamb was not completed by its death. It was completed by a meal, by *eating the flesh of the lamb* that had been slain.[5]

At least he begins his argument with "perhaps." Once he writes that the slaughtered sacrificial lamb was "crucified," the rest is highly questionable; unique, to be sure, but hyperbole nonetheless. One other theological interpretation is intriguing for it being, if unknown to itself, suggestive. "In the Eucharist the incarnate meaning of Christ is revealed in the symbol of the sacrificial meal. The meal offers human beings a participation in the sacrificial attitude of Christ, of which the cross is the proper symbol. The meaning of the cross and the meaning of the Eucharist are the same."[6] Leaving aside the question of Jesus's sacrificial self-understanding, there is indeed a profound connection between the Eucharist and the cross—one, however, not imagined by Mudd. The enduring presence of animals in the life of Jesus has been neglected. The meaning of the animals in his life remains to be made essential, and for reasons that go from the birth of Jesus to his execution, from the manger to the crucifix.

Albert Schweitzer writes, "The problem of the Last Supper is the problem of the life of Jesus."[7] Stated otherwise, and in the context of the Christians who were executed in the Roman amphitheater, a relevant

5. Pitre, *Jesus and the Jewish Roots of the Eucharist*, 74.

6. Mudd, *Eucharist as Meaning*, 201.

7. Schweitzer, *Problem of the Lord's Supper*, 137.

comment, for the following, could be: the problem of the Last Supper is the problem for the Roman magistrates and for the death of Christians. At the moment, however, Jesus has announcements to make that, for his Jewish disciples, would have been stunning. The significance of eating the body of Jesus and, most especially, drinking his blood, was completely outside the comprehension of the disciples around the table and for the covenant made between Noah and God. As for the announcement of a "betrayal," one that seems (for readers) obvious and related to Judas, Jesus may be referring to much more than himself. The event, and the words preserved of the moments of the Last Supper, continues to exert pressure on the reader; intimations are experienced but only vaguely sensed as to their meaning. The metaphysical internalization of Christ is antithetical to (and a substitution for) the sacrificial ritual slaughter of an animal at the Jerusalem temple and the act of commensality. Is there a similar relation between *betrayal and eating*? Is there a connection between internalizing Christ and handing Jesus over to the authorities? Does this sacrament of *eucharistia*, of "thanksgiving," nullify both sacrifice and the betrayal?

"Truly I tell you (*amen lego*), one of you will betray me, one who is eating with me" (Mark 14:18). Although the individual involved is too well known in tradition, Jesus's words are to be understood as a betrayal during the act of eating. The judicial sense cannot be avoided. There is treachery here. Jesus will be handed over—to the authorities, to the law—to be executed by crucifixion and suffer, at the same time, a more ignoble fate than death.

The fate of the crucified *after their death* has not been sufficiently considered.

During the meal, betrayal and eating are inseparable and *apocalyptic*. All the events from a mythic past have, for Jesus, the immediate sense of a fully present *logos* for him, most especially when he begins to imagine, as they share a now sacred meal, the fate of his body.

He fears he will be eaten and "buried" in the body of an animal.

The moment is not coincidental. Jesus is betrayed and handed-over to the law during a shared meal. Judas's act has *historical* consequences. The creation of the Eucharist, immediately after announcing his betrayal, has implications none of the disciples could possibly fathom and would only be realized during a gruesome end and finality consistent with the administration of the death penalty in the future. Jesus was not at the time thinking only about his own death, though the apprehension must have been as extreme as the experience in the garden of Gethsemane shows. He had the prophetic insight to imagine the suffering of those who would dedicate their lives to emulating him. Paul comments on the moment. "The Lord Jesus on the night when he was betrayed took a loaf of bread, and when he had given thanks, broke it and said, 'This is my body that is for you. Do this in remembrance of me'" (1 Cor 11:23–24). The interpretation of the meaning of the Eucharist—in the case of Paul, as prayer, thanksgiving, and commemoration—gives us a sense of the importance of the sacrament in the early community. Others have defined it in relation to sacrifice. "The Eucharist is the Sacrament of the sacrifice of Christ."[8]

Despite the theological interpretation of Jesus's acts, Girard's "nonsacrificial reading of the Gospel Text" is compelling. "The Gospels only speak of sacrifices in order to reject them and deny them any validity. . . . There is nothing in the Gospels to suggest that the death of Jesus is a sacrifice."[9] To now extend the argument and recall Girard's difficulty in the introduction, a preliminary definition, based on all the previous readings and examples, can be made. Girard writes,

> It is necessary to have legal forms in a universe where there are legal institutions, to give unanimity to the decision to put a man to death. Nonetheless, the decision to put Jesus to death is first and foremost a decision of the crowd, one that identifies the crucifixion not so much with a ritual sacrifice but (as in the case of the servant) with the process that I claim to be at the basis of all ritual and all religious phenomena. (167)

While "the crowd" can be conveniently blamed for the death of Jesus (and the entire scene of the assembled crowd being given a choice between two condemned men is historically dubious), the one certainty is far different and well known to us. Jesus was sentenced to death on the orders of Pontius Pilate. Girard simultaneously recognizes the connection, but because of his total theory ("*all* ritual and *all* religious phenomena") cannot make the affirmation that is all too clear to him. Jesus is sentenced to death because of his condemnation of sacrifice as a religiopolitical ritual sanctioned both by the Jerusalem Sanhedrin and the Roman imperial authorities. This is the reason for the sentence of crucifixion and for the site of the sentence to be carried out on Golgotha—"the place of the skulls."

8. Mazza, *Celebration of the Eucharist*, 7.

9. Girard, *Things Hidden*, 180. See the entire section of book 3, chapter 2, 180–223.

The *remnants* of the condemned were the indication of a final and abject humiliation.

One resists his death *as* a sacrifice because of the burden of its theology; and even more as an act done so as to forgive the sins of *all*. The blood being poured out "for many for the forgiveness of sins" (Matt 26:28) is inseparable from the equally necessary ingestion (internalization) of his body represented by the bread of life. For the present purposes, the theological interpretation of the Eucharist by Christian tradition and the church are set aside. Instead, an equally important *reaction* has to be taken into account. How did the Romans respond to this fledgling sect of seeming fanatics and outlaws who had neither regard for the sacred laws of the state nor the divine status of the emperor?

Historically, we now enter Rome during the reign of Nero. The historian Seutonius gives a summary of the reign of Nero, and writes, "Punishments were also inflicted on the Christians, a sect professing a new and mischievous religious belief."[10] One specific detail in the description of the martyrdom of Christians by Tacitus in *The Annals* will be much more elaborate and give us a complete sense of the Roman response to Christians. Its relation, for us, to God's first killing as a sacrificial act in Genesis could not be more poignant. In the meantime, Christians have become a well-known and highly suspicious sect. Roman reactions are consistent and are reflective of their understanding of piety, so different from Christians who seemed completely independent of any traditional observances.

> Originally the word piety was used to designate the honor and respect one showed to members of one's family, children to parents, children to parents and grandparents, and everyone to one's ancestors. But the term came to be used in a wider sense, designating loyalty and obedience to custom and traditions of Rome, to inherited laws, and those who lived in previous generations. . . . As time went on, the term acquired a more specifically religious sense, meaning reverence and devotion to the gods and to *the ritual of cultic acts* by which the gods were honored.[11]

Noticeably, the assessment by historians and others concerned with the period and the Roman/Christian relations have been *too general.*

10. Seutonius, *Twelve Caesars*, 221.

11. Wilken, *Christians as the Romans Saw Them*, 56, my emphasis.

The perspective has been broad, ill-defined, and often focused on social and political implications. Jesus had no interest in simply changing the political *status quo*. However, one particular interpretation has been overlooked: it is specific and related to one belief, a *pistis* that cannot be reduced to *faith*, with all the vulnerabilities the term conveys for the modern mind today. Once the sacrament of the Eucharist was specifically emphasized by the Romans as an outrageous act, and compared, in the imagination of the superstitious and malicious, as a form of *cannibalism*, we have suddenly entered into the realm of fantasy—one that demanded a lawful response. Christianity became a despised religion because it had repudiated animal sacrifice as a form of politico-religious belief and substituted it with a new covenant with a much more all-encompassing *metaphysical* sense. Politics, in time, would be an effect. Jesus now reveals what has been hidden since the beginning of the world, as Paul's letters had announced and then repeated in Matthew 13:35.

The Eucharist will replace animal sacrifice. The ingestion of *corpus Christi* will be a substitute for sacrificial commensality.

The presence of animals has never been sufficiently emphasized in the life and teaching of Jesus. Since Genesis, animals have been taken for granted, used instrumentally, disavowed for their inherent meaning and instead made to submit to the founding relationship of "dominion." Once the Last Supper and the creation of the Eucharist is recognized as an unprecedented event—as a revelation seemingly, still, to be *perceived*, as all disclosures must—then it can be anticipated with two historical events, one imminent, the other to be fulfilled in the context of Roman law.

The discussion of the Last Supper as a commentary, for Jesus, on both the observance of the Jewish Passover and (for his present) the relationship between betrayal in the context of a shared meal, now takes us to the moment of his death on the cross. The event of the crucifixion[12] itself or its meaning in Christian theology is, for us, not significant at the moment. Instead, the animals hovering in proximity to the cross become all-important. Has anyone noticed the birds circling above the cross and the packs of dogs wandering around below it in the expectation of what is to come? Domestic animals were present at his birth; birds and dogs will be near him as Jesus dies on the cross. For a crucified man, the body was not going to receive the same attention as prescribed by Jewish law and by the responsibility of the family. The site of the crucifixion,

12. Any study on the history of this particular form of the death penalty can begin with Hengel's *Crucifixion*.

Golgotha, was called "the place of the skulls" for a reason—and one that, now, takes us back to the foundation of civilization in the transition from the inside and the outside of the garden of Eden. God killed and sacrificed the first animal(s) in order to make clothes for Adam and Eve. They in turn invented religion and the first ritual founded on the reciprocity of sacrifice. Human disobedience and punishment led to the slaughter of an animal and the creation of a religious piety founded on violence, death, and meat-eating. Normally, the body of someone crucified would simply be left as *food* for birds and stray dogs. The deceased would not be buried. Or, rather, the body would be buried, in morsels, *within* the bodies of other animals as they fed on the carcass—an ignominious fate not ignored by the Romans who were witnesses to the death penalty and its aftermath. The gospels are filled with allusions to the death-watch. The sooner the condemned died, the sooner the Roman soldiers could be relieved of their duty. At the same time, the animals in close proximity to the crucifixions are led on by their own anticipations, one assured by the scent, waiting in anticipation for sustenance most especially for the roaming packs of dogs that, in antiquity, were more often than not both ignored and abused. In no time, nothing of his body would be left but bones, unpalatable viscera; whatever remained might have been disposed of on a large heap of garbage south of the city called *Gehenna*, the word in the gospels translated as "hell"—in part because, once more, the site was filled with maggots that fed on any organic matter they could find, including the remains of executed criminals and the parts of animals that could not be consumed after sacrificial feasts.

The detritus of animal sacrifice and human executions ended up in the same place.

On the heap of *Gehenna*, "hell," human beings, animals, and garbage were thrown together haphazardly and exposed to the most primitive aspect of nature, maggots feeding on the remnants of life. In the case of Jesus, the intervention by a follower who had the social influence to request the dead body for burial, also made it possible to create the testimony of the resurrection. Giving the body a burial by the intervention of Joseph of Arimathea makes it possible for the resurrection, in fact, or in testimony, to take place. Being fed to birds and dogs would have made the resurrection more graphic, if even conceivable, than can possibly be imagined. All metaphysical aspirations would have been negated by the sight of the body consumed by animals and, if anything at all had remained, dumped unto the garbage heap of Gehenna. Brute matter, the inevitability of organic decomposition, vermin feeding on rotten meat: hell is visceral, foul-smelling, abject. Some of the remains of Jesus's body might have ended up in the "hell" of Gehenna if not for the intervention of a man, Joseph, who was given permission to arrange a proper burial.

The body of Christ of the Eucharist and post-crucifixion had to remain intact in order for Christians to understand how their future would only be possible with the preservation of the sacraments. And this is now where the most formidable confrontation with the Roman Empire, and its judicial system, properly begins. Once some Romans understood the power of the Eucharist as a substitute for animal sacrifice and as the repudiation of all violence and, of course, the death penalty, such an idea could not remain unopposed; it represented the greatest single threat to the metaphysical foundations of the whole empire—one where land and geography was, in the end, irrelevant because what was ultimately at stake was a completely new conception of reality. Once we recognize that "capital power was the most jealously guarded of all the attributes of government,"[13] Jesus's teaching was an effrontery to the metaphysical foundations of social life—for the Romans as well as for his fellow Jews. Once he was sentenced to death and crucified, one other significant detail can now be affirmed and related to the events that are historically evident for us to examine.

What happened in Rome in 64 CE? While the history of the events as they have been described by Roman historians gives us nothing more than an impression—except for a precise sentence written by Tacitus that will be compared to Genesis 3—turning to the letter written by Paul to one or more of the churches in Rome is much more detailed. The situation is urgent, the problems are many, and despite all the support he gives them, in terms of faith, hope, and love, one reality seems to be overwhelming and soon to lead to extraordinary judicial events. There are many reasons for Paul writing the letter; some of them have been the source of sustained debate. Other points are much more evident. "His main aim in writing to the Romans was to achieve reconciliation within the community."[14] Others identify a problem and schism within the community, one noticed in other churches, most especially in Asia Minor. "Paul has an urgent need to write to Rome because he had learned that Judaizers are at work among the Roman Christians."[15] If true, if there

13. Sherwin-White, *Roman Society*, 36.

14. Green, *Christianity in Ancient Rome*, 36.

15. Stuhlmacher, *Paul's Letter to the Romans*, 5.

was an ongoing debate about the future of the identity of the church, Christianity as a whole would soon face much more grave problems. "The body of the letter serves to address the circumstances in Rome."[16] These "circumstances" appear to be much more political than theological. The Christian communities are obviously facing severe external pressure. Jesus's warnings have become all too real.

Since the sayings of Jesus to his disciples have been interpreted here from the perspective of a warning about their vulnerable future instead of any "end of days" scenario, one incomparable source informs us about the precarious situation of early Christians and more specifically in the city of Rome. Jesus's expectations have become reality; the followers of a man crucified for sedition under Roman law has come to the attention of the general population and, more dangerous to them, Roman law; neighborhood gossip about child sacrifice, cannibalism, and bacchanals have led the authorities to begin investigating this unusual group of religious outsiders. The Letter to the Romans gives us innumerable insights into the mind of Paul the apostle, the importance of Christian concepts he mentions throughout the correspondence, and the relationship he attempts to more firmly establish despite not yet meeting them in person; the letter hopes to minimize the distance before his long-awaited visit. Following Jesus's concern for his disciples and followers during the last part of his life, Paul's letter repeatedly discusses the law. One aspect of the law is unmistakable: as someone who has dedicated his life as an apostle to everyone—the Jews, Greeks, other Gentiles, and the "barbarians" he also mentions in the letter—the Mosaic law, most especially its rituals and observances, continues to be essential to pious Jewish converts, but neither necessary nor mandatory for others. There is, however, another law of utmost concern for Paul. It is not a law related to Judaism or Christianity; it has nothing to do with observing the imperative of the Sabbath, for example. The theological content of the letter, for all its foundational importance for belief and doctrine, cannot (for our purposes) overlook an equally important feature.

The letter is filled with allusions and direct references to Roman law, the justice system, and its consequences for Christians everywhere within the empire, and more specifically, for his first readers, in the city of Rome. Once we begin to see the social situation of Christians in the city and, then, anticipate the first persecution under the emperor Nero, when Paul himself was executed (along with Peter—the man to be so foundational

16. Fowler, *Structure of Romans*, 15.

for that Christian city), we can better understand the letter's urgency and the sense of its encouragement by first telling the Christian community in Rome that "your faith is proclaimed throughout the world" (Rom 1:8). The "proclamation" is as significant as their faith. They have a reputation *throughout the world*; they are acknowledged for being able to withstand the considerable pressure of living in the capital city of the empire and, despite the temptation of apostasy and reintegrating themselves back into ancient beliefs, they are prepared to withstand the ostracism. Paul is well aware that many different groups of philosophers, throughout the city's history, had been expelled for various reasons. More recently, during the reign of Claudius (41–53) and immediately prior to Nero, Jews too had been expelled from Rome. The circumstances were vague, the reasons unknown. Some speculate that the confrontation between Jews and Christians had led to some disturbances. Sectarian skirmishes were not unheard-of. In the coming years, they would only get much worse. In cities like Alexandria, for example, and despite the reputation for being open to syncretism, riots resulted in numerous deaths. Religion had suddenly become sectarian and unmanageable, a development that had to be of concern to the Roman authorities who were managing an increasingly complicated empire, both within its massive jurisdiction and at its vulnerable frontiers.

We begin to get an indication of Paul's knowledge of the judicial experience of the Roman community when he turns to their faith and "this grace in which we stand" (Rom 5:2). This is the "reckoning" mentioned in the letter; they "stand," firm and accounted for, enduring whatever is given for them to experience. If the Jewish law has earlier been mentioned as an important reminder of the community's choices and responsibilities, the *Roman law* is a strangely unifying force. Jew or Gentile, Roman law regards Christians as an entirely new group of people; there appears to be no context for understanding them despite the long-held view by the Roman of more or less religious toleration. The Roman ability to allow religious freedom, of course, within reason, was seriously strained and was on the verge of experiencing its own limit—a circumstance that, strangely, infuriated the authorities to no end. Toleration came face to face with dogma.

For reasons that may not be entirely clear, at least as stated by Romans (this despite some prejudice, the commonplace suspicion of outsiders) Paul now addresses the community of the city and supports the difficulty of their situation by inverting what has been usually accepted as normal—no different than his adoption of the virtues of a slave, for when we he tells them to "boast in our suffering, knowing that suffering produces endurance, and endurance produces character, and character produces hope" (Rom 5:4), the three-times repeated "produces" is related to proof and a test of character under duress. Their "suffering," though not attributed to anyone directly, as if minimizing its real impact, has specific causes. The development of Paul's judicial language is offset, absolutely, by the idea of *grace*. Paul's theology confronts Roman law and judges it to be active in the world and irrelevant for the one who is committed to an idea. The letter is written as a consequence of reports he has received, from the Roman community or others, that they are enduring judicial persecutions. They are being arrested, interrogated, urged to offer sacrifices in the name of the emperor and, upon refusal, suffering the consequences; this is the reason Paul appeals to the significance of the death of Jesus for all his followers. "Do you not know that all of us who have been baptized into Christ Jesus were baptized into his death?" (Rom 6:3). The knowledge of the martyr as a witness cannot be excluded from his words; if arrests have been made, perhaps due to *delatores* or those who judicially denounced others as a precondition of prosecution, Paul is writing to them in part to appease them. His words are *parakletic* insofar as the letter attempts to comfort them during a time of hardship, uncertainty, and persecution. Paul expresses his anguish for not being there with them and directly supporting their causes by sharing in their everyday experience. Although Paul does not yet use the language of the martyr ultimately to become essential in the development of Christian identity, he must somehow interpret the deaths suffered by the community of believers as, if not a desired experience, at least essential to the faith. He seems to be preparing a doctrine of grace inseparable from the martyr—an idea demanding utmost fortitude; a theology of grace had to be a powerful incentive when it was directly connected to the crucifixion. The theology in the Letter to the Romans is therefore developed, and strengthened, in relation to the judicial punishments (and, perhaps, the early executions) of Christians.

In the context of Christians being killed by the laws of Rome, the doctrine of the resurrection overcomes the singular experience of death; for just as Jesus was "raised from the dead," they too will be "alive" in a completely new way "since you are not under law but under grace" (Rom 6:14). The Greek *charis* and Roman *gratia* are ideas that supersede any law—and certainly any law that pronounces the Christian guilty of *being*.

Christian existence will be made illegal.

The existence of the Christian has become a crime; and the most effective way of pronouncing judgment after establishing guilt is to affirm the *law of nature* and the irreducibility of death. Paul's grace not only confronts Roman law; it affirms the possibility of utterly overcoming the finite conditions of the world and to reveal what he calls the "newness of life" (Rom 6:4), concepts that are readily understood both by the most simple reader and someone who had been philosophically instructed. The confrontation between the Christian and the Roman judiciary is ultimately a metaphysical encounter, each side—God and the state—determined to define, unequivocally, the meaning of life. Once the Roman judicial system fully understood what their confrontation meant, they had to devise (theoretically, and fully consciously) a death penalty that would absolutely *invert* Christian theology of grace and the spirit and nullify it with an example so extreme it would reduce the Christian to a body in the state of nature—the one the Romans dominated—and exposed to a bestiality they both abhorred and controlled with repeated examples of *dominion*. The Roman domination of the animal world was the foundation for the order and control of all other life. Roman power had become absolute; all biology and matter was at their disposal and used at their discretion. Without here entering into a discussion on Roman ingenuity as to their *technical* ability, all transformations of the natural world by feats of engineering, for example, was one more testament to their domination of the totality of the world; and that is the reason a new religion—a new form of piety and its resulting self-understanding—could not be allowed to exist that put into doubt the entire edifice of Rome's consciousness of its own power. Paul was clear about the status of the Christian: "But now we are discharged from the law, dead to that which held us captive, so that we are slaves under the old written code but in the new life of the Spirit" (Rom 7:6). The law Paul writes about now cannot be the Jewish law. The Roman law as it accuses, judges, and condemns Christians is the one most preoccupying him. They may in fact be killed; but the "old written code" so well known as one of the pillars of Roman society, most especially in that absolute punishment of the death penalty, cannot be compared to "the new life of the Spirit." Paul has begun to create formidable theological principles; once human law and the spirit are contrasted, they can no longer be limited to their historical context and immediacy. This is what Karl Barth called "the doctrine of Inspiration," a hermeneutic of the spirit that attempted to "see through and beyond history."[17] While this would appear self-evident for Christians, it was the Roman response (politically, judicially) that would only serve to more firmly sustain the meaning of such a belief.

When Paul tells the listeners of the letter that there is "no condemnation" for those who "are in Christ Jesus" (Rom 8:1), now using the language of in-dwelling and an ontological reciprocity to offset the reality of the law, he makes them aware of their new status of being human beings *above* the law. The implications of his words and argument are not without their ambivalence; by making the Christian above the law, he must disavow positive law and begin to consider another law altogether, one obviously familiar to him if not worked out systematically much less philosophically. In any case, that is not his concern; he has more preoccupations with the health of the Roman community than whether his arguments could be defended in front of the philosophers he met in Athens the first time he visited the city (Acts 17).

"I consider that the sufferings of this present time are not worth comparing with the glory about to be revealed to us" (Rom 8:18). Whether the *pathe* is physical or emotional, Paul believes it cannot be compared to the *revelations* they will experience. Who does he mean by "us"? Is it the people who will be executed and who will experience postmortem glory? Or is he addressing those who remain to continue their life as Christians? His response is not unambiguous: "For the creation waits with eager longing for the revealing of the children of God" (Rom 8:19). Once again using the language of revelations, Paul seems to intimate that there will be two kinds of births—those who will *die* in Roman custody as witnesses and those who will be *born* into a new self-conception. Both are necessary. He has essentially created a conception of the Christian able to defy the experiences of life or death. His words are intended to be a source of support and strength. The letter does seem as if it is responding to recent events of hardships; the judicial language is unmistakable. Paul anticipates how the suffering of the individual soon to be called martyrs (as they had been in Jerusalem with the opposition of the Maccabees to the rule of Antiochus IV Epiphanes) will lead to revelations. What does he mean? Whether Paul was fully conscious of the implications of the persecutions, arrests, and executions of Christians is not certain. The Letter to the Romans does, however, give us a sense of a certain anticipation of the times and how Christians were heading toward an unavoidable confrontation with the Roman Empire and with

17. Barth, *Epistle to the Romans*, 1.

a choice: the law of Caesar or the law of Christ. No reconciliation was possible. The letter is filled with constant reminders to his readers of an unavoidable experience of "hardships, or distress, or persecution" (Rom 8:35). The letter has been written with deliberation and with urgency. Paul has been informed of the difficulties of the Roman churches; far from his consistent arguments against the efficacy of Jewish law, he is much more preoccupied with the Christians and their precarious social and legal position in Rome. Although there are no specific incidents or the names of individuals who are being persecuted (as, for example, in the Apologies of Justin Martyr written in Rome circa 150) Paul nevertheless makes his readers aware of his full knowledge of the situation. This accounts for his desire to be with them. He is not avoiding them; he has to reassure them that his inability to come to Rome is not due to prudence or fear; on the contrary, he has been fully prepared, as he has throughout his missionary journeys, to face whatever danger was necessary for his apostleship to be fulfilled. It was important for Paul's credibility as a renowned minister to be more than willing to come to Rome despite the obvious danger of arrest and execution. Ironically, if he had forsaken some of the pressing responsibilities detaining him away from Rome, his life might have had a different outcome.

Paul's reflection on the law of the world, of "principalities," cannot compare with his understanding of what Jesus has accomplished, "for Christ is the end (*telos*) of the law" (Rom 10:4), its end and consummation. By telling the Romans this, Paul has in fact explained precisely why they are facing such dire persecutions from the Romans. The authorities have finally realized that the threat posed by Christianity is absolute; it threatens the entire foundation of Roman life insofar as all its supports (polytheistic worship and animal sacrifice) are not only repudiated. The Christian sacraments, surely understood by some Romans who were not simply ideologues, directly confronted the rituals of Rome. Although we have no Roman testimony, by a historian, for example, who made the attempt to understand the profound significance of the Eucharist—and how it represented a radical alternative to the *do ut des* of sacrifice, the "I give so you may give"—it must have dawned on a few minds that Christian doctrine was an altogether different way of thinking about the divine, one that had to have extensive consequences for society. "Neither slave nor free," to name but one idea, was inconceivable for the majority Romans. A cosmopolitan citizen was socially acceptable; any attempt to abolish distinctions of rank was unheard-of and preposterous.

In the context of a vulnerable Roman community experiencing hardships, Paul's advice is filled with encouragement and consolation—and perhaps, too, founded on a Jewish attitude toward the Roman authorities that was part of his training as a Pharisee. They are to submit, as he urges, to the prevailing powers, either to minimize their vulnerability to the absolute discretion of the law or as an attitude that, ultimately, recognized the powers of the world to be nothing more than instances of God's overall intention, however mysterious it seemed. "Do you have to have no fear of authority? Then do what is good, and you will received its approval" (Rom 13:3). Unfortunately, from the historical events that are soon to unfold, his advice did not reflect the reality of the Roman churches; he would experience the absolute law of Rome firsthand. Even if Christians acted with circumspection, as can be imagined, they were still perceived as suspicious outsiders by everyday Romans and a disruptive sect to those who were entrusted with securing the stability of the state. Despite being fully conscious of the vagaries of the law of the world, he nevertheless insists on advising fellow Christians in Rome to be obedient. Any other alternative was out of the question; the communities of Christians were hardly in a position to become a self-conscious opposition and act in defiance of Roman law and order. "For the authority does not bear the sword in vain" (Rom 13:4), he tells his readers, now as direct as possible and emphasizing coercive power to exercise its will, at will. He knew firsthand precisely what any *lawful* authorities were capable of. After all, the memories of his own persecutions of Christians could not be distant from his mind as he wrote the letter.

Paul's letter to the Roman communities of churches has made us aware of the difficult experience of those living in the city and their vulnerability. Before turning to the first known event of a systematic persecution and martyrdom during the reign of Nero and more than likely coinciding with Paul's execution, we must first turn to a brief assessment of Roman law and society. "Violence was omnipresent in Roman society and history. From animal sacrifice and slaughter to the disciplining of slaves and children to the brutalities of ancient warfare, the Romans had long accustomed to regarding creatures of lowly status, others and outsiders without reason or rights, as legitimate objects of violence."[18] Kyle's study provides an extensive representation of violence in Roman society as a whole and in the amphitheater; in the case of Christians, however, and despite recognizing how the Romans especially abhorred them as

18. Kyle, *Spectacles of Death in Ancient Rome*, 5.

antisocial, does not explain how the Romans in charge of judicial executions condemned the Christians and with a specific form of punishment.

This is now my principal argument after assessing Paul's Letter to the Romans. The specific circumstances of the first martyrdoms are less important than the attempt to understand Christian self-possession from the mind of a Roman magistrate. All previous consideration of the martyr have been, originally, written by its defenders, i.e., Augustine and, more personally, from the martyrologies,[19] or from more or less impartial historians. In the *Confessions*, Augustine may make a brief reference to "the ordeals of martyrdom,"[20] but once we enter into the mind of the Roman magistrate who condemned Christians to death, it is their *logic* that becomes most revealing and gives us a glimpse into their metaphysical conception—one that will be a confrontation between sacrifice and the Eucharist.

The writings of Cicero on law, the state, or philosophy give us indication of attitudes to capital crimes and the death penalty routinely used. The difference between the guilt of an *honestiores* as opposed to an *humiliores* again tells us about the class of people who drafted the law and who it would benefit most. There were, as could be expected, different penalties even if the judgments and guilt were precisely the same. Individuals of wealth and influence could be given, for example, the choice of exile as opposed to anyone else who suffered the ultimate penalty. As to the supposed influence of *humanitas*, historians are unconvincing.

> The death sentence is a lurid beacon right across our period—and beyond. But although capital punishment was never abolished, it presents differently in different epochs. In the Late Republic there was, both in public opinion and in the minds of legislators, a desire to reduce the incidence of death sentences. The desire was inspired by *humanitas*, the civilizing instinct that is one of the hallmarks of the Roman ethos, both in the Later Republic and, at times, in the Principate.[21]

19. See, e.g., Farina's *Perpetua of Carthage*.

20. Augustine, *Confessions*, 35.

21. Bauman, *Crime and Punishment in Ancient Rome*, 6. I am much less confident in what Bauman calls the "civilizing instinct" of *humanitas* as an ethos of the Romans. The disjunction between the writers who give us an impression of Roman *humanitas* and the history of the empire is an issue worth emphasizing—as Bauman readily admits, for example, in the case of Seneca, the Stoic philosopher and the teacher of the emperor Nero.

As Bauman hints, with an *apologia* for Seneca as well as pointing to Stoic conflict in doctrines, Nero furnishes one example of the irrelevance of *humanitas* either in the day-to-day running of the empire or in the judicial consequences for those singled out for persecution.

Prior to their executions, Christians were reduced to the abject state of the slave, and with one more judicial consequence. "Those condemned to death," Lewis tells us, "became slaves from the moment of condemnation, their property forfeited to the state."[22] The forfeit of property was one more important consequence for the Roman state's attempt to interfere with this new fledgling sect. Since their *ekklesia* was a private dwelling, in many cases one large enough to hold a gathering of the faithful, the confiscation of the property effectively shut the doors to their place of worship. Although there has been no research on the matter, it must be at least considered that the Roman judicial system targeted a certain class of Christians who, by virtue of their social status and wealth, could host a gathering in their homes. Their arrest and execution had many consequences: the confiscation of property was devastating to the whole family and to any heirs who now would be destitute. The state therefore dissuaded would-be Christians by enforcing a law that had *generational* consequences. The warning was precise: return to the gods of the Roman pantheon, the ones that had always ensured tradition and continuity, or face the full extent of the law—in the form of a gruesome public execution and, in effect, the destruction of the entire family's identity and fortunes. Faces with such an outcome, the power of Christian faith can hardly be underestimated. Converts were willing to lose *everything*.

What makes the Christians unique as victims of the Roman judicial system, "none of the protagonists were seeking an acquittal."[23] Those arrested were immediately forced to make one decision: the renunciation of their faith and providing the only proof acceptable by law, that is, the observance and participation in the ritual of sacrifice in honor of the emperor. The Christians who were *damnati ad bestias* were considered unlike any other "criminal." Robinson's argument, and noticeable throughout, that the Christians were treated no differently than others accused of a capital crime is indefensible. "Treatment of prisoners was brutal in the Roman world, but there is no reason to think it was more so for Christians than for others. . . . In general, indeed, the Roman authorities acted

22. Lewis, "Slavery, Family, and Status," 154.

23. Robinson, *Penal Practice*, 191.

with correctness, sometimes even with restraint, although mob pressure might be an important factor."[24] While the writers of martyr biographies have often been accused of sensationalizing the plight of accused Christians, with assessments ranging along a wide spectrum, the same can be said by historians who align themselves to a seemingly impartial and "objective" argument.[25] If an account of the martyrdoms is to be provided, the extremes of either the Christian depiction or the modern historian's objectivity are best set aside to imagine the consciousness of the Roman magistrate most especially during his interrogations.

"The sheer persistence of Christians in their beliefs would have been seen by many Romans as *contumacia* (arrogance, meaning, in this context, wilful refusal to obey a judicial order), naturally meaning chastisement by the magistrate's *coercitio* (power to administer summary punishment)."[26] There was only one judicial order for the Christians to obey if they wanted to avoid punishment. All Christians were required to do, as a sign of their renunciation of their belief, was to offer a sacrifice in the name of the emperor and to share in a communal meal of the sacrificial meat. Christians had to participate in the ritual of animal sacrifice and share a communal meal with others to reconfirm their allegiance both to the Roman gods and the divinity of the emperor who was the guarantee of the *pax Romana*. The refusal to *sacrifice and eat* led directly to the death penalty; the refusal to kill and eat was perceived as a crime. To refuse both sacrifice and commensality was a sign of extreme stubbornness and, for the presiding magistrates, an astonishing sign of defiance.

The overwhelming evidence for the argument to execute Christians was almost always attributed to their unwillingness to sacrifice. Along with their *contumacia*, additional legal definitions and charges could also have been brought against them. In his *Roman Law and the Legal World of the Romans*, Andrew Riggsby does not deal in any way with the law as it effected Christians. In one place he writes, "Committing a crime always involved an overt act. You cannot be convicted for omission or bad intentions."[27] Not true. The Christians were convicted of a crime precisely of omission. They refused to sacrifice. As Riggsby himself notes but does

24. Robinson, *Penal Practice*, 129. After the quite elaborate descriptions of punishments, torture, and executions, Robinson is unconvincing.

25. As, e.g., Moss, *Myth of Persecution*.

26. Bryan, *Render to Caesar*, 116.

27. Riggsby, *Roman Law*, 196.

not develop, if one of the crimes punishable by death was *maiestas*, it became a capital crime under the empire when the charge had changed from a general "diminishing the majesty of the Roman people" to the much more grave accusation of showing disrespect for the emperor. Such disrespect amounted to treason. The overt reasons demanded by the law had been established. Historians then provide an assessment of the actual situation of punishment and the situation in the amphitheater. Details are important for the information about the make-up of Roman society and its general attitude to criminals and, as is well known, the "entertainment" of the amphitheater.

"Despite all extenuations we may urge, the Roman people remain guilty of deriving public joy from their capital executions by turning the Colosseum into a torture-chamber and a human slaughter house."[28] Although a moral assessment of the Roman justice system is not without its pertinence, particular attention to the executions of Christians within the amphitheaters of the empire gives us a glimpse of the consciousness of the judiciary. Far from being an arbitrary decision and merely a method of execution consistent with traditional Roman practices, putting Christians into the arena to be attacked by wild animals was not some form of entertainment for the always-demanding Roman audience.

The punishment of Christians was reflective of their *theology*.

All consideration of the social meaning of the Roman amphitheater, while historically pertinent, in itself, is irrelevant when the death penalty inflicted on Christians is the issue. No one has yet considered how the death of martyrs as a spectacle for Romans was a *metaphysical* event. Sociological insights are historically relevant but they cannot recognize the confrontation between the meaning of the Eucharist and being eaten by wild animals.

While historical research into the history of the Roman amphitheater is instructive, consulting works on the nature of the amphitheater is ultimately not a concern. At issue is not the origin of the practice, the matter of the audience and their relation to the spectacle, the role of the emperor, or any other number of reasons. One problem concerns us: the relation between Roman law (and the magistrates who represent it) and the Christians who are condemned to death. In terms of gladiatorial shows and public executions, they are described as "political theatre" and

28. Carcopino, *Daily Life in Ancient Rome*, 254.

as the "wilful slaughter of men and animals as popular entertainment."[29] Of all the studies consulted, none of them concern themselves with the specific form of capital punishment as devised by Roman magistrates. Various studies concentrate on different aspect of the role and function of the amphitheater.[30] Nor is the seating arrangement and status of the spectators of any concern.[31] Of course the members of the imperial family, senators, and various members of the Roman bureaucracy were given privileged places for all to see. From our modern sensibility, the judgment of cruelty and barbarism is understandable; and yet the morality of the punishments are far less important, for the conclusion of this study, than what its meaning still can reveal to us. After all, while the *thanatography* of the Roman amphitheater is unquestionable, as is a moral response, there are other, even more compelling meanings requiring an analysis of the experience of the martyrs and the Roman magistrates who condemned them.

The references above are an indication of the relationship of scholars to the history examined. Unfortunately, it seems as though the individuals in question related to the events of the past as facts without pursuing the more necessary interpretation. The fact of the martyrdoms is unquestioned. If the Roman judiciary had begun to focus on the Christians as a seditious sect that had to be punished with the most gruesome executions possible, then the death sentence of *ad bestias* is inseparable from the interpretation of the law that was appropriate to the group of individuals who refused to sacrifice and eat meat collectively as a form of politico-religious worship to the gods and the emperor. Since they refused to sacrifice animals and to declare themselves as part of the Roman community by eating with others, then they would be sentenced to a death penalty for who they *were*. By now the sacrament of the Eucharist was so well known that Christians were the subject of both mockery and accusations—including being cannibals and eating their own children. While such "wives' tales" were probably common, Roman magistrates who had been educated were far less likely to indulge in superstitious fancies and instead concentrate on the problem at hand—Christians who were so single-minded about their belief that they refused to apostatize even if it meant certain death and under the most cruel conditions. The

29 Hopkins, *Death and Renewal*, xiv. As for the "lesson," Hopkins believes the spectacle contributed to the consolidation of sovereign power.

30. Welch, *Roman Amphitheatre*.

31. Momgardner, *Story of the Roman Amphitheatre*.

Roman magistrates who condemned Christians *ad bestias* were assigning them to a death penalty consistent with their *faith*. The Eucharist had replaced animal sacrifice. The internalization of the body and blood of Jesus was intended to be the new covenant that would do nothing less than initiate, in part, a new "kingdom," a new way of being in the world. The Roman magistrates who were in charge of administering punishment to Christians understood the logic of the death penalty in the arena. Christians would be exposed to wild and ravenous animals in the arena and *eaten*.

Ultimately, the specific judicial accusation, charge, and conviction of a specific crime (or how the verdict was reached) are less pertinent than the form of punishment—though Cicero does give us a sense of the *personal* nature of the confrontation between anyone charged with a crime and a magistrate. They expected deference and obedience. Obeying Roman laws meant "not only that the citizens be obedient and dutiful towards the magistrates, but also that they love and honour them."[32] Given the self-conception of Roman law and society as directly guided by the gods of the pantheon, magistrates were intermediaries; they were responsible for ensuring the peace between humans and the gods. One indication of how the Romans with governmental and judicial authority dealt with Christians can only be understood when two forms of belief confronted each other, each with particular claims about the divine and themselves. Again, in *Laws*, Cicero writes,

> Law is not a product of human thought, nor is it any enactment of peoples, but something eternal which rules the whole universe by its wisdom in command and prohibition. Thus they have been accustomed to say that Law is the primal and ultimate mind of God, whose reason directs all things either by compulsion or by restraint. Wherefore that Law which the gods have given the human race has been justly praised; for it is the reason and mind of a wise lawgiver applied to command and prohibitions. (381)

Once the law is supported by the divine, then any confrontation with the state is no longer simply a political one; it threatens the foundations of the entire order of a world.

Condemning Christians to be slaughtered by wild animals reveals much more about the Roman relationship to this group of people and their beliefs than any merely legal definitions. Still, in his compendium

32. Cicero, *De Legibus*, 463.

of martyr accounts, Musurillo writes, "A study of the authentic texts does not help clear up the problem. The legal basis of the persecutions remains vague; and this precisely corresponds with the actual state of things. Even the Romans themselves would have been hard put to explain the foundations of what they did."[33] Although the "legal basis" might be uncertain, the most severe of the sentences handed down by the Roman magistrates is most revealing; they knew precisely what they were doing. To understand their state of mind, it is necessary to delve deeper into the form of the punishments and understand it from the magistrate's point of view.

To understand the *meaning* of sending Christians into the amphitheater to be devoured by animals was inseparable from two foundational doctrines: one, the sacrament of the Eucharist and, two, the belief in postmortem resurrection. The lack of judicial records on the entire proceedings does not preclude us from reconstructing how it took place, beginning with the interrogations by the magistrates who knew, well before, the extent of Christian theology. The metaphysical meaning of the events that are soon to take place in the Roman amphitheater are inseparable from the historical confrontation between two incompatible worldviews. The confrontation, as Paul understood it, was between the reality of the Roman world and the faith of Christians insofar as they believed in the "newness of life." The Roman magistrates were not merely superstitious polytheists who made up fantastic accounts of Christian rituals. It dawned on a few Romans within the judicial system that the most far-reaching difference between them came down to an irreducible reality: the Eucharist above all represented the abolition and a replacement of the whole edifice of a sacrificial culture. One judicial response was appropriate. Just as the entertainment of the games or "*ludi* can be seen as offerings to the gods provided by public officials on behalf of the entire community,"[34] so too did the executions of Christians take on all the appearances of sacrifice to the gods, though with one additional factor: eating sacrificial meat was now to be completely inverted.

No historian or, for that matter, a theologian, has entered the amphitheater with the *damnati ad bestias* to understand not so much the experience of the martyrs, but the *logic* of Roman magistrates. Being among the wild animals of the Roman amphitheaters and the Christians both is a specific historical event and, so as to conclude my overall argument,

33. Musurillo, intro to his translation of *The Acts of the Christian Martyrs*, lxi.

34. Beacham, *Spectacle Entertainments of Early Imperial Rome*, 13.

brings a long history of animal sacrifice and the death penalty to its conclusion insofar as they were interrelated and mutually influential in ancient society. Once animal sacrifice and the death penalty are essential to each other in the events surrounding the experience of the martyrs, then we are in a better position to understand the metaphysical confrontation between Romans and Christians. There was one reason and one reason only that the Christians were sentenced to death: they refused to perform a sacrifice in honor of the emperor. Their "stubbornness" was perceived by the magistrates as willful, reckless, and to them incredulous; they were merely asked to *perform an act*; and they refused, from some principle impossible for them to understand. The spectacle about to take place would have far-reaching results for some of the people who *witnessed* it. We too one-dimensionally refer to the martyrs as witnesses. True enough; equally important was being seen by others, as examples. A "witness" is, in legal terms, someone who testifies; in their case, Christians refused to fulfill the one command of sacrificing in the name of the emperor and then provided their testimony by doing more than representing themselves without saying a word.

There is a convergence in the Roman amphitheater that now allows us to recall the whole of the preceding arguments. Not a few of the magistrates who were called to respond to the accusations against Christians soon learned that the Eucharist was nothing less than a substitute for animal sacrifice and therefore, by implication, a complete rejection of the most significant politico-religious ritual of Roman society, one that also repudiated the divinity of the emperor. There is one reason and one reason only for the repeated references in the literature of Christians being offered unconditional release: all they had to do was perform a sacrifice, nothing more. The magistrates were more than aware that Christians could easily act, *hypocritically*, in order to save their own lives. Roman magistrates were indifferent to the idea of conscience. They only wanted proof of submission. The refusal of Christians to submit to this very easy demand infuriated Roman magistrates to no end; they were unable to comprehend their attitude. They had never seen such a level of resistance and noncompliance. Christians were offered the choice of simply offering a sacrifice in the name of the emperor and they would be released. The magistrates knew that they could then simply go on about their daily lives and continue to be Christians. And yet, despite this seemingly magnanimous offer, as the magistrates saw it, which saved them from a brutal fate in the amphitheater, they refused, giving them no choice but to sentence them to death. The magistrates could not understand how the Christians were making a "rational choice."[35]

The metaphysics of the earliest Christians in Rome, who eventually came to the attention of the authorities, created a bureaucratic response expected from the ruling powers, from what Paul called "principalities." The metaphysics of the Eucharist was inconceivable for the Romans. The Eucharist was no mere ritual, to be *acted out* in a temple along with so many other observances, a public display; it had nothing to do with the religiopolitical rituals of the Romans or any other people, most especially their relationships to their various gods and all the attendant acts done as a binding service to them. The Eucharist was eventually seen by the Romans magistrates, who had to adjudicate their cases, as an absolute effrontery to them as representatives of a binding law. The Eucharist made every single Christian equal, undermining all social distinctions; but much more than that, it also unified the Christian into a whole and equal with God. Such an idea could not be accepted by the Romans, because their theology and society had been founded on erecting hierarchies, beginning with the divine/human being separation. More significantly, Christian metaphysics made the place of the emperor in Roman society no longer dominant or privileged. Once the Eucharist, as the internalization of the body of Jesus, made everyone equal among each other and as part of one body, internally for every human being and externally insofar as they were in the body of Christ in church, then the privileged place of the emperor became irrelevant. The Romans had no choice but to admit that the Christians's refusal to sacrifice at the temple was seditious. The internalization of the body and blood of Jesus was an abolition of animal sacrifice and therefore a rejection of the violence inherent in the sacred as the necessary reality unifying the whole of society and empire. As soon as Christians internalized the Eucharist, then they became coterminus in responsibility with all other members of the church and who, as a unity, were all identified with the idea of the divine. Such a sharing made Christians, ultimately, superior to the emperor. More to the point, the emperor was no longer divine. The Roman emperor had been displaced from his preeminent social position as a leader by virtue of his divinity. Once Christians also became related to the divine and due to the creation of a completely different relationship with God—one separated from the reciprocity or gift-giving of sacrifice—then the emperor could be seen as

35. Chapter 8 of Stark's *The Rise of Christianity* is called "The Martyrs: Sacrifice as a Rational Choice."

nothing but a second-class citizen. As soon as the Romans realized what the metaphysics of Christian doctrine implied for the whole of society, they had no choice but to act. Perhaps not accidentally, one of the first widespread periods of persecutions begins at virtually the same time as Paul is being held in a Roman prison awaiting his trial and, eventually, his execution by beheading—a death accorded to him because of his Roman citizenship.

The executions of Christians were soon to be perceived symbolically. The metaphysics of the Eucharist had to be, somehow, destroyed. The Romans could not tolerate its meaning. How did they do this? The imagination of the law knew no bounds. If the man Jesus was crucified for his attempt to abolish the sacrificial system in the temple—which the Romans understood as seditious and by no means restricted to a Jewish interpretation of their law—then to overturn such a revolutionary theology required the most intense response possible. It had to be materially brutal and without restraint. Political power would be unleashed on a metaphysical truth. Now that Christian doctrine had been developed and was well known, the Roman authorities understood the relation between the abolition of animal sacrifice and its substitution by the Eucharist. A few of the more intelligent among the Romans in the judiciary had to be astounded by the implications of the teachings of Christians. In the end, the events to unfold during the reign of Nero in 64 CE are decisive for all subsequent Christian history. The Roman judiciary metaphysically confronts Christian teaching on the Eucharist with a corporeal punishment and a method of execution that fully shows the extent of Roman logic and brutality. The Romans will attempt to destroy the metaphysics of the Eucharist by feeding Christians to the wild animals in the Roman amphitheater.

Every single interpretation of the meaning of the Eucharist by theologians does not consider how the Romans understood the ritual—though we know how the gossip of everyday Romans could be both imaginative and malicious. The magistrates, on the other hand, had a more pragmatic understanding. The Eucharist was a *substitute* for animal sacrifice and the shared meal. When the first Christian martyrs were released into the Roman amphitheater to be ripped apart and eaten raw by wild animals, the logic of the judicial punishment was premeditated and logical to the extreme. By putting groups of Christians into the amphitheater and making their death, as executions, a source of entertainment and sacrifice, they were simultaneously making legitimate Roman culture and history and consigning Christian thought into a state of nature; more precisely, the ingestion of the Christian body into a wild animal was the antithesis of Roman *religio* that had founded the state upon its relationship to the gods and the meal shared as part of the sacrificial ritual.

It would be relatively easy, and quite wrong, to simply dismiss such a form of execution as the perverted imagination of one or more Roman magistrates or the executioners associated with carrying out punishments; nor can it be reduced to a convenient form of entertainment for the common Romans who, seeing the mutilation of other human beings, might more readily accept the relative hardship of their everyday lives. The punishment had several meanings and consequences, beginning with a counter to the logic of the sacrament whereby the body of Jesus, as bread, and his blood, as wine, was consumed—that is, internalized such that its presence would thereby transform the individual. Sacrificing Christians to wild animals was the Roman rejection of the Eucharist insofar as it represented the spiritual transformation of the individual; the eaten Christian was not simply relegated out of the world of the spirit, according to the Roman judge, but also out of the human world and back into a natural state whereby animals necessarily attacked, killed, and ate each other in order to live. Being eaten raw by a wild animal was to place the Christian body not simply in nature, outside culture or the city of Rome; it was, equally important for its symbolic value in a culture that treated the familial dead with the greatest of circumspection, to *temporarily bury* the Christian body inside a living animal. Again, the Romans who were responsible for such judicial punishment did so by being fully conscious of one of the fundamental doctrines of early Christianity: the turn away from polytheistic worship, the rejection of animal sacrifice, and the refusal to eat sacrificial meat.

There is no more appropriate way to end the interlaced history of animal sacrifice and the death penalty than to recall our beginnings most especially in Genesis and to lead the readings of our texts to the first full-scale martyrdoms in Rome. In *The Annals*, Tacitus gives us just enough detailed information to recognize a stunning similarity between the act of God in Genesis 3 (as God gives the hides of one or more animals for Adam and Eve to wear as clothing) and the experience of the Christians dying in the amphitheater.

"And as they perished, mockeries were added, so that, covered in the hides of wild beasts, they expired from mutilation by dogs."[36]

In a recollection that, for us, emphasizes the first act on the part of God to provide Adam and Eve with clothing made from animal skins, the Christians condemned to the amphitheater were first made to "wear" animal pelts soaked in blood, which were then sown together to cover them before being put into the amphitheater; once inside, wild dogs were unleashed and, no doubt ravenous with hunger and distressed by abuse, threw themselves on the victims. The magistrates who condemned Christians to such a scene of carnage, even if they were not aware of the passage in Genesis 3, nevertheless knew exactly what they were doing insofar as the Christians who refused to sacrifice animals and then eat them in an act of commensality, were exposed to a complete inversion of the natural order of the world. Human beings were reduced to the most barbaric state imaginable; since they refused to acknowledge their own culture and civilization, then they would suffer the most ignoble death possible. The death was terrifying enough. The wounds were not always the immediate cause of death: shock, loss of blood, a gradual death from the number of wounds, made death long and drawn out. The magistrates had one last vindication: not only was the sentence to be a complete repudiation of the Eucharist as the alternative to animal sacrifice, the death of the condemned would nullify any hope in one of their central beliefs—the resurrection. The method of execution was a double-penalty: it imposed the death sentence on them by being exposed to a ravenous animal and would prevent, after being ingested and therefore temporarily internalized, both a burial and resurrection. The magistrates conceived the finality of the whole process with one last consequence: not only would the Christian be killed by an animal, forego a human burial, and so be prevented from achieving any resurrection at all, the final, irreducible proof would lie in the sand and dirt of the Roman amphitheater.

The transcendence of the resurrection would be denied absolutely by the excrement of an animal.

36. Tacitus, *The Annals*, 326.

Bibliography

Achtemeier, Paul J. *An Introduction to the New Hermeneutic*. Philadelphia: Westminster, 1969.

Adamson, Peter. *Classical Philosophy: A History of Philosophy without Any Gaps*. Oxford: Oxford University Press, 2014.

Aeschylus. *Prometheus Bound*. In *Aeschylus II*, translated by David Greene. Chicago: University of Chicago Press, 1942.

Agamben, Giorgio. *Homo Sacer: Sovereign Power and Bare Life*. Translated by Daniel Heller-Roazen. Stanford: Stanford University Press, 1998.

Allen, Danielle S. *The World of Prometheus: The Politics of Punishing in Democratic Athens*. Princeton: Princeton University Press, 2000.

Allen, R. E. *Socrates and Legal Obligation*. Minneapolis: University of Minnesota Press, 1980.

Alter, Robert. *Genesis: Translation and Commentary*. New York: Norton, 1996.

Anderson, Paul N. *The Riddles of the Fourth Gospel: An Introduction to John*. Minneapolis: Fortress, 2011.

Annas, Julia. "Plato's Myths of Judgment." *Phronesis* 27 (1982) 119–43.

Apollodours. *Library*. In *Gods and Heroes of the Greeks*, translated with introduction and notes by Michael Simpson. Amherst: University of Massachusetts Press, 1976.

Armstrong, Karen. *In the Beginning: A New Interpretation of Genesis*. New York: Ballantine, 1996.

Arnold, Bill T. *Encountering the Book of Genesis*. Grand Rapids: Baker, 1998.

Augustine. *Confessions*. Translated by R. S. Pine-Coffin. London: Penguin, 1961.

Balthasar, Hans Urs von. "Jesus, the Absolutely Singular." In *The Von Balthasar Reader*, edited by Medark Kehl and Werner Löser, 129–31. Edinburg: T. & T. Clark, 1982.

Barrett, C. K. *The Gospel according to John: An Introduction with Commentary and Notes on the Greek Text*. 2nd ed. London: SPCK, 1978.

Barton, Bruce C., et al. *John*. Wheaton, IL: Tyndale, 1993.

Bataille, George. *The Theory of Religion*. Translated by Robert Hurley. New York: Zone, 1992.

Baukham, Richard. *Jesus and the Eyewitnesses: The Gospels as Eyewitness Testimony*. Grand Rapids: Eerdmans, 2006.

Bauman, Richard A. *Crime and Punishment in Ancient Rome*. London: Routledge, 1996.

Beacham, Richard C. *Spectacle Entertainments of Early Imperial Rome*. New Haven: Yale University Press, 1999.

Beall, E. F. "Hesiod's Prometheus and Development in Myth." *Journal of the History of Ideas* 52 (1991) 355–71.

Beatrice, Pier Franco. "Le Tuniche di Pelle: Antiche letture di Gen. 3,21." In *La Tradizione dell'enkrateia: Motivazione ontologiche e protologiche*, edited by Ugo Bianchi, 433–84. Rome: Edizioni dell'ateneo, 1985.

Beck, Randy, and David VanDrunen. "The Biblical Foundations of the Law: Creation, Fall and the Patriarchs." In *Law and the Bible: Justice, Mercy and Legal Institutions*, edited by Robert F. Cochran Jr. and David VanDrunen, 23–48. Downers Grove: InterVarsity, 2013.

Benko, Stephen. *Pagan Rome and the Early Christians*. Bloomington: Indiana University Press, 1984.

Berrigan, Daniel. *Genesis: Fair Beginnings, Then Foul*. Lanham, MD: Rowman & Littlefield, 2006.

Bingham, D. Jeffrey. "Christianizing Divine Aseity: Irenaeus Reads John." In *The Gospel of John and Christian Theology*, edited by Richard Bauckham and Carl Mosser, 53–67. Grand Rapids: Eerdmans, 2008.

Blenkinsopp, Joseph. *From Adam and Abraham: Introduction of Sacred History*. London: Darton, Longman & Todd, 1965.

Bloch, Ernst. *Natural Law and Human Dignity*. Translated by Denis J. Schmidt. Cambridge: MIT Press, 1986.

Blumenberg, Hans. *Work on Myth*. Translated by Robert M. Wallace. Cambridge: MIT Press, 1985.

Bonnechere, Pierre. "Divination." In *A Companion to Greek Religion*, edited by Daniel Ogden, 145–60. Chichester, UK: Wiley-Blackwell, 2010.

Borchert, Gerald L. *John 1–11*. Nashville: Broadman & Holman, 1996.

Borg, Marcus J. "Seeing Jesus: Sources, Lenses, Method." In *The Meaning of Jesus: Two Visions*, 3–14. New York: HarperCollins, 1999.

Boyarin, Daniel. *Dying for God: Martyrdom and the Making of Christianity and Judaism*. Stanford: Stanford University Press, 1999.

Boyele, Elizabeth Michael, and Carol J. Dempsey. *The Bible and Literature*. Maryknoll: Orbis, 2015.

Boys-Stones, G. R. and J. H. Haubold, eds. *Plato and Hesiod*. Oxford: Oxford University Press, 2010.

Breech, James. *The Silence of Jesus: The Authentic Voice of the Historical Man*. Philadelphia: Fortress, 1983.

Bremmer, Jan N. "Pandora and the Creation of Eve." In *Greek Religion and Culture, the Bible, and the Ancient Near East*, 19–34. Leiden: Brill, 2008.

Bruce, F. F. *The Gospel of John: Introduction, Exposition and Notes*. Grand Rapids: Eerdmans, 1983.

Brueggemann, Walter. *Genesis*. Atlanta: John Knox, 1982.

Bryan, Christopher. *Render to Caesar: Jesus, the Early Church, and the Roman Superpower*. Oxford: Oxford University Press, 2005.

Buber, Martin. *I and Thou*. Translated by Walter Kaufmann. New York: Touchstone, 1970.

Bultmann, Rudolf. *The Gospel of John: A Commentary*. Translated by G. R. Beasley-Murray et al. Philadelphia: Westminster, 1971.

———. *What Is Theology?* Edited by Eberhard Jüngel and Klaus W. Müller. Translated by Roy A. Harrisville. Minneapolis: Fortress, 1997.

Burkert, Walter. "Discussion." In *Violent Origins: Walter Burkert, René Girard, and Jonathan Z. Smith on Ritual Killing and Cultural Formation*, edited by Robert G.

Hamerton-Kelly, introduction by Burton Mack, commentary by Renato Rosaldo, 177–88. Stanford: Stanford University Press, 1987.

———. "Greek Tragedy and Sacrificial Ritual." *Greek, Roman, and Byzantine Studies* 7 (1966) 87–216.

———. *The Orientalizing Revolution: Near Eastern Influence on Greek Culture in the Early Greek Period.* Translated by Margaret E. Pinder and Walter Burkert. Cambridge: Harvard University Press, 1992.

———. "Sacrificial Violence: A Problem in Ancient Religions." In *The Oxford Handbook of Religion and Violence*, edited by Michael Jerryson et al., 437–54. Oxford: Oxford University Press, 2013.

Burn, Andrew Robert. *The World of Hesiod: A Study of the Greek Middle Ages, c. 900–700 B.C.* London: Kegan Paul, Trench, Trubner, 1936.

Burnyeat, M. F. "The Impiety of Socrates." *Ancient Philosophy* 7 (1997) 1–12.

Byron, John. *Cain and Abel in Text and Tradition: Jewish and Christian Interpretations of the First Sibling Rivalry.* Leiden: Brill, 2011.

Carcopino, Jérôme. *Daily Life in Ancient Rome.* Edited by H. T. Rowell. Translated by E. O. Lorimer. Harmondsworth, UK: Penguin, 1975.

Cassuto, U. *A Commentary on the Book of Genesis.* Translated by Israel Abrahams. Jerusalem: Magnes Press, Hebrew University, 1961.

Chaine, Joseph. *Le Livre de La Genèse.* Paris: Les Éditions du Cerf, 1949.

Charlesworth, James H. *The Historical Jesus: An Essential Guide.* Nashville: Abingdon, 2008.

Chilton, Bruce, and Craig A. Evans. *Authenticating the Activities of Jesus.* Leiden: Brill, 1999.

Cicero. *De Legibus.* Translated by Clinton Walker Keyes. Cambridge: Cambridge University Press, 1970.

———. *De re publica.* Translated by Clinton Walker Keyes. London: Heinemann, 1928.

———. *Tusculan Disputations.* Translated by J. E. King. Cambridge: Harvard University Press, 1927.

Cochrane, Charles C. *Jesus of Nazareth in Word and Deed.* Grand Rapids: Eerdmans, 1979.

Collins, Adela Yarbro. "The Origin of the Designation of Jesus as 'Son of Man.'" *Harvard Theological Review* 80 (1987) 391–407.

Collins, Derek. "Mapping the Entrails: The Practice of Greek Hepatoscopy." *American Journal of Philology* 129 (2008) 319–45.

Connor, W. R. "The Other 399: Religion and the Trial of Socrates." In *Georgica: Greek Studies in Honour of George Cawkell*, edited by Michael A. Flower and Mark Tower, 49–56. London: Institute of Classical Studies, 1991.

Crossan, John Dominic. *God and Empire: Jesus Against Rome, Then and Now.* San Francisco: HarperSanFrancisco, 2007.

———. *In Parables: The Challenge of the Historical Jesus.* New York: Harper & Row, 1973.

Daniélou, Jean. *In the Beginning . . . Genesis I–III.* Montreal: Palm, 1965.

Daquino, Piertro. *Lettura Cristiana della Genesi.* Turin: Elle di Ci, 1972.

De Romilly, Jacqueline. *A Short History of Greek Literature.* Translated by Lilian Dougherty. Chicago: University of Chicago Press, 1985.

Derrett, J. Duncan M. *Law in the New Testament.* London: Darton, Longman & Todd, 1970.

Detienne, Marcel. "Culinary Practices and the Spirit." In *The Cuisine of Sacrifice among the Greeks*, translated by Paula Wissing, 1–20. Chicago: University of Chicago Press, 1989.

———. *Dionysos Slain*. Translated by Mireille Muellner and Leonard Muellner. Baltimore: Johns Hopkins University Press, 1979.

Detienne, Marcel, and Jean-Pierre Vernant. *Cunning Intelligence in Greek Culture and Society*. Translated by Janet Lloyd. Sussex: Harvester, 1978.

Dibelius, Martin. *From Tradition to Gospel*. Translated by Bertram Lee Woolf. New York: Scribner, 1935.

Diller, Hans. "Hesiod und die Anfänge der griechischen philosophie." *Antike und Abendland* 2 (1946) 140–51.

Dodd, C. H. *The Interpretation of the Fourth Gospel*. Cambridge: Cambridge University Press, 1953.

Dougherty, Carol. *Prometheus*. London: Routledge, 2006.

Duggan, Michael. *The Consuming Fire: A Christian Introduction to the Old Testament*. San Francisco: Ignatius, 1991.

Edwards, C. P. *The Language of Hesiod in Its Traditional Context*. Oxford: Blackwell, 1971.

Ekroth, Gunnel. "Bare Bones: Zooarchaeology and Greek Sacrifice." In *Animal Sacrifice in the Ancient Greek World*, edited by Sarah Hitch, 15–47. Cambridge: Cambridge University Press, 2017.

Faraone, Christopher A., and F. S. Naiden, eds. *Greek and Roman Animal Sacrifice: Ancient Victims, Modern Observers*. Cambridge: Cambridge University Press, 2012.

Farina, William. *Perpetua of Carthage: Portrait of a Third Century Martyr*. Jefferson, NC: McFarland, 2009.

Farley, Lawrence F. *The Gospel of John: Beholding the Glory*. Ben Lomand, CA: Counciliar, 2006.

Fishbane, Michael. *The Exegetical Imagination: On Jewish Thought and Theology*. Cambridge: Harvard University Press, 1998.

Flood, Derek. *Healing the Gospel: A Radical Vision of Grace, Justice, and the Cross*. Eugene, OR: Cascade, 2012.

Fowler, Paul B. *The Structure of Romans: The Argument of Paul's Letter*. Minneapolis: Fortress, 2016.

Fredriksen, Paula. *From Jesus to Christ: The Origins of the New Testament Images of Jesus*. New Haven: Yale University Press, 1988.

Freud, Sigmund. *Totem and Taboo*. In *The Origins of Religion*, translated by James Strachey, edited by Albert Dickson. Pelican Freud Library 13. Harmondsworth, UK: Penguin, 1985.

Funk, Robert W. *The Acts of Jesus: The Search for the Authentic Deeds of Jesus*. San Francisco: HarperSanFrancisco, 1998.

Gernet, Louis. *Anthropologie de la Grèce antique*. Paris: Flamarrion, 1982.

Gilhus, Ingvild Saelid. "Ritual Meals and Polemics in Antiquity." In *Commensality: From Everyday Food to Feast*, edited by Susanne Kerner et al., 203–16. London: Bloomsbury, 2015.

Girard, René. *Evolution and Conversion: Dialogues on the Origins of Culture*. With Pierpaolo Antonello and João Cezar de Castro Rocha. London: Bloomsbury, 2008.

———. *I See Satan Fall like Lightning*. Translated by James G. Williams. Maryknoll: Orbis, 2001.

———. *The One by Whom Scandal Comes*. Translated by M. B. DeBevoise. East Lansing: Michigan State University Press, 2014.

———. *The Scapegoat*. Translated by Yvonne Freccero. Baltimore: Johns Hopkins University Press, 1986.

———. *Things Hidden since the Foundation of the World*. Translated by Stephen Bann and Michael Metteer. Stanford: Stanford University Press, 1986.

———. *Violence and the Sacred*. Translated by Patrick Gregory. Baltimore: Johns Hopkins University Press, 1977.

Good, Edwin M. *Genesis 1–11: Tales of the Earliest World*. Stanford: Stanford University Press, 2011.

Gregory, C. R. *Canon and Text of the New Testament*. Edinburgh: T. & T. Clark, 1907.

Green, Bernard. *Christianity in Ancient Rome: The First Three Centuries*. London: T. & T. Clark, 2010.

Greenblatt, Stephen. *The Rise and Fall of Adam and Eve*. New York: Norton, 2017.

Guardini, Romano. *The Death of Socrates: An Interpretation of the Platonic Dialogues; Euthyphro, Apology, Crito and Phaedo*. Translated by Basil Wrighton. New York: Sheed & Ward, 1948.

Gunkel, Hermann. *The Legends of Genesis: The Biblical Saga and History*. Translated by W. H. Carruth. New York: Schocken, 1964.

Halbertal, Moshe. *On Sacrifice*. Princeton: Princeton University Press, 2012.

Hamerton-Kelly, Robert G. *Pre-existence, Wisdom, and the Son of Man: A Study of the Idea of Pre-existence in the New Testament*. Cambridge: Cambridge University Press, 1973.

———, ed. *Violent Origins: Walter Burkert, René Girard, and Jonathan Z. Smith on Ritual Killing and Cultural Formation*. Introduction by Burton Mack. Commentary by Renato Rosaldo. Stanford: Stanford University Press, 1987.

Hamilton, Victor P. *The Book of Genesis, Chapters 1–17*. Grand Rapids. Eerdmans, 1990.

Hanks, Gardner C. *Against the Death Penalty: Christian and Secular Arguments against Capital Punishment*. Scottdale, PA: Herald, 1997.

Hanson, Richard S. *The Serpent Was Wiser: A New Look at Genesis I–II*. Minneapolis: Augsburg, 1972.

Hartley, John E. *Genesis*. Peabody: Hendrickson, 2000.

Hauerwas, Stanley. "Punishing Christians: A Pacifist Approach to the Issue of Capital Punishment." In *Religion and the Death Penalty: A Call for Reckoning*, edited by Erik C. Owens et al., 57–72. Grand Rapids: Eerdmans, 2004.

Havelock, Eric A. *Preface to Plato*. Cambridge: Belknap, 1963.

Hearne, Vicky. *Adam's Task: Calling Animals by Name*. New York: Knopf, 1986.

Heath, Malcolm. "Hesiod's Didactic Poetry." *Classical Quarterly* 35 (1985) 245–63.

Heidel, Alexander. *The Babylonian Genesis: The Story of the Creation*. Chicago: University of Chicago Press, 1942.

———. *The Gilgamesh Epic and Old Testament Parallels*. Chicago: University of Chicago Press, 1946.

Heinisch, Paul. *Problemi di Storia Primordiale Biblica*. Cremona, Italy: Morcelliana, 1950.

Hénaff, Marcel. *The Price of Truth: Gift, Money, and Philosophy*. Translated by Jean-Louis Morhange, with the collaboration of Anne-Marie Feenberg-Dibon. Stanford: Stanford University Press, 2010.

Hengel, Martin. *The Charismatic Leader and His Followers*. Translated by James Greig. New York: Crossroad, 1981.

———. *Crucifixion: In the Ancient World and the Folly of the Message of the Cross*. Translated by John Bowden. Philadelphia: Fortress, 1977.

———. *Studies in the Gospel of Mark*. Translated by John Bowden. Philadelphia: Fortress, 1985.

Henry, Michel. *I Am the Truth: Toward a Philosophy of Christianity*. Translated by Susan Emanuel. Stanford: Stanford University Press, 2003.

Hesiod. *Theogony*. Translated by Stanley Lombardo. Indianapolis: Hackett, 1993.

———. *Theogony*. In *The Poems of Hesiod*, translated with introduction and comments by R. M. Frazer. Norman: University of Oklahoma Press, 1983.

———. *Works and Days*. In *The Poems of Hesiod*, translated with introduction and comments by R. M. Frazer. Norman: University of Oklahoma Press, 1983.

Hiebert, Theodore. *The Yawhist's Landscape: Nature and Religion in Early Israel*. New York: Oxford University Press, 1996.

Hobbs, Hershel H. *The Origin of All Things: Studies in Genesis*. Waco, TX: Word, 1975.

Hopkins, Keith. *Death and Renewal*. Vol. 2, *Sociological Studies in Roman History*. Cambridge: Cambridge University Press, 1983.

Horsley, Richard. *The Liberation of Christmas: The Infancy Narratives in Social Context*. Eugene, OR: Wipf & Stock, 1989.

Hubert, Henri, and Marcel Mauss. *Sacrifice: Its Nature and Function*. Chicago: University of Chicago Press, 1981.

Hyman George. *The Power of Sacrifice: Roman and Christian Discourses in Conflict*. Washington, DC: Catholic University of America Press, 2007.

Jaeger, Werner. *Early Christianity and Greek Paideia*. Cambridge: Harvard University Press, 1961.

Jaki, Stanley J. *Genesis I Through the Ages*. New York: Thomas More, 1992.

Kanagaraj, Jey J. *John: A New Covenant Commentary*. Cambridge, UK: Lutterworth, 2013.

Keiser, Thomas A. *Genesis 1–11: Its Literary Coherence and Theological Message*. Eugene, OR: Wipf & Stock, 2013.

Keith, Chris. *The* Pericope Adultarae, *the Gospel of John, and the Literacy of Jesus*. Leiden: Brill, 2014.

Kissling, Paul J. *Genesis*. Vol. 1. Joplin, MO: College Press, 2004.

Klawans, Jonathan. *Purity, Sacrifice, and the Temple: Symbolism and Supersessionism in the Study of Ancient Judaism*. Oxford: Oxford University Press, 2006.

Knust, Jennifer Wright, and Zsuszanna Vàrhelyi. *Ancient Mediterranean Sacrifice*. Oxford: Oxford University Press, 2011.

Kraut, Richard. *Socrates and the State*. Princeton: Princeton University Press, 1984.

Kyle, Donald G. *Spectacles of Death in Ancient Rome*. London: Routledge, 1998.

LaCocque, André. *The Trial of Innocence: Adam, Eve, and the Yahwist*. Eugene, OR: Cascade, 2006.

Lambden, Stephen N. "From Fig Leaves to Fingernails: Some Notes on the Garments of Adam and Eve in the Hebrew Bible and Select Early Postbiblical Jewish Writings."

In *A Walk in the Garden: Biblical, Iconographical and Literary Images of Eden*, edited by Paul Morris and Deborah Sawyer, 74–90. Sheffield: SJOT, 1992.

Lamberton, Robert. *Hesiod*. New Haven: Yale University Press, 1988.

Lännström, Anne. "A Religious Revolution? How Socrates' Theology Undermined the Practice of Sacrifice." *Ancient Philosophy* 31 (2011) 261–73.

Latourelle, René. *Finding Jesus through the Gospels: History and Hermeneutics*. Translated by Aloysius Owen. New York: Alba House, Society of St. Paul, 1978.

Léon-Dufour, Xavier. *Life and Death in the New Testament: The Teachings of Paul and Jesus*. Translated by Terrence Prendergast. San Francisco: Harper & Row, 1986.

Levinas, Emmanuel. *Totality and Infinity: An Essay on Exteriority*. Translated by Alphonso Lingis. Pittsburgh: Duquesne University Press, 1969.

Lewis, Andrew. "Slavery, Family, and Status." In *Roman Law*, edited by David Johnston, 151–74. Cambridge: Cambridge University Press, 2015.

L'Hereux, Conrad E. *In and Out of Paradise: The Book of Genesis from Adam and Eve to the Tower of Babel*. New York: Paulinist, 1982.

Lightfoot, R. H. *St. John's Gospel: A Commentary*. Edited by C. F. Evans. Oxford: Clarendon, 1956.

Lim, Johnson T. K. *Grace in the midst of Judgment: Grappling with Genesis 1–11*. Berlin: de Gruyter, 2002.

Lincoln, Bruce. "Violence." In *The Cambridge Companion to Ancient Mediterranean Religions*, edited by Barbette Stanley Spaeth, 199–219. Cambridge: University of Cambridge Press, 2013.

Lindars, Barnabas. *The Gospel of John*. Grand Rapids: Eerdmans, 1972.

———. *Jesus Son of Man: A Fresh Examination of the Son of Man Sayings in the Gospels in the Light of Recent Research*. Grand Rapids: Eerdmans, 1983.

Lohr, Joel N. "Righteous Abel, Wicked Cain: Genesis 4:1–16 in the Masoteric Text, the Septuagint, and the New Testament." *Catholic Biblical Quarterly* 71 (2009) 485–96.

Longman, Temper, III. *Genesis*. Grand Rapids: Zondervan, 2016.

Longman, Tremper, III, and David E. Garland. *Genesis-Leviticus*. Grand Rapids: Zondervan, 2008.

Maahs, Kenneth A. *The John You Never Knew: Decoding the Fourth Gospel*. New York: Lang, 2006.

Marion, Jean-Luc. *God Without Being*. 2nd ed. Translated by Thomas A. Carlson. Chicago: University of Chicago Press, 2012.

———. *The Visible and the Revealed*. Translated by Christina M. Gschwandter. New York: Fordham University Press, 2008.

Martin, George. *Bringing the Gospel of John to Life: Insight and Inspiration*. Huntington, IN: Our Sunday Visitor, 2016.

Matthews, Kenneth A. *Genesis 1—11:26*. Nashville: Boardman & Homan, 1996.

Mazza, Enrico. *The Celebration of the Eucharist: The Origin of the Rite and the Development of Its Interpretation*. Translated by Matthew J. O'Connell. Collegeville: Liturgical, 1999.

McClymond, Kathryn. "Don't Cry over Spilled Blood." In *Ancient Mediterranean Sacrifice*, edited by Jennifer Wright Knust and Zsuszanna Vàrhelyi, 235–50. Oxford: Oxford University Press, 2011.

McDermott, Brian O. *Word Become Flesh: Dimensions of Christology*. Collegeville: Liturgical, 1993.

McLelland, Joseph L. *Prometheus Rebound: The Irony of Atheism*. Waterloo, ON: Wilfred Laurier University Press, 1988.

Melzer, Arthur M. *Philosophy Between the Lines: The Lost History of Esoteric Writing*. Chicago: University of Chicago Press, 2014.

Milgrom, Jacob. *Leviticus: A Book of Ritual and Ethics*. Minneapolis: Fortress, 2004.

Miller, William T. *The Book of Genesis, Question by Question*. New York: Paulist, 2006.

Moltmann, Jürgen. *The Crucified God: The Cross of Christ as the Foundation and Criticism of Christian Theology*. Minneapolis: Fortress, 1993.

Momgardner, David, M. *The Story of the Roman Amphitheatre*. New York: Routledge, 2000.

Moss, Candida. *The Myth of Persecution: How Early Christians Invented the Story of Martyrdom*. San Francisco: HarperOne, 2013.

Mudd, Joseph C. *Eucharist as Meaning: Critical Metaphysics and Contemporary Sacramental Theology*. Collegeville: Fortress, 2010.

Munteanu, Dana LaCourse. *Tragic Pathos: Pity and Fear in Greek Philosophy and Tragedy*. Cambridge: Cambridge University Press, 2012.

Musurillo, Herbert. Introduction to *The Acts of the Christian Martyrs*, translated by Herbert Musurillo, xi–lxiii. Oxford: Clarendon, 1972.

Nancy, Jean-Luc. *The Inoperative Community*. Edited by Peter Connor. Translated by Peter Connor et al. Minneapolis: University of Minnesota Press, 1991.

Neusner, Jacob. *From Politics to Piety: The Emergence of Pharisaic Judaism*. Englewood Cliffs, NJ: Prentice-Hall, 1973.

Neyrey, Jerome H. *The Gospel of John in Cultural and Rhetorical Perspective*. Grand Rapids: Eerdmans, 2009.

Nietzsche, Friedrich. *Human, All Too Human: A Book for Free Spirits*. Translated by R. J. Hollingdale. Cambridge: Cambridge University Press, 1986.

———. *Philosophy in the Tragic Age of the Greeks*. Translated by Marianne Cowan. Chicago: Gateway, 1962.

Novak, David. "Can Capital Punishment Ever Be Justified in the Jewish Tradition?" In *Religion and the Death Penalty: A Call for Reckoning*, edited by Erik C. Owens et al., 31–47. Grand Rapids: Eerdmans, 2004.

Nussbaum, Martha C. *The Fragility of Goodness: Luck and Ethics in Greek Tragedy and Philosophy*. Cambridge: Cambridge University Press, 1986.

Pancaro, Severino. *The Law in the Fourth Gospel: The Torah and the Gospel, Moses and Jesus, Judaism and Christianity according to John*. Leiden: Brill, 1975.

Pelikan, Jaroslav. *Whose Bible Is It? A Short History of the Scriptures*. New York: Penguin, 2006.

Perrin, Norm. *Jesus and the Language of the Kingdom: Symbol and Metaphor in New Testament Interpretation*. Philadelphia: Fortress, 1980.

Philips, F. Carter. "Narrative Compression and the Myth of Prometheus in Hesiod." *Classical Journal* 68 (1973) 289–305.

Pitre, Brant. *Jesus and the Jewish Roots of the Eucharist: Unlocking the Secrets of the Last Supper*. New York: Image, 2011.

Plastaras, James. *Creation and Covenant*. Milwaukee: Bruce, 1968.

Plato. *Apology*. In *The Last Days of Socrates*, translated by Hugh Tredennick and Harold Tarrant, 31–70. London: Penguin, 1993.

———. *Critias*. Translated and annotated by Desmond Lee. Translated, revised, introduced, and annotated by T. K. Johansen. London: Penguin, 1965, 2008.

———. *Crito*. In *The Last Days of Socrates*, translated by Hugh Tredennick and Harold Tarrant, 71–96. London: Penguin, 1993.

———. *Euthyphro*. In *The Last Days of Socrates*, translated by Hugh Tredennick and Harold Tarrant, 1–30. London: Penguin, 1993.

———. *Gorgias*. Translated with an introduction by Walter Hamilton. Harmondsworth, UK: Penguin, 1960.

———. *Ion*. In *Early Socratic Dialogues*, translated by Donald Watt. Harmondsworth, UK: Penguin, 1987.

———. *Laches*. In *Early Socratic Dialogues*, translated by Iain Lane. Harmondsworth, UK: Penguin, 1987.

———. *The Laws*. Translated with an introduction and notes by Trevor J. Saunders. London: Penguin, 2004.

———. *Lysis*. In *Early Socratic Dialogues*, translated by Donald Watt. Harmondsworth, UK: Penguin, 1987.

———. *Minos; or, On Law*. Translated by Thomas L. Pangle. In *The Roots of Political Philosophy: Ten Forgotten Socratic Dialogues*, edited by Thomas L. Pangle, 53–66. Ithaca: Cornell University Press, 1987.

———. *Phaedo*. In *The Last Days of Socrates*, translated by Hugh Tredennick and Harold Tarrant, 97–200. London: Penguin, 1993.

———. *Philebus*. Translated with an introduction by Robin H. Waterfield. London: Penguin, 1982.

———. *Protagoras*. Translated by W. K. C. Guthrie. Harmondsworth, UK: Penguin, 1965.

———. *Republic*. Translated by G. M. A. Grube. Indianapolis: Hackett, 1974.

Propp, William H. "Eden Sketches." In *The Hebrew Bible and Its Interpreters*, edited by William Henry Propp et al., 189–203. Winona Lake, IN: Eisenbrauns, 1990.

Rhoads, David, and Donald Michie. *Mark as Story: An Introduction to the Narrative of the Gospel*. Philadelphia: Fortress, 1982.

Ricoeur, Paul. Paul. *The Conflict of Interpretations: Essays in Hermeneutics*. Edited by Don Ihde. Evanston, IL: Northwestern University Press, 1974.

———. *Freud and Philosophy: An Essay in Interpretation*. Translated by Denis Savage. New Haven: Yale University Press, 1970.

———. *Hermeneutics and the Human Sciences: Essays on Language, Action, and Interpretation*. Edited and translated by John B. Thompson. Cambridge: Cambridge University Press, 1981.

Ridderbos, Herman. *The Gospel of John: A Theological Commentary*. Translated by John Vriend. Grand Rapids: Eerdmans, 1997.

Riggsby, Andrew M. *Roman Law and the Legal World of the Romans*. Cambridge: Cambridge University Press, 2010.

Robert, Christian-Nils. *L'impératif sacrificiel: Justice pénale: au-delá de l'innocence et de la culpabilité*. Lausanne: Editions d'en bas, 1986.

Robinson, John Mansley. *An Introduction to Greek Philosophy*. New York: Houghton Mifflin, 1968.

Robinson, O. F. *Penal Practice and Penal Policy in Ancient Rome*. London: Routledge, 2007.

Rosenberg, David, trans. *The Book of J*. Interpreted by Harold Bloom. New York: Grove Weidenfeld, 1990.

Rowe, C. J. "Archaic Thought in Hesiod." *Journal of Hellenic Studies* 103 (1983) 124–35.

Rutherford, Ian. "Hesiod and the Literary Traditions of the Near East." In *Brill's Companion to Hesiod*, edited by Franco Montanari et al., 9–35. Leiden: Brill, 2009.

Sailhamer, John H. *The Meaning of the Pentateuch: Revelation, Composition and Interpretation*. Downers Grove: IVP Academic, 2009.

Sarna, Nahum M. *Understanding Genesis*. New York: Shocken, 1970.

Schillebeckx, Edward. *Interim Report on the Books of Jesus and Christ*. New York: Crossroad, 1981.

Schleiermacher, Friedrich D. E. "The Aphorisms on Hermeneutics from 1805 and 1809/10." In *The Hermeneutics Tradition: From Ast to Ricoeur*, edited by Gayle L. Ormiston and Alan D. Schrift, 57–84. Albany: State University of New York Press, 1990.

Schwartz, Regina M. *The Curse of Cain: The Violent Legacy of Monotheism*. Chicago: University of Chicago Press, 1997.

Schweitzer, Albert. *The Problem of the Lord's Supper*. Translated by A. J. Mattill Jr. Edited by John Reumann. Macon, GA: Mercer University Press, 1982.

Sedley, Douglas. "Sacrifice, Transcendence, and 'Making Sacred.'" *Royal Institute of Philosophy Supplement* 68 (2011) 257–67.

Seutonius. *The Twelve Caesars*. Translated by Robert Graves. London: Penguin, 1957.

Sherwin-White, A. N. *Roman Society and Roman Law in the New Testament*. Oxford: Clarendon, 1963.

Sloyan, Gerald. *John*. Louisville. Westminster John Knox, 2009.

Smith, Jonathan Z. *Relating Religion: Essays in the Study of Religion*. Chicago: University of Chicago Press, 2004.

Solmsen, Friedrich. *Hesiod and Aeschylus*. Ithaca, NY: Cornell University Press, 1949.

Sommerstein, Alan H. "Hesiod and Tragedy." In *The Oxford Handbook of Hesiod*, edited by Alexander C. Loney and Stephen Scully, 279–94. Oxford: Oxford University Press, 2018.

Sordi, Marta. *The Christians and the Roman Empire*. Translated by Annabel Bedini. Norman: University of Oklahoma Press, 1986.

Stark, Rodney. *The Rise of Christianity: How the Obscure, Marginal Jesus Movement Became the Dominant Religious Force in the Western World in a Few Centuries*. San Francisco: HarperOne, 1997.

Stauffer, Ethelbert. *Jesus and His Story*. London: SCM, 1960.

Stowers, Stanley. "The Religion of Plant and Animal Offerings Versus the Religion of Meanings, Essences, and Textual Mysteries." In *Ancient Mediterrean Sacrifice*, edited by Jennifer Wright Knust and Zsuszanna Vàrhelyi, 35–56. Oxford: Oxford University Press, 2011.

Stratton, Beverly J. *Out of Eden: Reading, Rhetoric, and the Ideology in Genesis 2–3*. Sheffield: Sheffield Academic, 1995.

Strauss Clay, Jenny. *Hesiod's Cosmos*. Cambridge: University of Cambridge Press, 2003.

Strauss, Leo. *Natural Right and History*. Chicago: University of Chicago Press, 1953.

———. "On the Minos." In *The Roots of Political Philosophy: Ten Forgotten Socratic Dialogues*, edited by Thomas L. Pangle, 67–79. Ithaca: Cornell University Press, 1987.

———. *Persecution and the Art of Writing*. Chicago: University of Chicago Press, 1952.

———. *Studies in Platonic Political Philosophy*. Chicago: University of Chicago Press, 1983.

Strenski, Ivan. *Theology and the First Theory of Sacrifice*. Leiden: Brill, 2003.

Stuhlmacher, Peter. *Paul's Letter to the Romans: A Commentary*. Translated by Scott J. Hafemann. Louisville: Westminster John Knox, 1994.

Tacitus. *The Annals*. Translated, with introduction and notes, by A. J. Woodman. Indianapolis: Hackett, 2004.

Towner, Wayne Sibley. *Genesis*. Louisville: Westminster John Knox, 2001.

Turner, Laurence A. *Announcements of Plot in Genesis*. Eugene, OR: Wipf & Stock, 2008.

Ullucci, Daniel. "Sacrifice in the Ancient Mediterranean: Recent and Current Research." *Currents in Biblical Scholarship* 13 (2015) 388–439.

Van Noorden, Helen. *Playing Hesiod: The "Myth of the Races" in Classical Antiquity*. Cambridge: Cambridge University Press, 2015.

Vermes, Geza. *Jesus the Jew: A Historian's Reading of the Gospels*. Minneapolis: Fortress, 1981.

Vernant, Jean-Pierre. *Mortals and Immortals: Collected Essays*. Edited by Froma I. Zeitlin. Princeton: Princeton University Press, 1991.

———. *Myth and Society in Ancient Greece*. New York: Zone, 1990.

———. "Théorie générale du sacrifice et mise a mort dans la ΘΥΣΙΑ grecque." In *Le sacrifice dans l'antiquité*, 2–21. Genève: Vandoeuvres, 1980.

Vernant, Jean-Pierre, and Pierre-Vidal Naquet. *Myth and Tragedy in Ancient Greece*. New York: Zone, 1990.

Vidal-Naquet, Pierre. *The Black Hunter: Forms of Thought and Forms of Society in the Greek World*. Translated by Andrew Szegedy-Maszak. Baltimore: Johns Hopkins University Press, 1986.

Vos, Howard F. *Genesis*. Chicago: Moody, 1982.

Watts, James W. "The Rhetoric of Sacrifice." In *Ritual and Metaphor: Sacrifice in the Bible*, edited by Christian A. Eberhart, 3–16. Atlanta: SBL, 2011.

Weiss, Roslyn. *Socrates Dissatisfied: An Analysis of Plato's* Crito. New York: Oxford University Press, 1998.

Welch, Katherine E. *The Roman Amphitheatre: From Its Origins to the Colosseum*. Cambridge: Cambridge University Press, 1983.

Wells G. A. *The Jesus of the Early Christians*. London: Pemberton, 1971.

Wenham, Gordon J. *Genesis 1–11*. Waco: Word, 1987.

West, M. L. "The Prometheus Trilogy." In *Aeschylus*, edited by Michael Lloyd, 359–96. Oxford: Oxford University Press, 2007.

Westermann, Claus. *Genesis 1–11: A Continental Commentary*. Translated by John J. Scullion, SJ. Minneapolis: Fortress, 1994.

Wiles, Maurice F. *The Spiritual Gospel: The Interpretation of the Fourth Gospel in the Early Church*. Cambridge: Cambridge University Press, 1960.

Wirshbo, Eliot. "The Mekone Scene in the Theogony: Prometheus as Prankster." *Roman and Byzantine Studies* 23 (1982) 1–10.

Wollheim, Richard. *The Sheep and the Ceremony*. Cambridge: Cambridge University Press, 1979.

Wright, N. T. *Who Was Jesus?* Grand Rapids: Eerdmans, 1992.

Yoder, John Howard. *The Christian and Capital Punishment*. Newton, KS: Faith and Life, 1961.

www.ingramcontent.com/pod-product-compliance
Lightning Source LLC
LaVergne TN
LVHW050628100826
845148LV00011B/1785

* 9 7 8 1 6 6 6 7 0 3 8 7 0 *